# GOALS, NO-GOALS AND OWN GOALS

# GOALS, NO-GOALS AND OWN GOALS

A debate on goal-directed and intentional behaviour

*Edited by*

Alan Montefiore & Denis Noble

*Balliol College, Oxford*

LONDON
**UNWIN HYMAN**
BOSTON    SYDNEY    WELLINGTON

© A.C.R.G.Montefiore, D.Noble, K.V.Wilkes, D.J.McFarland, D.C.Dennett, S.Lockery 1989.

This book is copyright under the Berne convention. No reproduction without permission. All rights reserved.

This volume was prepared, proofed and passed for press at the University of Oxford.

Published by the Academic Division of

**Unwin Hyman Ltd**
15/17 Broadwick Street, London W1V 1FP, UK

Unwin Hyman Inc.,
8 Winchester Place, Winchester, Mass. 01890, USA

Allen & Unwin (Australia) Ltd,
8 Napier Street, North Sydney, NSW 2060, Australia

Allen & Unwin (New Zealand) Ltd in association with the Port Nicholson Press Ltd, Compusales Building, 75 Ghuznee Street, Wellington 1, New Zealand

First published in 1989

---

British Library Cataloguing in Publication Data
Montefiore, Alan
    Goals, no goals, and own goals: a debate on goal-directed and intentional behaviour.
    1. Intention, — Philosophical perspectives
    I. Title II. Noble, D. (Denis)
    128'.4
ISBN 0-04-445341-8

---

Library of Congress Cataloging-in-Publication Data

Goals, no-goals, and own goals

    Bibliography: p.
    Includes index.
    1. Action theory. 2. Agent (Philosophy). 3. Intentionality (Philosophy)
I. Montefiore, Alan. II. Noble, Denis.
B105.A35G63 1989                   128'.4                       88-33932
ISBN 0-04-445341-8 (alk. paper)

---

Printed and bound at the University Press, Cambridge

# CONTENTS

*Preface* vii

*Acknowledgements* ix

## PART I   INTRODUCTION

1 General Introduction   *Alan Montefiore and Denis Noble*   3

2 Philosophical Background   *Alan Montefiore*   14

3 Scientific Introduction   *Denis Noble*   28

## PART II   THE POSITIONS STATED

4 Goals, No-Goals and Own Goals   *David McFarland*   39

5 Intentions and Causes   *Alan Montefiore*   58

6 Intentional Action and Physiology   *Denis Noble*   81

7 Cognitive Ethology: Hunting for Bargains or a Wild Goose Chase?   *Daniel C. Dennett*   101

8 Representation, Functionalism, and Simple Living Systems   *Shawn Lockery*   117

9 Representation and Explanation   *Kathy Wilkes*   159

## PART III  THE POSITIONS DEBATED

10  Narrow Intentions  *Shawn Lockery*  185

11  Explanation — How Not to Miss the Point  *Kathy Wilkes*  194

12  The Teleological Imperative  *David McFarland*  211

13  Comments  *Daniel C. Dennett*  229

14  Round Two  *Alan Montefiore*  238

15  What Do Intentions Do?  *Denis Noble*  262

## PART IV  A CHALLENGE RENEWED

16  Swan Song of a Phoenix  *David McFarland*  283

*Bibliography*  295

*Further reading*  302

*Notes on authors*  303

# PREFACE

We hope this book will be of interest to a very wide range of readers, many of them students in philosophy, psychology, computing and in the behavioural and physiological sciences. But even those of our readers who may not think of themselves as students may nevertheless find it helpful to know what to expect in this book and how it might best be read.

The book is organised into four parts. Part I consists of three introductory chapters. There are three chapters here, because we are aware that readers with very different backgrounds will require different kinds of introduction. The first explains how the book came to be written and what are its purposes and organisation. The second provides a brief account of some of the relevant philosophy, while the third acts as a more scientific introduction. We hope these chapters will make the book more accessible to those readers who require some introduction to our debates, but we are aware that much of the material here may be unnecessary for many others. Those who are already familiar with the kind of interdisciplinary debate to be found here, may find it possible to embark straight away on Part II where the positions to be debated are laid out. In Part III the initial positions outlined in Part II are discussed, and finally in a single chapter, in Part IV, one of the authors presents his reactions to the debate.

Those who embark directly on Parts II–IV may later wish to read some of Part I as a concluding overview of the book.

Certainly, parts of these introductory chapters may only be fully appreciated *after* having engaged in the debate itself. That also means that, read as introductions, some of the points made there will have to be taken 'on trust', waiting for the real debate to begin to see what we are trying to say.

A word about bibliographies. Wherever it has seemed that it might be appropriate and helpful, the contributors have added a few suggestions for further reading at the ends of their own chapters with a note of explanation as to what might be expected of the books suggested. At the end of the book, we have appended a much longer list of all those works to which reference has been made in the main text; in a separate section we have also added a short list of works to which reference has not been made, but which might prove of further interest to readers wishing to pursue the discussion in one direction or another. Many of the works mentioned under one or other of these heads themselves contain helpful and sometimes extensive bibliographies and/or suggestions for further reading on specific topics.

A book of this kind is almost impossible to index since the items that might be indexed are diffused throughout the book. Each index item would have required reference to a very large number of pages. We have instead indicated in the bibliography the pages on which each reference is cited. This should be useful to those who wish to find where a particular paper or book is discussed.

Inevitably the debates do not follow a single straight line. It may sometimes be found necessary to weave back and forth between the chapters in Parts II & III to get the full flavour of the discussion. The significance of some of the arguments will only become fully clear when the other chapters have been read — or perhaps re-read — in the light of a later argument. If you find you need to do this, then you will be retracing the spirit of the original university seminars and the many associated less formal discussions that led to this book being written.

*Alan Montefiore and Denis Noble*

# Acknowledgements

We should like to thank many of our colleagues for their helpful and critical comments at various stages in the work for this book, and in particular Dr Susan Greenfield and the anonymous publishers' readers for their valuable suggestions, nearly all of which have been acted on in revising the book for publication.

The Wellcome Trust has been helpful in two ways. First, by providing Shawn Lockery with a research grant during his work in Oxford and, second, through a Major Equipment Grant for the SUN computer system on which the text was typeset using TeX and Textcode. (TeX is a trademark of the American Mathematical Society, and Textcode is a trademark of Oxsoft Ltd.)

# PART I
# INTRODUCTION

CHAPTER 1

# GENERAL INTRODUCTION
*Alan Montefiore and Denis Noble*

This volume is intended to provide an interdisciplinary approach to some of the many intertangled problems connected with the identification, characterisation, understanding and explanation of goal-directed and intentional behaviour. In fact, this very opening sentence of what is 'intended' as our own introduction to our own volume also presents itself as a telling example of the problems with which we are concerned; for it contains what appears as an unabashedly straightforward declaration of would-be intention. But one of the most intricate set of issues addressed in the discussions that follow turns around the disputed significance (or lack of significance) of the fact (if it is indeed a fact) that we human beings, we speakers and writers of language, seem to be unable to argue or even to think ourselves free of such reliance on reference to or signalling of our own intentions.

This volume has, then, six authors, half of them professional scientists, half of them professional philosophers. Their contributions are not, however, to be found aligned on opposite sides of some imaginary line separating the 'scientific' from the 'philosophical' point of view. On the contrary, on just about every major issue the scientists were to be found tending towards disagreement with other scientists just as the philosophers with other philosophers, while members of each 'professional group' could look to find allies as well as dissentients from among members of the other. The lines of debate cross and re-cross that of any boundary that might be drawn to distinguish scientists from philosophers. That boundary is here more discernible in the differing experience and expertise of those who have been trained to work in either one field or the other. But even this boundary contains numerous crossing points. The scientists here involved are well read in at least some major areas of the professional philosophical literature — indeed, one of them has contributed to it; while the philosophers have been particularly concerned, so far as they are competent to do so, to take the findings of the relevant scientific disciplines into account.

However, this situation is not, it should be stressed, accidental; the interdisciplinary nature of this volume does not consist in its simply having been put together on the basis of *ad hoc* contributions specially invited from representatives of different disciplines. Rather it has its origins in successive series of seminars, together with many surrounding discussions, in which all but one of the present authors have been engaged in Oxford over the last two decades. This is not to say that any one of those five has taken part in all of those seminars and discussions. Still less should it be taken as either forgetful or unappreciative of all those many other participants who have appeared in these ongoing debates — colleagues and students alike, philosophers, psychologists, physiologists, animal behaviourists and many others — whose criticisms, objections, questions, suggestions and general stimulus have so much contributed to their enrichment. Moreover, not only is our sixth contributor, Daniel Dennett, well known to all the rest of us through his writings on our common topics; to a number of us he is known through personal encounter as well. In short, this book has grown out of a whole series of discussions between a number of people of very different backgrounds and experience but with common and overlapping concerns, and in particular the common conviction that none of those concerns has any sensible likelihood of finding satisfactory pursuit other than in such cross-disciplinary co-operation and debate. It goes without saying that the end of this book is in no way the end of our discussions. It is rather, we hope, the occasion for others to join in.

The discussions that form the background to this book have, then, been going on for what is by now a long time. For a number of the present contributors they had their origins in our several reactions to Charles Taylor's *The Explanation of Behaviour* (Routledge and Kegan Paul, 1964). The earlier seminars led to publication in various forms, including the *Analysis* debates in 1967 between Noble and Taylor, the Aristotelian Society symposium of 1971 on 'Final Causes' between Timothy Sprigge and Montefiore and parts of Anthony Kenny's *The Five Ways* (Routledge and Kegan Paul, 1969). The present book, though clearly influenced by those earlier debates, takes a largely new look at the issues, being more directly based on a renewed set of seminars (and some intensive related discussions) held in Oxford over the last three or four years.

These seminars provided an extended opportunity in which to try out ideas in a context of critical discussion. However, it did not seem sensible to try to recreate in this book the atmosphere of the seminars themselves by way of some sort of reconstructed transcript — even supposing that we might have been able to present a plausible reconstruction. We decided, therefore, to start more or less from the point that the seminars had reached. Each author was asked to write an opening chapter presenting the position that he took himself to have reached at that stage and the problems with which he was most immediately preoccupied. Once these chapters had been circulated and discussed in draft form, second chapters were written in which each had an opportunity to react to what had been produced by the others or to elaborate further on any points of his or her own which he or she wished to develop. Those draft first chapters have here been modified only to the extent of seeking to eliminate sources of distraction or unfruitful misunderstanding and to improve their presentation. In general, even though some of us may subsequently have been led to modify or even to retract some of our first chapter views or formulations, they have nevertheless been allowed to stand here in the interest of preserving the onward movement of debate. For, as will be evident enough, much of what has been written in the second chapters takes the form that it does as direct response to what had been written in the first.

What of the order in which the different contributions have been placed? It would be a mistake to attribute too much importance to it. None of us set out to write either his or her first or second contribution with any particular order already in mind, and the order on which we have finally settled was established entirely *ex post facto* in primary response to the evident necessity of having some order or another. Nevertheless, we do see real significance in our decision to place David McFarland's opening statement first, because, as a strikingly bold and articulate expression of a set of views that, in some largely unexpressed form or another, are probably taken for granted by a wide variety of working scientists, it represents a standpoint that did in fact serve as a main organising or focusing principle for many of our more recent discussions, and that still so serves in many of the discussions that are to be found in this book. Alan Montefiore's opening statement comes second because it represents, on many of the central issues at any rate, a diametrically opposed view. From there on we have simply continued by way of an alternation between scientists and philosophers that conveys very fairly the thoroughly interdisciplinary nature of our debates.

The same broad considerations apply to the ordering of the second round contributions. Its inevitable overall linearity may be somewhat misleading, however, in as much as these second round contributions are not simply and straightforwardly responses to the whole set of opening statements, but, in the case of those participants resident in Oxford at any rate, reflect also the fact that discussion among them has naturally proceeded as they have continued to work on these matters. Indeed, the best way to read these second round contributions is as both the record and the continuation of a multilateral debate, with all the internal cross-currents that any such discussions are bound to generate. If anyone should ask why any particular second round contribution takes up the particular issues that it does, while failing to take up others which, no doubt, it might equally well have taken up, the answer is again to be found in the nature of discussion itself; one inevitably tends to respond to what seems most immediately pertinent or challenging in the light of one's own immediate preoccupations. (It may also be, of course, that points are sometimes not taken up because the author concerned — wrongly perhaps — takes his agreement with them for granted, and for granted also that, in the light of his general position, his agreement must here be transparent to all.) All of us — indeed, this has been one of our main editorial troubles — keep on having further thoughts on old thoughts, or thinking of new things to say in further reaction to what has been said by one or another of our fellows. But this too is of the nature of an on-going discussion; there would be little point in inviting others to join in if one did not know it to be essentially incomplete.

Our final section differs from the first two in that it consists of one third round contribution alone. The reason for this is not — it need hardly be said — that David McFarland is the only one among us to feel the urge to return to the argument, to take up the points that have been urged against him and, in so doing, to carry forward the working out of his own position. But just as we have placed his first contribution first in recognition of the pivotal role which his (as some of us have thought, rather extreme) views have played in the development of the rest of our discussions, so it has seemed appropriate to ask him to conclude the volume with what is, very clearly, not a summing-up sort of conclusion, but rather the opening thrust of the next round of debate. For, to repeat, the topics of this debate are urgent, the discussion remains very much open and if there are here no third round contributions from the other five participants concerned, that is certainly not because they would have nothing to say in further reply.

While the results of all this, and in particular, of course, the opening statements as they here stand, reflect many of the seminar discussions, they also differ from them in certain quite substantial ways. These differences lie primarily in the fact that by the time that the contributors got down to preparing their opening statements many of the arguments that they had earlier been pursuing in the seminars themselves had virtually disappeared. These were arguments that those concerned felt to have been settled, or to have been shown to be of no substantial importance. Nevertheless, the issues in question include some on which it is important to comment here in order to help the reader pick up the threads at the point at which the published debate takes off.

A major issue of the earlier seminars, and one that remains on the surface of even much later debate, was whether the choice between teleological and non-teleological forms of explanation for the occurrence of behaviour that might in principle be specified in descriptively neutral terms, could be decided on straightforwardly empirical grounds. This question figured very largely in the debate on Taylor's *The Explanation of Behaviour*, and echoes of that debate are still to be found in Noble's opening chapter (chapter 6). It no longer, however, figures as a key issue; for there now seems to be common agreement that the distinction between the conceptual and the empirical cannot usefully or plausibly be made hard and fast in any general or overall way. Thus, in trying to develop criteria for the identification and characterisation of goal-directive behaviour, and in analysing the peculiar nature of intentional behaviour in particular, the empirical–conceptual dichotomy no longer seems to be of central importance. Still, it would be unwise to conclude from this that the earlier debate had been irrelevant. On the contrary, we have arrived at the positions that we now (however transitionally) occupy in part by virtue of having sought to work that discussion through, and of having thus been brought to believe that the question that it may always be relevant to push at appropriate moments is not so much 'Is this an empirical or a conceptual matter?' as 'Should this matter be treated in this context as depending on primarily empirical or conceptual considerations?'.

We are, hopefully, all of us much more aware than we may have been to start off with of the ways in which the uncertain delicacy of this interplay between the 'conceptual' and the 'empirical' is bound to render any working distinction between them always provisional and, in the last resort, not fully determinable. It follows from this that the ways in which we order our concepts is bound to impinge on what we may take to be the outcome of observation and experiment when we come to test our theories against the 'reality' that we are trying to identify, to understand and to explain. It may also follow that philosophers, as they work primarily on their analyses of concepts, and scientists, as they work primarily on their investigations of 'reality', have more regular and thoroughgoing need of each other's participation than present institutional habits and arrangements can easily provide for.

A second and not altogether unrelated issue that featured frequently in our earlier discussions turned around questions concerning the classification of different forms of behaviour. Is it in principle possible to draw lines between goal-directive and non-goal-directive, or more specifically intentional and non-intentional, behaviour so workably clear-cut as to enable one to say, on the basis of the most detailed observation, of any given piece of behaviour that it fell fairly and squarely into either the one class or the other? If there is in principle any way of so classifying behaviour as to achieve this result, we certainly did not find it. Perhaps it is too early for such a venture to succeed; maybe we need much more 'hard' scientific information before the basis of any such classification could be constructed. But it may also be that intentionality does not reside in particular strictly observable forms of behaviour at all, in particular kinds of feed-back loops or in certain characteristic sets of equations. At all events, even if problems of classification have not altogether disappeared, we now find ourselves much more inclined to ask not so much '*What* precise forms of behaviour, if any, are intentional?' as '*Why* are we led to make use of such intentional concepts as we do, and do we really need them for the satisfactory characterisation and explanation of certain human and perhaps other animal forms of behaviour?'

There is a third cluster of problems about which it is harder for us to be sure whether or to what extent they may have survived as a source of potential confusion for ourselves and our readers. Every specialist professional group — psychologists, physiologists, philosophers or whatever — are bound over the course of time to develop their own special vocabularies, their own bodies of authoritative texts, to which compressed reference can easily or even 'must' be made, their own technical procedures, their own peculiar use of otherwise quite common words. (Not to mention the fact that only too often members of one and the same family of specialists may use the same words in significantly different ways, the differences being rooted, as often as not, not merely in careless discrepancies of surface usage but in deep underlying differences of theoretical analysis and understanding.)

Inevitably, quite a large part of the seminar discussions between partners coming from such different disciplines was devoted simply to explaining ourselves to each other. In writing our first chapters for this book we have tried to disentangle ourselves from avoidable misunderstandings between ourselves, while yet making use of that earlier experience to enable newly participant readers to avoid falling into similar misunderstandings. How far we may have been successful in achieving this aim is for us hard to tell. On the one hand, we may have gone so far in taking for granted the elimination of sources of earlier misunderstanding as to leave them in effect as unmarked booby traps for the unwarned reader, relatively unfamiliar as he or she is almost bound to be with at least one or other set of our originally disparate assumptions. On the other hand, we may, almost certainly and despite all our previous efforts, ourselves have persisted in certain mutual misunderstandings. Some of these, indeed, actually emerge on the explicit surface of our second chapters; others, no doubt, remain for the reader to detect, if he or she can.

Part of these difficulties lies in a phenomenon of which we have become increasingly aware as we have gone along. We have already noted the impossibility in principle of establishing any hard and fast overall boundary between the empirical and the conceptual. But this difficulty is not wholly independent of one that we have noticed in trying to keep track of our own mutual disagreements and in determining the extent to which they may be 'merely' terminological or, on the other hand, substantial. In so doing we have become aware of a tendency, perhaps more natural to scientists than to philosophers, to soften the threatening outlines of looming substantial disagreement by way of an implicit mutual agreement to treat it as one of merely discrepant terminology. We would urge our readers to be similarly aware of this temptation and of this problem.

If this is a temptation that comes naturally to scientists, it may be because of the common and understandable assumption that the natural sciences are to be thought of as together contributing to one internally coherent account of the universe as a whole, and that if, therefore, two scientists actually disagree on a matter of substance, one of them must be wrong. Not all philosophers would feel themselves so sustained or constrained by any comparable view of the 'objectivity' of their branch of learning. Be this as it may, readers of this book should be warned that they must not take it too easily for granted that all of the contributors have always succeeded in using the same terms in the same consistent way as each other, even when they appear to be most directly in mutual agreement or at mutual loggerheads. Indeed, the interplay between fact and terminology is one of the most fascinating and tricky aspects of this whole area of debate.

We have already noted that in the course of the discussions to be found gathered together in this volume we have had, scientists and philosophers alike, both to spell out certain things that we should not normally feel the need to spell out at such a level of debate with 'mere' fellow professionals, and yet also at times to limit ourselves to highly abbreviated and virtually unargued statements of our own particular views on what are in fact complex and controversial matters. We have also had to leave more or less unmentioned whole bodies of debate on topics closely interconnected with those at the heart of our present concerns, but which for one reason or another have not come to the forefront in our discussions. So far as the primarily philosophical literature is concerned, one may think, for example, of the debate surrounding the mind–brain identity thesis, of the discussions concerning the analysis of such notions as 'function' and 'role', of the arguments that have been presented both for and against the hypothesis of a so-called 'language of thought', of the various theories that have been put forward and attacked as to the best way of understanding the relations between the concepts of 'reason' and 'cause' (and their analogues in other languages). There are also, of course, topics in what more generally comes under the title of moral philosophy, such as that of 'the freedom of the will', and related problems concerning the nature of responsibility, which likewise touch very closely on the issues under present discussion and around which a vast literature has built up.

It is not that such topics are not touched on, if not explicitly then at any rate implicitly, in the discussions that follow; but we should say clearly that we make no pretence of trying to engage with the extensive established literature that has been devoted to them. (Reference to that literature can, however, be tracked down by judicious use of the suggestions for further reading and by the bibliography provided on pp. 295–301, either directly or, more often, by onward reference from the works that are listed in one or the other.)

Our main aim, then, has been to forward discussion of the matters of our common concern, each with colleagues of other disciplines as well as with those of his or her own. Consequently, we should on the whole expect those of our readers with prior experience of the philosophical literature to find greatest immediate interest and stimulus in the contributions by the scientists amongst us and *vice versa*; though, from our own point of view, we take the main interest of these debates to lie in how each reacts to the other, and in the directions in which the subject is taken when philosophers and scientists of different convictions and experience discuss it seriously together. What should not be expected, however, are scholarly articles of the sort for which one might very properly look in the distinctive specialist journals of psychology, philosophy, physiology or animal behaviour. We have not here sought to advance the 'strictly professional' aspects of our subjects in that way.

But let not this disclaimer be misunderstood. We *do* believe that in the longer run each of our own professionalisms stands to benefit in essential ways from serious exchange with each others'. That is to say, we do *not* believe in the long term viability of strictly compartmentalised approaches to the understanding of human nature and the human situation.

There is another general point to which it may be helpful to draw preliminary attention. This introduction opened with a declaration of intention, a declaration that cannot, one might think, be understood other than on the supposition that those who issue it take their intention to have had at least some effective guiding influence on their production of the texts that follow. Physiological psychologists and animal behaviourists would, in the present state of the art, regard it as being an already very considerable achievement to be able to provide sufficient explanations of even relatively simple instances of apparently goal-directive behaviour of relatively simple organisms such as bees or spiders or birds. (Such organisms are already complicated enough.) Here, there are three tendencies: either actually to define those purposive concepts which one might want to apply to such behaviour in terms of those special patterns of causal interaction that seem to explain its occurrence; or to maintain that the whole concept of an intention is confused and unnecessary; or to argue that whatever intentions we may ascribe to ourselves or to others in fact play no part whatsoever in the production of the behaviour that we observe. (This is the tendency so forcefully expressed by David McFarland in his contributions to this volume.) The hope is then expressed — indeed, it may be held to as a matter of scientific faith — that in the long run all observable behaviour, including linguistic behaviour and even such linguistic behaviour as may be made manifest in the self-ascription of intentions, may be shown to be explicable in the same general ways.

Those who feel most uneasy and uncertain as to what sense may be made of such claims tend to start from the opposite end of the spectrum, and hence to argue in characteristically different ways. That is, they tend to *start* from a consideration of linguistic behaviour, from an attempt to show in what ways concepts of intentionality may be indispensable to any adequate characterisation of it (and hence to any adequate explanation of its occurrence), and then to ask whether it may perhaps turn out to be more appropriate to characterise certain forms of *non*-linguistic behaviour in nevertheless analogously intentional ways. (Alan Montefiore provides a clear example in this volume of this form of argument.)

Thus, there are at least two clearly distinguishable ways of approaching the problems. One — which may be called, more provocatively than accurately no doubt, the 'normal' scientist's way — is to start by working with familiar tools on such relatively simple areas as are most amenable to immediate study in the hope that the same methods and patterns of explanation may subsequently be extendable to all other cases, including even the most complex. The other — which, in a spirit of similar provocation and disdain of strict accuracy, may be called the more typically philosophical — is to start by reflecting on the worst, i.e. the most complex, case in an effort to establish, inevitably by conceptual rather than by experimental means, what are the minimum conceptual conditions that any adequate account must satisfy; and then to speculate on whether there might turn out to be good reason to extend the use of whatever concepts might be found to be indispensable in the worst case back down the spectrum, so to speak, to help in the better understanding of cases in which it might have seemed more possible to get by without them.

What is striking in the discussions recorded and pursued in this book is the way in which both 'sides' to this aspect of the debates have tended to move not perhaps towards agreement, but at any rate towards taking better account of each other's primary concerns; and how, in partial consequence no doubt, questions of linguistic behaviour have taken on an increasingly central role in the discussions between them.

A word should also be said about the apparent absences from our discussions. Why are there no contributions from a physicist, an expert in artificial intelligence, a psychoanalyst, for example? Part of the answer is that physicists *have* taken part in our discussions at more than one point; that while the artificial intelligence specialists whom we had hoped would be able to join us found themselves in the end unable (for practical reasons) to do so, more than one among the contributors has had more than a passing experience of the theoretical as well as the practical world of computers; that at one stage, indeed, we even had a practising psychoanalyst taking part in our meetings (and at another stage an ex-psychoanalyst now turned philosopher). Another and equally important part of the answer lies in the reminder that these discussions are simply what they present themselves as being: that is, the summing up and continuation of an on-going debate between a particular group of people, who feel the need, at the stage at which they now find themselves, to open up their debate to a wider range of participants than those to whom they happen to have easy personal access. Certainly we hope that there may be physicists, artificial intelligence people, psychoanalysts, etc. among this wider range.

If we once again mention what may fairly be called the immensity and immense variety of the specialist background to our own discussions, it is not exactly to apologise for not having tried to bring it into more explicit play. Indeed, had each of us tried first, or at the same time, to address himself or herself to his or her fellow physiologists, psychologists, philosophers or whatever, it is more than doubtful whether our own cross-disciplinary discussions could ever have got going at all. Still, we cannot but remain conscious of how much better equipped we should all be to engage in discussions of this kind of complexity and importance were each of us able to speak (and to think) out of a full and confident acquaintance with the literature and techniques of each other's special disciplines. For many practical reasons this may be a largely impossible ideal, no doubt; it is, for all that, one which it is salutary, perhaps even necessary, to keep before us.

CHAPTER 2

# PHILOSOPHICAL BACKGROUND

*Alan Montefiore*

Of the three philosophical contributors to this volume, two have written contributions which present themselves as being essentially self-explanatory, that is to say as standing in no need of any especial introduction. The ways in which they do this are to some extent different. In presenting her own explanation and discussion of the nature of the controversies in which we are all engaged, Kathy Wilkes manages at the same time to explain the terms of her own presentation; Daniel Dennett, on the other hand, finds ways of presenting and discussing the problems, as he sees them, which hardly appear to rely on or to presume any special previous philosophical experience whatsoever. I myself am thus largely alone in finding myself here relying on, even abbreviating whole stretches of my argument into, what are in effect exceedingly condensed allusions to the history of philosophy. Those who are already familiar with that history are unlikely to have any difficulty in picking them up, even if they may not necessarily agree with my reading of this or that author, this or that thesis or argument. For readers who are not familiar with that history, however, who may even have no prior knowledge of it at all, I should try to provide some clue as to how these allusions are to be taken. It goes without saying that no clue to the understanding of what are by any standard complex and controversial matters can be itself uncontroversial. Often, no doubt, the degree of controversiality of a matter may be taken as one measure of its importance. Moreover, the simpler and sparser the account, the more controversial it is likely to be. No matter; it is better to say something, however brief and simplified it may be, than to provide no clue at all. For those who are interested to discover more, there is plenty of ancillary literature to help them on their way; and even the original sources themselves often make a much better read than many may have supposed. For immediate purposes, however, only the barest of pointers must suffice.

There is one other preliminary point, however, which may also be worth making. The great majority of contemporary analytic philosophers have probably been brought up to take what is known as a 'problems approach' to philosophy. That is to say that they would find it, as it were naturally, conducive to clarity to distinguish between the articulation, analysis and discussion of philosophical problems on the one hand and, on the other hand, the history of their discussion by previous philosophers. Reference to what the greatest of previous philosophers have had to say may, no doubt, be helpful to us in our own discussions, but it is in principle no more indispensable to their successful pursuance than is a knowledge of the history of mathematics or physics to the successful teaching, learning or pursuit of those subjects. There is another philosophical tradition, however, from whose perspective the idea that philosophical problems exist 'timelessly' or outside the context of their own history, so to speak, may sometimes have some provisional pragmatic utility, but in the end involves always an illusion. For a variety of reasons, into which it would be inappropriate to enter here, I find myself in increasing sympathy with philosophers writing from this perspective; and so, speaking simply for myself, I should be inclined to see my attempt to provide some brief background unpacking of my own historical allusions as being of some potential relevance also to my colleagues' much less historically self-conscious contributions. But *that*, as I say, is an argument into which there is no call to enter here.

We may start, then, with the man whose work is often regarded as marking the birth of modern philosophy, René Descartes. In the first paragraph of page 60 I refer to the experience of 'a present which in some not fully Cartesian sense it must nevertheless deem to be undeniably its own'. What is this sense?

Descartes is famous for having sought to base the whole ordered structure of our knowledge on foundations of such certainty that no-one who contemplated them could fail to recognise them as being secure beyond all possible doubt. Such a foundation he found in the utter certainty which anyone whose attention is turned to the matter must acknowledge in his or her own existence as a consciously thinking being at each present moment at which he turns his thought thus back upon himself. 'I think, therefore I am.' Everything else, however subjectively convinced I may feel of its truth or reality, is in principle open to some kind of doubt or another. Let me try to doubt my own present existence, however, and the very gesture or act of my own self-conscious doubt, as I turn to reflect upon the problem, provides me with the irrefutable proof of its own baselessness. Such certainty cannot, on the other hand, attach to any thought that I may entertain of either my past or my future. Probable as short-term memory or prediction may be, they are, notoriously, not infallible. Similarly, I can never be one hundred per cent sure of the real existence, independently of my own apparent consciousness of them, of anything or anybody else of which or whom I seem to be aware. Of my own immediately present existence as a (self-)consciously thinking being, however, I can be utterly and indubitably certain. The 'fully Cartesian sense' in which one's own present existence is undeniable is that in which it may thus seem to be directly and unproblematically present to one's own immediate consciousness.

This Cartesian thesis is undoubtedly one of great power. Embedded within it, moreover, are a number of further equally powerful implications. One of these concerns the fundamental nature of our own temporal experience of ourselves — as, indeed, of everything else of which we may seem to become aware as falling within our field of consciousness: namely, that this experience, whatever it may happen to *feel* like, has to be thought of as essentially discrete.

The line of reasoning which leads to this conclusion can be indicated in very simple terms. As we have just noted, memory and prediction are both in principle fallible. It follows that I can never be one hundred per cent sure *either* that I have had a past — maybe God has just created me, or maybe I have simply just come into existence, at this immediately present moment, along with whatever may be my present thoughts, apparent memories and all — *or* that I shall experience a future. My present experience of myself presents me with a striking contrast to these uncertainties. It alone cannot be doubted, inasmuch as it stands by itself. It is, that is to say, whatever it is, independently of whatever the past or the future may have been or may be, independently indeed of whether there has been or will be any past or future at all. And every present moment of experience is necessarily in the same case. As Descartes himself said in his third Meditation, 'every moment of our lives is independent of every other moment'.

The British Empiricists — according to the well-established roll-call, Locke, Berkeley and Hume — in effect accepted, if with varying but increasing degrees of consistency, the two following Cartesian assumptions: (i) that all 'direct' experience is limited to the contents of our own conscious awareness, and, (ii) that each such moment of experience is strictly independent of whatever might have occurred or might occur at any other moment — that is to say that each moment of experience is complete in itself and is recognisable as such. To these they added the characteristically empiricist assumption that all the contents of our mind, all our perceptions or ideas or impressions as they were variously called, have to be understood as either constituting some 'original' aspect of experience, as thus construed, or as derived from it.

It was Hume, it is broadly fair to say, who, of the classical British Empiricists, pushed the consequences of these assumptions to their furthest limits, seeking to display the origins of even our most complex organising ideas in the 'impressions' of immediate experience and in what he took to be the natural tendency of the human mind to form habitual associations. 'Ideas' Hume took to consist of either simple copies of the 'original impressions' or more or less complex juxtapositions of such copies. In the case of 'causation', which he took to be a quite notably complex idea, and which is of course of particular relevance to our own present concerns, he sought to show its origin to lie essentially in the repeated experience of sequences of events (or, as he himself more often said, of objects) following each other with such thoroughgoing regularity as to set up settled habits of expectation that such regularities of succession would continue in the future — that is, that whenever the first member of such a sequence occurred, the second would duly follow.

It was, Hume thought, absurd to suppose that one could ever experience, as a matter of observable fact as it were, anything that might conceivably serve to link the first event, A, of such a sequence (as cause) to the following event, B, (as effect) by a tie of any greater necessity than the 'mere' *de facto* regularity of the sequence and our consequent psychologically accompanying feelings of settled expectation. For suppose that one did come to register a further impression of some sort as presenting itself with equal regularity between the occurrences of some such sequentially linked As and Bs. Given that every moment and item of experience has still to be taken as being fully independent of every other, that our perceptions are all, as Hume put it, 'separate and distinct existences', what else could the regular experience of any such intervening impression show other than that this particular regularly occurring sequence of essentially discrete but contingently associated events contained more members than supposed?

If the nature of causal connection is thus to be understood as consisting at bottom in nothing more than contingent regularity, in what Hume called 'constant conjunction', and causal explanation of particular events as consisting in their being placed in the context of whatever appropriate regularities, the Humean view that there is simply no incompatibility between the discourse of intentional action, of free will and of moral responsibility and that of thoroughgoing causal explicability or causal determinism, follows as a matter of course. For, as he points out, the freedom of intentional choice stands opposed to compulsion or constraint, while the opposite of consistent regularity in the onward course of events lies in mere randomness or chance. Mere regularity in the repeated occurrence of sequences of in themselves wholly independent events can obviously neither constrain nor compel any one event to occur rather than any other. Indeed, such regularity of *de facto* connection between the occurrence of desire or decision and that of the action desired or decided upon, far from being incompatible with deliberate or responsible agency, is, Hume points out, a necessary condition of it. For what sort of responsibility or even sanity could one attribute to an agent whose actions stood in no relation of regular connection to his own acknowledged desires or intended decisions?

Modern Humean-type analyses of the nature of causal explanation and associated Humean-type doctrines of the compatibility between causation and free intentional action have, of course, become extremely sophisticated. What I have provided here is but a thumb-nail sketch of their ancestry and their rationale. However, it may, I hope, help to clarify the sense of my allusions, on page 61 and again on page 78, to 'Humean compatibilisms'.

It is, inevitably, far harder to provide any acceptable clue — acceptably clear and yet acceptably brief — to the sense of my allusions to Kant (starting with that on page 61); for Kant's writings are, notoriously, among the most difficult of any philosopher of the Western tradition. In sketchy outline, however:

Kant saw that there had to be something wrong with the programme of showing how all our ideas are to be understood in terms of their derivation from an experience consisting of nothing but essentially discrete perceptions. Indeed, Hume himself had virtually come to realise this, as he makes clear in his Appendix to his great *Treatise on Human Nature*, where he looks back on the analysis that he had attempted in the main body of his text of the idea of personal or self-identity, and recognises that it will not do. Hume, however, caught as he was within a framework of what seemed to him to be clearly unrenounceable assumptions, could see no way out of the impasse in which he nevertheless acknowledged himself to be. For if the series of perceptions, the series of which the whole of our conscious experience is made up, is really one of radical discontinuity, from what element within it can our ideas of continuity, and most notably that of a self or subject of experience, continuous or identical with itself over the time of its own experience, ever arise?

The reply that Hume himself had attempted in the main body of his *Treatise* was that such ideas must have arisen as a result of an illusion, rather in the way in which the cinema-goer experiences an illusion of continuous movement as a result of having a series of discrete stills projected onto the screen before him with what Hume would have called an 'inconceivable rapidity'. The problem with this solution, however, is that it, the problem, immediately recurs. The very account of how such an illusion arises makes implicit but indispensable reference to some idea of an observing subject who must, of course, be one and the same (that is, continuous with itself) throughout the time of its observation of the series of discrete but rapidly successive stills. If there was no such subject, continuously identical with itself from one moment of its experience to another, there would be nobody or nothing in whom the series might produce the illusion of being itself a continuity. Only an already self-identical subject, one might say, could experience the alleged illusion of its own continuous self-identity.

Hume, as I have said, saw, or largely saw, the problem, but could envisage no solution to it. (He did express the hope that he might be able to work it out at some later moment; or thought, alternatively, that it might be something that he would have to leave to his successors.) Kant, on the other hand, may be understood as having made the radical move of taking the reference to a unitary and unifying subject to be a necessary *presupposition* of any meaningful experience whatsoever. Such a subject must be taken as unitary in the sense of being one and the same throughout the whole extent of its own experience, and unifying in that it is to be presupposed as capable of holding the different elements of that experience together in relation to each other; in so doing, it is presupposed as being itself the generative source of the continuity not only of the content of experience but, even more fundamentally, so to speak, of its own temporality and hence of its own continuous identity through time. As a presupposition of the very possibility of (any self-conscious) experience, the idea of such a subject could not itself be derived from the experience which presupposes it — any more, of course, than it could be met with as some sort of empirical content of that experience. This is the very point of treating it as a presupposition.

But this is only a start of the Kantian story. The next stages of the argument attempt (among many other things) to substantiate the following claims: (a) That the necessary presupposition of a unitary and unifying subject of all self-conscious (or potentially self-conscious) experience in turn presupposes the subject's ability to distinguish itself from its own experience; (b) That this distinction is inseparably bound up with a crucial distinction within experience between that which is subjective and that which is objective; (c) That such an objectivity cannot be understood as if it were the objectivity of a world of 'things-in-themselves', as it were, a world somehow lying behind and never directly accessible to the actual content of consciousness — for it was the absurdities inherent in any such conception that eventually led a thinker such as Hume to abandon any serious account of objectivity whatsoever, other than as a fiction (Hume's own word) of the human imagination; (d) That the objectivity of the experienciable world has therefore to be understood as resting on those powers of structural organisation which the thinking subject itself, that first necessary presupposition of all self-conscious experience, brings to the otherwise unstructured manifold of its own sense experience; (e) That these powers are simply those by which a rational being, by virtue of its very rationality, organises the contents of its thought, whatever their nature, relating one element to another — the elements here in question being those of spatio-temporal experience; (f) That we cannot think (of) the experienciable world other than in terms of these organising structures or categories; (g) That foremost among these categories, and a crucial element in the objectivity of experience, are those of a thoroughgoing causal connection and interconnection of everything that is or could even in principle be thought of as presentable to us as belonging to the world of our spatio-temporal experience; (h) That the causal relation is, therefore, not be thought of, *à la* Hume, as nothing but a matter of contingent regularity of sequential relationship between essentially independent events that may themselves be identified in wholly non-causal terms, but rather as a matter of a priori and necessary principle, a principle that is, as such, internal to the very identifiability of every experienciable object and event.

All this is, of course, nothing more than a bare list of some of the principle elements of a view of the nature of the human subject and its relations to itself and the world which demands to be argued out in complex, and inevitably controversial, detail. Clearly, there can be no question of embarking on such a project here. What is of immediate relevance, however, is to note how considerations such as these may lead very naturally to the further contention that, though our 'theoretical' knowledge is necessarily restricted to the (causally — or perhaps causally-statistically) orderable world of our experience, including even such 'theoretical' knowledge of ourselves as we may acquire through introspective observation, we nevertheless cannot coherently think of ourselves as of creatures wholly and exhaustively contained within this world.

For — apart from all other reasons which Kant also cites — the exercise of those powers of rational ordering, that active holding together of what would otherwise be the ever evanescent and hence unnoticeable moments and elements of our time and our experience, those powers, as Kant calls them, of synthesis and pure spontaneity, cannot themselves be thought of as straightforwardly equivalent to activities taking place *within* the already constituted world of temporally ordered experience. For they are activities — if 'activity' is the proper word, if there is any 'proper' word — through which that very ordering is made possible. Hence, Kant argues, although we can have no theoretical knowledge of ourselves in this way, we have nevertheless to think of ourselves as essentially dual aspect beings: not such dual aspect beings as might be part one thing and part another, but rather such as belong wholly to the natural, causal order, while yet belonging also and at the same 'time' to that other rationally self-directing order, in response to whose principled activity the natural order itself appears as the locus of our natural being.

Against this background Kant is now able — even, perhaps, constrained — in effect to argue that the 'compatibility' of a thoroughgoing causal determinism and freedom lies not in their referring simply to two quite different aspects of one and the same natural order, but rather in their reference to two quite different realms of human being, one the natural, causally fully determinate realm of everything that exists or happens in time and space and the other the realm of rational, essentially non-temporal (or pre-temporal) ordering and self-ordering spontaneity and synthesis. Kant has a whole complex of interrelated arguments devoted to showing how and why we human beings cannot but take ourselves to belong to both these two realms — at once crucially complementary and yet apparently incommensurable. We are also clearly committed to the assumption that the two realms must somehow interact, even though it seems equally impossible to understand in any convincing or even coherent detail just how this action might take place. Hence all sorts of problems, not to say, indeed, paradoxes. Hence, too, a whole history of attempts to rework the main Kantian theses in such a way as to deprive them of their combined power to force one to conclusions so uncomfortable to what is normally taken to be a rational or scientific mind. (Kant himself would have said, no doubt, that it was reason itself which led us to the recognition of its own limits, at any rate in human beings 'such as us'.) And hence also my own various references to Kant in chapter 5.

The reference to Wittgenstein on page 65 also calls for a great deal of careful unpacking, of course; but again only the most schematic of indications will have to do here. Wittgenstein is celebrated for (among many other things) the way in which in his later writings he assembles a whole battery of arguments designed to show the impossibility of a 'purely private language'. Exactly how these arguments are to be understood as working together in Wittgenstein's text is a matter of extensive, even sometimes rather fraught learned debate. However, the line of argument that is most relevant to our present purposes may be reconstructed briefly as follows.

The difference between the production of a mark or noise as a mere natural phenomenon, so to speak, and its production as a meaningful symbol lies in the fact that while natural phenomena just are whatever they are, the production of symbols is always necessarily subject to assessment as appropriate or inappropriate. That is to say that wherever meaningfulness is involved, one is committed to the presumption that one's production of whatever mark or noise may be in question may in principle be assessed by reference to some norm or rule of usage, however relatively indeterminate or open-ended such a rule or norm may be. If it made no difference to the meaning of my utterance that I should have produced one noise rather than another, if anything would go as well as anything else, then my production of a noise would be just one natural phenomenon among others and there would be no meaning to be attached to it beyond the mere fact of its occurrence (and such causal explanation of the occurrence as one might care or be able to provide).

No sense, however, can be given to this crucial idea that it must make a difference of appropriateness or inappropriateness to my production of one mark or noise rather than another, if sense cannot also be given to the possibility of my encountering some sort of check on any such (in)appropriateness. A check is not, it should be emphasised, to be thought of as any sort of certificate of guaranteed correctness. No such certificates or guarantees are in principle available. A check is not only a test, however; it is also, quite crucially, something that may *prima facie* hold me up, something that may prevent my production of any old mark or noise going through as 'appropriate' simply by virtue of my having made it. This is why a purely private system of meaning or language is in principle impossible. Only something that confronts me from outside of myself, as it were, can in principle hold me up. More specifically, according to the Wittgensteinian-type argument, only an encounter with another speaker, another participant in the same form of discourse, could provide such a check. For the non-linguistic world, left to itself, can do no other than provide a *de facto* setting for any noise or mark that I may happen to make; it is simply what it is, but, in simply being so, can do nothing to suggest that there may be anything wrong with the meaningfulness of my performance.

It is often thought that one's own memory should be able to provide all the check that is needed. But this must be a mistake. For what is memory if not a reference to the past that makes claim to be correct? But if, once again, I can give no sense to the possibility of encountering a *prima facie* check on such a memory claim, I can give no sense to any would-be distinction between the making of any old statement about the past and a genuine memory claim. The argument takes the same form as before. Without the possibility in principle of a check, there is no sense to be given to the very concept of memory.

I mention in chapter 5, but let me re-emphasise the point in advance, that this reference to the possibility of a check is to be understood as a reference not to what may be in fact practical but to conceptually envisageable possibilities. To use a term meaningfully is implicitly to know, i.e. to be capable in principle of recognising the fact, that I might have misused it. To know this it is enough for me to know that something could in principle count as *prima facie* evidence of misuse. But if this condition is sufficient, it is also, according to the Wittgensteinian argument, necessary. It is not something that one might have thought up as a possible hypothesis; it is rather a necessary *presupposition* of meaningfulness. And so, too, whatever further conditions may be necessary to my being able to conceptualise a check as a check are necessary presuppositions of meaningfulness. This is, in effect, the structure of one of the arguments that I rely on and further develop in my two contributions to this book.

It should be stressed, no doubt — for misunderstanding of this point is both natural and frequent — that the Wittgensteinian argument carries with it no suggestion that people may not think quite meaningfully 'to themselves', that they may not quite meaningfully choose not to communicate their thoughts to anybody else, or that they may not be able to do so, or that all their thinking must, if it is to be meaningful, take fully explicit symbolic form. The claim is simply that thought that is 'private' in this straightforwardly contingent sense must, if it is to be understandable as being meaningful, be connectable up with forms of expression that are open to 'public' check. Just what varied forms these connections might take is, of course, another and very complicated story.

There are two other references to named philosophers which may well seem improperly cryptic to those who may not have come across them before. On page 68 I note in brackets that 'I am here ignoring possible Parfitian complications of maybe conceivable fission and fusion and of ancestor and successor selves'. Since I am indeed here ignoring them, it might have been less confusing to have passed them over in silence. However, since I was concerned in that part of chapter 5 with what I argue to be very fundamental necessary presuppositions relating to the identity of participants in discourse over time, it seemed better to make reference, however allusive and condensed, to Derek Parfit's sustained and ingenious probing of the concept of personal identity in his book *Reasons and Persons* (and many associated papers). Parfit pursues his discussion through an elaboration of a whole series of intricate speculations as to how men might have been led to structure their ways of conceiving of such matters had the world been, or should it become, very different indeed from the way we actually take it to be now — for example (one among many), had men not only behaved like amoebae in splitting from time to time into halves each qualititatively identical with the whole which they had previously formed, but also at other times come together in transformations of fusion as those of raindrops running down a window pane and merging into each other. Anyone interested in following up such lines of thought will find amply fascinating material in Parfit's book.

On page 73 I make reference to Husserl's attempt 'to account for the nature of our inner time-consciousness in terms of retention and protention'. Again, any attempt to explain the nature of Husserl's theory of phenomenology would go wildly beyond all presently feasible limits; and likewise again, it might have been simpler to leave out any reference to Husserl. However, for those to whom the reference will mean nothing, it is enough to say that Husserl sought to show how within every act of recognition of a present moment of experience as present, there lies an inextricable implicit reference to both the other moments of time, time past and time future, with respect to the moment that is now present. There is thus, according to Husserl, no such thing as an exclusively present consciousness of the present.

Finally, I should refer to a point on which I seem to have led the publisher's (excellent) reader of the penultimate draft of this book into some (what I hope to be nevertheless avoidable) confusion. At the very beginning of her first contribution Kathy Wilkes draws attention to the distinction between intentionality and what philosophers know technically as 'intensionality'. The reader noted that I start out by focusing on intentions, but felt that I then 'rapidly allowed "intentionality" to be used in the more general technical sense (so that meaningfulness is subsumed).' My reply must be that a central part of my argument turns around the claim that the production or interpretation of meaningfulness is only possible to creatures capable of forming and following intentions — or at any rate incapable of *not* taking themselves to be capable of forming and following intentions. (My reasons for making this claim lie in the thesis that behaviour that is either productive or interpretive of meaning contains an irreducibly normative aspect, and that there is strictly no sense in ascribing normative behaviour to creatures that one takes to be wholly incapable of forming intentions.) One might put this quasi-epigrammatically, I suppose, by saying that my argument amounts to the claim that intensionality presupposes intentionality. I do not in fact put it this way in chapter 5; but the more important point is that my sticking to the term 'intentionality' was, whether right or wrong, at any rate intentional. (See also Kathy Wilkes, chapter 11, p. 195)

**Suggestions for further reading.** In theory, no doubt, the very best way of further exploring the philosophical background, for someone as yet largely unfamiliar with it, must be to go to the texts themselves and to form their own opinions from them. Even the best of historians and commentators can only introduce you to or inform you about the subject in the light of their own vision of it. In practice, most people are unlikely to have either the time or the minimum necessary initial experience to be able to find their way around the texts on their own in such a way as to be able to sort out what is of most relevant interest to them. For entry to the historical background, then, it seems most sensible to suggest a (highly selective) scatter of first-rate commentaries, all of them containing their own suggestions for yet further reading as well as guidance, each in their own way, to the bodies of the relevant texts themselves. They should at least provide accessible starting points. It goes without saying that from within the whole wide range of the currently available literature it would have been possible to suggest an entirely different and no doubt equally satisfactory list.

Anthony Kenny, *Descartes: A Study of his Philosophy* (Harmondsworth, 1968). This is a very well organised explication and discussion of Descartes' philosophy, with most useful suggestions for further reading appended at the end of each chapter. There have, of course, been twenty years of further writing since this book was first published. It remains, however, one of the greatest clarity.

J. A. Passmore, *Hume's Intentions* (Cambridge University Press, 1952). This is an even older book (and does not, in fact, contain any further bibliography of its own). It remains, however, clear and accessible, and is well focused on topics appropriate to the concerns of this book. Nevertheless, anyone interested in a more recent account may like to be referred to Barry Stroud's *David Hume* (Routledge and Kegan Paul, 1977), which also provides a readable and reliable way into the subject.

Kant is, as already noted, a far from easy philosopher and it is not at all easy to write books about him that are at once genuinely introductory and yet adequate to the complexity of the subject. Moreover, while my own view would be that the only adequate way to gain a proper sense of any major part of his enterprise is to see at least all the main works as so interrelated as to mean that the assessment of any one of them calls for some sort of reference to the others, many of the best books on Kant written in the more recent Anglo-Saxon tradition tend to concentrate almost exclusively on either one part of his writings or another. So far as his so-called theory of knowledge is concerned, Henry Allison's *Critique of Pure Reason (Kant's Transcendental Idealism)* (Yale University Press, New Haven, 1983) and Paul Guyer's *Kant and the Claims of Knowledge* (Cambridge University Press, 1987) are both excellent (although I myself do not totally agree with them) and, though by no stretch of imagination could they be regarded as 'introductions', they are both very clearly written. A book that *is* written as an introduction, and an introduction, moreover, to Kant's critical philosophy as an overall whole, is Gilles Deleuze's *Kant's Critical Philosophy*, first published in French in 1963, but translated by Hugh Tomlinson and published in English in 1984 by Athlone

Press. This is a starkly brief book, not relaxing reading, certainly, but brilliant in its overall conception and grasp. Another, perhaps more approachable if slightly less exciting introduction of similar length and scope is John Kemp's *The Philosophy of Kant* (O.U.P., 1968); Roger Scruton's *Kant*, in O.U.P.'s 'Past Masters' series (first published in 1982) is also remarkably clear and helpful as a first way in. These three introductions are written from very different points of view, and one could do a great deal worse than start by reading any two, or even all three, of them together.

For Wittgenstein and the anti-private language argument I should once again suggest Anthony Kenny and his *Wittgenstein* (Harmondsworth, 1973). This too is a work of notable clarity on a notably difficult topic. And the best way of finding out more about Derek Parfit's philosophy would be to read his own *Reasons and Persons* (Clarendon Press, 1984),

On Husserl I should suggest *Husserl, Intentionality and Cognitive Science*, a quite first rate collection of essays edited by Hubert Dreyfus in collaboration with Harrison Hall (M.I.T. Press, 1982). Again, these are very professional essays and, inevitably given the nature of the subject matter, are not easy reading. But they contain much that is relevant to the discussions of this book, and provide a very good idea of what there is that is worth further exploration in this area of the subject.

Finally, mention should be made of Charles Taylor's *The Explanation of Behaviour* (Routledge and Kegan Paul, 1964), which is the book from which many of our own discussions took off. The subject may have moved on somewhat since then; but this was a seminal book, and is still very much worth reading as such.

CHAPTER 3

# SCIENTIFIC INTRODUCTION

*Denis Noble*

'The proper study of mankind is man.' In one way or another the pursuit of curiosity in the organised form of scientific enquiry inevitably touches our understanding of ourselves. The questions become most acute at the extremes of the spectrum of sciences: theoretical physics and biology. The first raises questions about the limits of our understanding or imagination, including the extent to which we can escape from, or at least fundamentally reformulate, the categories we use. At this end of the spectrum, the 'bounds of sense', to use Strawson's description of Kant's idea that there are a priori limits to what we can say or conceive, concern the concepts of time, space, energy, mass with which we categorise the physical world. At some point we are bound to ask to what extent these depend on the fact that we are the subjects of understanding.

At the other end of the spectrum — the biological end — we become also the objects of understanding. The questions then acquire added reference to ourselves. For it is here that the issues concern the contexts in which we can meaningfully analyse ourselves while also retaining the position of the subject of understanding. This is a theme that will recur at various points in this book. It can be broken down into three questions:

1. What is it that we can infer about the basis of our own behaviour from the fact that we can meaningfully discuss the matter at all;
2. What limits might this impose on the application of the principles of the study of animal behaviour to ourselves; and

3. How might these inferences or limits alter our perception of the analysis of animal behaviour?

This introductory chapter is written in part as a guide to the way in which the scientific contributors see the issues and where their own technical language may need some explaining. This may interest our more philosophical and general readers. The chapter also acts as an introduction for scientific readers to explain why a philosophical analysis of the problems cannot be avoided. In doing this, I shall try to identify the other major themes of the discussion, to relate them to the three questions above, and to put the debate into a more general scientific context.

First it is worth asking why it should be necessary to put the scientific issues into a philosophical context at all. Indeed, many of my scientific colleagues may think not only that it is unnecessary but that it is either confusing or even condescending, depending on their point of view. Surely, some will say, the application of scientific ideas to the problems of behaviour, including that of intentionality, cannot require anything beyond an intelligent pursuit using the conceptual tools that science itself has already developed? Some would go further and say that the less we have to do with the (to them) contorted language of professional philosophy the better. Science, after all, separated itself from philosophy for good reason.

My own discipline, physiology, is one that benefited very directly from this separation. It was the insistence on experimental method and the clearing away of a legacy of a long philosophical tradition that led, via William Harvey and his successors, to the flowering of modern physiological science.

It is important, though, to realise that there is a natural limit to this process. The limit arises from the fact that we must adopt a particular philosophical position, though we may not be aware of the fact either that we are doing so, or at least that others have done so for us, in order to experiment at all. Science is not a neutral activity. It involves a highly developed set of philosophical presuppositions. In very many areas of science that may not be very evident. We feel, for example, that the range of chemical substances available to us, either naturally or by chemical synthesis, hardly depends on how we came to identify or classify them or understand their reactions. And it is significant that chemistry and its related subjects tends not to produce extensive philosophical analysis, whereas theoretical physics and biology produce philosophers and philosophical problems in abundance. One has only to think of C.S. Sherrington (*Man on his Nature*), J.Z. Young (*Introduction to the Study of Man*), P.B. Medawar (*The Art of the Soluble*) and François Jacob (*Logique du Vivant*), to name just a few of the twentieth century biologists who have made major contributions to the development of philosophical ideas. The theoretical physicists could produce a similarly impressive list.

Their existence indicates the strength of the demand for an analysis of some of the philosophical questions inevitably raised by the progress of science. And I have no doubt at all that the biology of the future will produce many more examples. They will not always declare themselves as actually doing philosophy, of course, but how else are we to fully interpret the work of, for example, the author of *The Selfish Gene* and *The Extended Phenotype*: Richard Dawkins? My purpose here is not to praise or criticise Dawkins, but rather to say that the issues about which he writes with such obvious enthusiasm as a scientist and with, I think reading between the lines, a certain impish suspicion of professional philosophy, are themselves inevitably in part philosophical questions. If you hesitate to accept this view then recall that many who we now regard as significant philosophers, including one of the modern archetypes, Wittgenstein, saw themselves at the time as reacting against what they regarded as the errors of philosophy and even, in the case of a school of thought originating with Wittgenstein (and echoed by Kathy Wilkes in this volume — see page 210), proposed its abolition. The idea was that when the problems had been satisfactorily analysed once and for all using their (linguistic) methods, the problems would disappear (the analysis therefore was better regarded as dissolving rather than solving the problems) and, if this programme could succeed across the board, the need for professional philosophy would cease.

My point in referring to this little piece of recent philosophical history in the present context is to remind some of our readers that the great majority of modern philosophy was itself a reaction against previous philosophy and that the reaction often goes so far as to identify itself as antiphilosophical. So, if you feel that the role of a scientist in these discussions is to express a certain impatience with and even separation from what you regard as philosophy, do remember that most of the major philosophers did just the same. You are not alone and you do not have to be a scientist to feel that way.

In part, this feeling, when it is expressed by scientists, is a reaction to the philosophical analysis of problems that we may feel, deep down, should more properly be regarded as 'our own'. Often, though, they are not 'our own'. They deeply concern others precisely because our activity as researchers is not a neutral one, and because it has its roots deeply set in particular philosophical traditions. That is why we cannot totally avoid philosophical questions when we start to think about the wider implications of our work. Once we start doing that we become, whether we recognise it or not, philosophers.

In doing what, inevitably therefore, is a kind of philosophy, we have two options: the first is to think that our scientific training must somehow be sufficient to the task and launch ourselves into the debate with no further preparation. Some of the worst examples of scientific speculation masquerading as philosophy have come via this route.

The other option is to recognise that there is at least a technical language that philosophers use, that it differs in its technicality from that used in science primarily in the fact that the technicality lies not so much in the addition of new vocabulary (though that does sometimes happen — an example relevant to this book would be the word intensionality spelt with an $s$ — see Wilkes, p. 159–60) as in the tighter use of existing vocabulary and modes of expression. This technicality is not arbitrary. Philosophers have developed it for good reasons. The scientists contributing to this book are well aware of that fact and that the concept of intentionality, while having its roots in ordinary discourse, is one that already has an extensive philosophical tradition that cannot be entirely ignored without risk of confusion.

The option of taking the language and tradition of professional philosophy seriously is the one that was adopted by, for example, P.B. Medawar and J.Z. Young, unquestionably two of the best biological essayists of this century. It will be evident from my own contributions to the present book where I stand with regard to these two options. Indeed, I submitted the first draft of my first chapter (*Intentional Action and Physiology*) to a professional philosopher (not one of the present authors) for a critical discussion. It did not surprise me in the least that he identified about a dozen points on which the way in which I had expressed the issues were either incoherent or would at the least have seriously misled a philosophically trained reader. On one or two points, he succeeded in convincing me to change significantly the point I was making.

The other two scientific authors of this book have also earned their philosophical credentials the hard way. David McFarland, whose position is a pivot around which much of the debate focuses, has succeeded, I think, in coming as close as anyone has to putting what many philosophers would regard as a view verging, at least, on incoherence into terms that properly engage in philosophical debate. Many scientists reading this volume will, if they are true to the traditions of their own disciplines, find strong echoes of their own position in McFarland's chapters. His is the most uncompromising position in that it takes a view (that intentions are not responsible for behaviour) that is used at least heuristically in his own and in many related areas of science. McFarland has been a member of the discussion group that gave rise to this book almost from its inception and the way in which he develops his case has its roots both in the development of his own area of science, in which he is an international leader, and in the interaction both with the philosophical authors of this book and with me as a scientist who takes a somewhat different position.

Shawn Lockery's position will be one with which many modern neuroscientists will identify. He represents a school of thought which, while it would be impatient with the dualism of the generation represented by Eccles and Sherrington, has not reverted to the simple historical alternative. On the contrary it has adopted a sophisticated and more professionally philosophical approach. During his two years at Oxford, Shawn Lockery carried out experimental research in neurobiology while also attending graduate courses in philosophy. The result is I think that the way in which he presents the modern neuroscientist's views speaks naturally to many philosophers. As he would himself readily admit, the roles of cellular neuroscientist and philosopher do not easily coexist. Indeed, the great majority of Lockery's and my professional scientific colleagues would regard our acquisition of some of the tools of the professional philosopher as a probable wasted effort. That feeling has, if anything, grown recently as many areas of neuroscience have become increasingly biochemical and molecular rather than cellular and integrative. That reflects the more strongly anti- (or non-) philosophical bias of the chemical sciences.

I am willing though to bet that by the turn of the century the tide will have turned again. As projects of the scale of the *human frontier* project (originating in Japan and aiming to let neuro- and biochemical science inform our development of the computers — if that is what we will call them — of the twenty-first-century) are developed, and as neuroscience, cognitive science and philosophy continue to interact, the interdisciplinary nature of a debate of the kind found in this book will become a strength. The problems we are discussing will not go away simply because some areas of neural biophysics have become indistinguishable from biochemistry. For the questions we are concerned with are naturally integrative.

Not surprisingly, therefore, the tension that exists between integrative and reductive approaches lies at the heart of the scientific background to the problems dealt with in this book. That tension has always existed. It was, for example, through defining the integrative concept of the internal environment (*milieu intérieur*) and its control that the nineteenth-century French physiologist, Claude Bernard, defended physiology as a discipline against the simple reductive approach of the organic chemists of the time (Holmes, 1974). A twentieth-century example of this debate centres on the tension between machine and software approaches to computer function. My own contributions to this book make extensive use of this theme.

It may therefore be helpful to comment here on 'hardware' and 'software' as technical terms used frequently in this book. Doubtless, most of our readers will understand already the distinction between the computing machine itself (the hardware) and the programs that tell it what to do (the software). What may not be so clear, but is nevertheless important to parts of our discussion, is that this distinction is not always easy to draw. Before it can control anything, software must be converted into machine states. Indeed some 'software' — such as the so-called co-processors, which are bits of hardware that greatly speed up the calculations, or greatly extend other facilities of the machine — is not actually found as software. It is as though the software to which these machine states correspond has been abandoned, while their machine-state equivalent has been permanently 'etched in' to the machine. Yet programs that make use of them are in a sense incomplete as programs without reference to a software version of what these co-processors are doing, just as pressing the 'ln' key on a pocket calculator is meaningless without an understanding of what natural logarithms are. This problem of drawing a line between software and hardware is not without its amusing aspects. Legal minds argue about what, if anything, can be copyrighted or patented. And it is significant that similar difficulties are beginning to appear as the new biotechnology industries seek to copyright or protect knowledge of bits of genetic code and cell structure.

This should warn us that the problems cannot be far away in any discussion of biological systems. Nature is opportunistic: if a hardware solution exists, it is hardly likely to develop a software solution to a developmental problem. Some neurophysiologists, such as J.-P. Changeux in his excellent *L'Homme Neuronal*, would even say that the hardware–software distinction does not apply to the nervous system.

Nevertheless, while it is necessary to bear in mind the difficulties in drawing a hard and fast line, the distinction between hardware and software is important. For it is only via software (whether left as such or etched into hardware form) that a machine can come to display rule-guided behaviour and rationality. And that is what makes the distinction important in discussing human or animal behaviour.

Moreover, calling the relevant material software does capture the essence of its nature. The softness lies precisely in the flexibility, that at the touch of a few keys it can be changed and developed. Indeed, debugging (the process of removing software faults) is precisely that: it involves selection of better and better versions until the behaviour it produces is optimal in meeting the specifications.

I used the word 'selection' here deliberately, for selection is also of central importance in biological science. And I believe the concept has a crucial role to play in some of the debates on intentionality (see p. 278). Yet it is hard to avoid some of the pitfalls of language here. The meaning of select normally implies an act of selection by a selector. Yet no such act, and certainly no such selector, is involved in the standard use of the term in evolutionary theory. We usually emphasise that fact by using the term 'natural selection'. But when does natural selection cease to be natural? What of the mechanisms that 'select' the neuronal patterns of behaviour during the lifetime of each individual? I have used the concept of selection myself in one argument of central importance to the differences to be found between my position and that of Alan Montefiore (see p. 278) but I am aware that we run close to some question-begging in using a concept that itself involves intentionality in at least some of its more natural uses: the most 'natural' use of the concept of selection is *not* involved in 'natural selection'!

It will already be clear, and not be at all surprising to most of our readers, that another group of concepts of central importance is that involved in evolutionary theory. Implicit in McFarland's use of optimality principles is that there is pressure for something, for example the efficiency of energy utilisation, to be optimised, and natural selection provides that pressure. The question that then arises is how many of the details of behaviour may be susceptible to this approach. Does intentional behaviour, for example, lie outside such pressure; or is it a mere 'cover' for such pressures — masquerading as real when it is simply a rationalisation, much as we might rationalise an act we had been 'forced' to perform hypnotically; or, again, is it possible that intentionality is itself of central importance to the recent evolutionary process? The end of my chapter 15 (p. 278) briefly broaches this issue.

Finally, there is the background of scientific use of the concept of causation. Readers will find that even the scientists here do not operate with exactly the same meaning of 'cause'. How else could two experimental physiologists, like myself and Shawn Lockery, appear to be close to conflict on the issue? He refers freely to the causal role of intentions, while a major theme of my first contribution is that they are not causes in the sense in which we talk, say, of the neural causes of movements. This is one of the discussions in this book (taken up explicitly in my second chapter) where the disagreement is at one and the same time less and more important than it may seem. Less important because Lockery and I will be found not to be in serious disagreement on the issue once certain arguments are taken into account. Yet it is also more important because in clarifying the matter we have come to take a more subtle view of the concept of causation. This is a theme that also emerges clearly in Kathy Wilkes' second chapter (chapter 11), which forms a valuable review of the way in which we have manipulated some of the central concepts of causation, explanation and laws, amongst others. Anyone who is puzzled by some of the ambiguities and possible contradictions in and between the other chapters would do well to refer to this chapter in order to stand back from the discussion and ask, as Kathy Wilkes does, what it is all about.

These then are some of the scientific issues and their philosophical counterparts that are relevant to an understanding of where this book draws some of its arguments. This introduction is not intended to cover all the matters that might, with profit, be laid before the reader in a tentative way before he plunges into the real debate. It is intended rather to indicate the kind of issue that is relevant, and to prepare the reader for the somewhat different scientific perspectives he will find in this book.

# PART II
# THE POSITIONS STATED

CHAPTER 4

# GOALS, NO-GOALS AND OWN GOALS

*David McFarland*

Animal (and human) behaviour often looks as though it is purposive in the sense that it appears to be aimed at a particular goal. In this essay I distinguish between goal-achieving, goal-seeking, goal-directed and intentional behaviour. These are all instances of purposive behaviour, some by design and others by cognition. I will try to clarify these distinctions, and will call into question the common-sense view that intentions influence behaviour.

## Preview

Examples involving animal behaviour often arise in philosophical discussions of teleology and purposiveness. To me these often seem somewhat naive, not because of inaccuracies of behavioural detail, but because the examples give a simplistic account of what is really a complex matter. For instance, Woodfield (1976) uses the following example:

> A man is standing on a river bank watching a rat swim across to the far side. The rat is steadily swimming towards that part of the bank which is nearest the food. The man frames the judgement that the rat is swimming across the river in order to get the food. For the man, this teleological judgement is a hypothesis ... The man is not judging that the rat will get the food, or even that it will reach the river bank. Another rat may reach the food first or the swimming rat may drown ... So if any prediction is entailed by the teleological description it is

one of the following nature, 'The rat will get the food provided that no obstacles prevent it' (Woodfield, 1976, p.92).

Whether or not the man forms a teleological hypothesis about the rat's behaviour may depend upon his philosophical outlook. It may also depend upon his attitude to animal behaviour. It would not be beyond the bounds of ethological credulity to postulate that the rat may decide, having experienced the strength of the current, that the food is not worth the effort. This possibility introduces an entirely new element into the discussion.

The simple teleological hypothesis implies that the rat aims to get the food at all costs and will fail only on account of insurmountable obstacles. This scenario has the advantage that the issue is compartmentalised. The food-seeking behaviour of the rat can be considered in isolation from the rest of the animal's behavioural repertoire. In real life this will never be the case, and a more realistic hypothesis is called for.

The more naturalistic hypothesis supposes that the rat will get the food provided that it is able to and provided that the rat continues to judge that the project is worthwhile. Here we have a new ingredient in the form of a different kind of goal. To be worthwhile an activity must be accountable in terms of some economic goal involving time and energy expenditure. Woodfield (1976) implies that the rat takes the shortest or quickest route towards the food. But this is not a necessary condition for attaining the food. If the rat's goal is simply to attain the food then it can take any route. If its goal is to attain the food by the most direct route then there are really two types of goal: (1) attaining the food, and (2) satisfying some economic criterion. In considering animal behaviour, the economic considerations should be taken seriously, because in real life no activity is undertaken in isolation from other possible activities. To assume that an animal's goal is simply to attain food is unrealistic. Even the guided missile, a favourite example of goal-directed behaviour, is not immune from economic considerations. Guided missiles working on negative-feedback principles are capable of goal-directed behaviour (see below). The design of the missile is, however, subject to strict performance criteria. For most missiles these criteria are designed to ensure that the target is reached as quickly as possible. The missile is thus goal-directed in two senses: (1) to reach the target, and (2) to minimise the flight time and fuel expenditure. The reason that missiles are designed this way is that the designers do not have to worry about only one missile, but the whole missile program. This program is in competition with other government programmes for the limited resources of money, manpower, and materials.

Just as the individual missile is tailored to fit into the missile program as a whole, so the individual item of goal-seeking behaviour is designed by natural selection to fit into the animal's overall behaviour program. In this essay I argue that, if we take the economic considerations seriously, we find that the traditional goal concept, which involves internal representation of a desired or required state of affairs, is unnecessary in accounting for animal behaviour. In other words, it is possible that this widely used type of model is incorrect, unverifiable, and misleading.

## Teleological hypotheses

People readily form teleological hypotheses about their own behaviour, about the behaviour of other people, and about the behaviour of animals. From introspection and observation they form judgements about the purpose of the behaviour. This is a commonsense approach to animal behaviour, not a scientific one. The common sense approach presupposes that the observer can identify the goal in advance. The observer's hypothesis about the goal is reinforced if the animal's behaviour changes when it reaches the goal. It is further reinforced if the animal took the shortest of various possible routes to the goal, if it appeared to overcome obstacles in reaching the goal, or if it appeared to be frustrated or disappointed in failing to reach the goal.

How can the observer identify the goal in advance? There are a number of generally recognised ways, including previous experience of the animal in similar situations, manipulation of the animal's situation, and preindications by the animal. Thus previous experience may lead to an inference about the predatory purpose of the fox approaching the chicken run. If the fox is initially observed some distance from the chicken run, and its footprints in the snow indicate that it took the shortest route to the run, then it might be reasonable to suppose that the fox went to the chicken run on purpose.

If the farmer's dog barks and growls in the direction of the chicken run at the time of night that the fox usually visits, then one possible hypothesis (among others) is that the dog is giving a preindication that, if released, it would dash to the chicken run with the purpose of chasing the fox. If, when released, the dog did just that behaviour, then the hypothesis would be reinforced.

If, woken by the barking dog, the farmer tells his wife that he intends to go to the chicken run to see about that fox, it would normally be supposed that the farmer was going with the purpose of investigating the possibility that the fox might be visiting. If the farmer then goes to the chicken run, we tend to assume that he goes on purpose, that is his behaviour is directed by the preconceived intention of checking the situation at the chicken run. We say that his behaviour is goal-directed, meaning that a (mental) representation of the goal (checking the chicken run) is instrumental in guiding his behaviour.

How are we to move from a commonsense approach to a scientific one? We have, somehow, to find a way of verifying hypotheses. There is a danger, here, of becoming mixed up over terminology. In this essay I use the term goal-directed to indicate behaviour (of a human, animal, or machine) that is directed by reference to an internal representation of the goal-to-be-achieved. By directed I do not mean that the behaviour is absolutely determined by reference to the (internally represented) goal. The behaviour will be subject to outside disturbances, which may or may not be corrected for. By directed I mean that the behaviour is guided or steered towards the goal.

By goal-representation I mean a physically (or physiologically) identifiable (in principle) representation that is 'explicit' in the sense of Dennett (1982–3) and Wilkes (this volume). By intention I mean that there is an explicit goal-representation which is in some way instrumental in controlling the behaviour of the animal, or person.

Let us now return to the fox's visit to the chicken run and look again at our reasons for supposing that the behaviour of the participants is goal-directed. Our past experience tells us that when the fox visits the chicken run it kills some chickens. If it fails to kill on one occasion then it soon visits the chicken run again. If it succeeds it does not visit the run again for some time. There is no question that chicken is the goal of the fox's behaviour. However, we have no real evidence that the fox is directed in its behaviour by a representation of this goal. The fox's behaviour is goal-achieving, it may even be goal-seeking, but we can claim it as goal-directed only if we can show that there is a goal-representation involved in the control of the behaviour.

When the dog senses the fox and gives an apparent preindication of its motivation to chase it, how can we be sure that its behaviour is goal-directed. If, when the dog is released it chases the fox, our hypothesis that the dog was barking because of the fox is confirmed, but are we justified in concluding that the dog's behaviour is goal-directed? If we can explain the dog's behaviour without postulating a goal-representation, then we would have an alternative to the goal-directed hypothesis, and we would have to think of some way of distinguishing among the possible alternatives.

When the farmer tells his wife that he intends to investigate the situation at the chicken run, and subsequently does just that, it would seem that we have a clear-cut case of pre-indication of goal-directed behaviour. Can we be sure, however, that the farmer's stated intention is sufficient evidence of intention, if we conclude that the dog's pre-indication is not sufficient evidence of goal-direction?

In order to move from a commonsense view to a scientific view of apparent intentional behaviour, we need to establish a number of things: (1) We need to establish the essential features of the goal-directed explanation of behaviour. (2) We need to establish whether alternative explanations are possible. (3) We need to establish the nature of the evidence that might enable us to distinguish between goal-directedness and its alternative(s). (4) We need to establish why the common-sense view is so prevalent and persuasive. In this essay I will attempt to address the questions raised here.

## Goal-directedness and doubts

A system can be goal-achieving or goal-seeking without being goal-directed. A goal-achieving system is one which can recognise the goal once it is arrived at (or at least change its behaviour when it reaches the goal), but the process of arriving at the goal is determined by the environmental circumstances.

A goal-seeking system is one which is designed to seek the goal without the goal being explicitly represented within the system. While it can always be said that the goal must be somehow represented, since there must be features of the system that are responsible for the goal-seeking behaviour, the representation is more apparent than real. This tacit form of representation (Dennett, 1982–3) is essentially a collection of distributed parameters, such as form the structure of any system. Tacit representations are not independent of the system being controlled in the way that explicit representations are.

Goal-achieving systems can be based upon a dynamic equilibrium of various forces operating within the system. In engineering terminology these are sometimes called passive control systems. In the biological sciences this type of system has often been suggested as an alternative to the goal-directed explanation of physiological regulation and animal behaviour (see McFarland, 1989 for details).

The goal-directed system has an explicit representation of the goal-to-be-achieved, which is instrumental in guiding the behaviour. An intentional system is a form of goal-directed system in which there is a mental representation of the goal-to-be-achieved. (note that this is a narrower definition of an intentional system than that of Dennett, 1987) In addition to its role in guiding behaviour, this representation may have other roles, and is probably particularly important as a basis for language. Despite the popularity of this model, I have doubts about its veracity. I will now attempt to draw together these doubts.

My first doubt is that when we see goal-achieving behaviour it is natural for us to assume that it is goal-directed. I suspect that we make this type of assumption because we normally communicate in teleological terms. Introspection tells us that much of our own goal-achieving behaviour is intentional, and we tend to assume that the behaviour of other people, of some animals, and even of some machines, is similar. Our introspection may be misleading, for good evolutionary reasons which I will discuss later. Even if our introspection is a good guide to our thinking on some teleological matters, it is certainly a poor guide on others. More than a hundred years after the publication of Darwin's *Origin of Species*, it is still necessary to convince many people that evolution is not purposive, but takes place as a result of a simple goal-achieving process, called natural selection. So pervasive is the tendency to assume that goal-achieving phenomena are purposive, that some biologists (e.g. Dawkins, 1986) go to considerable lengths to persuade the layman otherwise. It is not self-evident to me that introspection can be relied upon to point the way to the workings of human, or animal, motivation. I find it disturbing that so many writers on teleological matters take as their starting point the 'evident' goal-directedness of human behaviour.

My second doubt is similar to the first in that it concerns our predilection for goal-directed explanations. The problem is that many model-makers, having found one way of solving the teleological problem, namely the goal-directed, negative feedback model, proceed to apply it to all possible situations. Ever since Rosenblueth et al. (1943) discovered that goal-achieving behaviour could be readily explained in terms of negative feedback, this approach has become very fashionable. We see it in studies of animal motivation (e.g. Toates, 1986), human psychology (von Cranach and Harré, 1982), and artificial intelligence. The goal-directed model is used where it is difficult to think of an alternative, but this does not mean that there are no alternatives. What started as an heuristic, became a band-wagon, and is now in danger of becoming a dogma. My third doubt concerns the nature of the evidence for the type of explicit representation that is necessary for goal-directed behaviour. I do not think that it is possible to find conclusive evidence on behavioural grounds alone (basically, because a behavioural model can never be unique (McFarland, 1983, 1989)), and I know of no convincing physiological evidence. Indeed, I agree with Noble (this volume) that there are good reasons for doubting that physiological evidence can ever be found. It is sometimes argued that certain aspects of behaviour are in themselves evidence of goal-directedness. These include persistence, plasticity and disappointment. However, behaviour indicative of persistence and disappointment are easily accounted for without recourse to any notion of goal-directedness. When the consequences of behaviour differ from normal, the animal initially 'tries harder', persists, or shows 'behavioural inertia'. Such phenomena are commonplace, and various explanations have been offered (for a review see McFarland, 1989). The notion of differing from normal may seem to require an explicit representation of the normal. This is a feature of some explanations, but it is not a necessary feature. After the initial period of 'trying harder' animals often show signs interpreted as disappointment, frustration, etc. Again, there have been many explanations offered, and only some of these involve explicit representation of the 'expected' outcome of the behaviour.

A classic feature of goal-directed behaviour is plasticity. This is the ability to choose among alternative routes to the goal according to the prevailing circumstances. Many have regarded plasticity as evidence of purpose (e.g. Braithwaite, 1946–7, 1953), and the subject has aroused a diversity of opinions. Many of the arguments concerning plasticity and teleology are reviewed by Woodfield (1976). I do not wish to enter these here; but, because plasticity is regarded by others as an important issue, I will briefly outline my own position.

I am willing to accept plasticity as evidence that the behaviour has a goal, but because it can occur in both goal-achieving and goal-seeking systems, I do not see how it can be taken as evidence of goal-directedness. Plasticity shown by a goal-achieving system is nothing more than evidence of redundancy in the design of the system as a whole. Thus the embryo may take alternative developmental routes, a phenomenon called equifinality (Bateson, 1978). In this, and in other goal-achieving systems, natural selection has acted as a designing agent in providing the alternative routes.

Plasticity can also be shown by a goal-achieving automaton. For example, insects show plasticity of gait, and an individual can modify the pattern of leg movement according to the speed of locomotion, or in response to the loss of one or two legs. It has been discovered, however, that the coordination of leg movement follows a simple set of rules, which can account for a variety of gaits, even those shown by insects that have lost legs (Wilson, 1966). This is an example of a system designed (by natural selection) with built-in contingent behavioural alternatives.

These doubts would have remained dormant if there were no alternative ways of explaining goal-achieving behaviour. Not only do I maintain (above) that there are possible alternatives, but it seems to me that the goal-directed model seems to be incompatible with another important principle currently employed in the explanation of animal behaviour. This is the trade-off principle, to which I now turn.

## The trade-off principle

Ethological explanation of animal behaviour seeks an account in terms of both proximal cause and evolutionary function. The argument may be outlined as follows: We can expect natural selection to shape the decision-making mechanisms of animals in such a way that the resultant behaviour sequences tend to be optimally adapted to the current situation. On these grounds we would expect animal choices to be transitive and, therefore, some entity will be maximised as a result of decision-making processes in animals.

The maximised entity will be closely related to Darwinian (inclusive) fitness (McFarland, 1977; McFarland and Houston, 1981; Krebs and McCleery, 1984).

This is a brief outline of a complex argument which can easily be misunderstood. It is important to understand that the question 'What does it mean to say than an animal is behaving optimally?' has a number of different meanings.

Firstly, an animal may, or may not, be behaving optimally with respect to natural selection. There are good grounds for expecting animals to spend their time in a manner which is most likely to maximise their fitness (Maynard Smith, 1978). However, this does not mean that the individual animal will always behave optimally in its natural environment. Genetic variation between individuals, the patchy nature of the environment, and evolutionary lag, all combine to make it very unlikely that the individual animal could ever be perfectly adapted to its niche. Nevertheless it is useful to imagine an animal that is perfectly adapted, because we can then specify what an animal would have to do to be perfectly adapted. The answer, in general terms, is that the animal would have to employ a form of dynamic optimisation such that its behaviour always satisfied the optimality criteria embodied in the cost function (McFarland and Houston, 1981).

The cost function is characteristic of the environment, in the sense that it reflects the selective pressures that moulded the optimality criteria during the course of evolution. The cost function, therefore, specifies the instantaneous level of risk incurred by (and reproductive benefit available to) an animal in a particular internal state, engaged in a particular activity, in a particular environment (McFarland, 1977). The 'perfectly adapted animal', by deploying its behavioural options so as to continuously maximise a particular mathematical function (called a Hamiltonian and including the cost function), achieves that behaviour sequence which maximises its inclusive Darwinian fitness in the prevailing circumstances.

Secondly, the animal may or may not be an optimising machine in the sense that its behaviour conforms to a set of optimality criteria that are embodied within the animal itself. This has been referred to as the goal function (McFarland and Houston, 1981). The goal function is envisaged as a property of the individual animal, and can be expected to differ from one member of the species to another. The individual animal is seen as an optimising machine designed to maximise a particular entity (the Hamiltonian) which includes the goal function.

The goal function will include those properties of the animal which are relevant to the notional costs associated with the various causal states and with the various aspects of behaviour. These may include physical properties of the animal as well as evaluations represented in the brain. For example, a person travelling across town on foot has to make decisions as to when to rest, to walk, to jog, to pause, etc. The goal function will include factors associated with the person's energy reserves, the risks of crossing roads, etc. It would also include some more physical factors, such as the length of the person's legs (thus affecting the natural walking pace). Optimal decisions betwen jogging, walking, pausing and resting will inevitably be affected by all these factors, and will result in a trade-off between rates of energy expenditure and speed of travel.

Thirdly, let us now look at the situation from an investigator's point of view. We must suppose that the investigator has been able to characterise the system by means of a set of equations, which provide a description of the animal's state (at least in its important respects) and are capable of predicting what changes in state will result from a particular behaviour pattern. In asking whether or not the animal is an optimising machine, the investigator has various options. If it can be established that the choices made by the animal are transitive, then the way is open to investigate the (goal) function that is being maximised. An alternative approach is to assume that the animal is an optimising machine and to test hypotheses about the goal function by using optimality theory to predict the behaviour of the animal under the given circumstances. This is called the inverse-optimality approach (McFarland and Houston, 1981). In order to avoid confusion, the hypothesised goal function is called an objective function. The aim of the inverse-optimality exercise is to establish that a particular objective function can account for the observed behaviour of the animal. The question may then arise as to whether there is another objective function which could also account for the behaviour. We may call this the objective-uniqueness problem.

We can now return to the question of what it means to say that an animal is behaving optimally. There are three basic possibilities. Firstly, an animal may be supposed to be behaving optimally with respect to natural selection. This is tantamount to asking whether the behaviour conforms to a particular cost function. Secondly, an animal may or may not be an optimising machine in the sense that its behaviour conforms with some goal function. A further distinction, which is discussed below, is that the animal may be behaving in an overall optimal manner or may only be behaving optimally with respect to a given set of constraints. Thirdly, an animal may appear to be behaving optimally if its observed behaviour can be shown to conform to a particular objective function. Once again, there may be a distinction between the overall behaviour and the constrained optimum. The question also arises as to whether an animal that can be shown to be behaving optimally with respect to an objective function, is necessarily behaving optimally with respect to a goal function.

An inevitable consequence of the optimality approach to animal behaviour is that there will be trade-offs among alternative courses of action. The logic of this conclusion is fairly simple. If the conditions relevant to only one activity pertain at a particular time, then the optimal policy is straightforward. The animal engages in that activity and optimises its pattern of behaviour with respect to the use of energy, time, etc. For example, the optimal behaviour for a hungry pigeon faced with a source of food is to eat at a negatively accelerating rate (Sibly and McFarland, 1976; McCleery, 1977). If the conditions relevant to two (or more) activities apply simultaneously, then the animal has to choose between them. Moreover, its state when one activity is possible is not the same as its state when two activities are possible, and so the optimal behaviour for one activity in the presence of the other possibility is not the same as for that activity on its own.

The argument may be summarised as follows: Natural selection has designed animals not to pursue a single goal at a time, but to pursue a course of action which is optimal in relation to a large number of internal and external factors. The result of this design is a continual trade-off among the costs and benefits of various possible activities. This is probably accomplished by following a complex set of rules. The result is that behaviour is directed, not by any goal-representation, but in a holistic manner which takes into account all (relevant) aspects of the animal's internal state, and of the (perceived) external situation. It may help, at this point, to bring this line of argument to bear on a particular example. To avoid caveats relating to the special circumstances of particular species, I have chosen the domestic robot as the exemplar.

## The optimising robot

We can imagine a robot designed to carry out the cleaning and cooking chores in an American kitchen. The robot has to make decisions about its use of time: when to stop cleaning the floor, what chore to do next, etc. A well-designed robot will embody a goal function which relates the different options to a common currency. That is, it specifies the extent to which adopting each option contributes to the maximised entity. We can suppose that the robot is designed to maximise some notion of efficiency, involving work done per unit time, per unit of energy expenditure, etc. The goal function is a design feature of the robot, but this does not mean that it is explicitly represented in the robot's brain. Many aspects of the design are relevant to the goal function, such as the diameter of the wheels, length of arms, etc. In other words the goal function is tacitly represented, and is an emergent property of the design as a whole.

The robot can behave absolutely optimally, with respect to its goal function, only if it has complete freedom of action. In reality there will generally be constraints upon the robot's behaviour. The amount of energy available may be limited so that energy spent on one activity is subtracted from that spent on another within a given time period. The rate at which chores can be performed may be limited both by the nature of the environment and by the physical features of the robot.

The state of the robot in conjunction with the goal function specifies the optimal course of action, but because of the constraints inherent in the situation, the robot may not be able to follow that course of action. Therefore we have to distinguish between the optimal solution to the problem presented by a particular situation, and the optimal attainable solution. The robot may be doing its best, but its best may not be the best possible behaviour relevant to the situation.

The robot is designed to operate in a completely standardised American kitchen. The kitchen is an unvarying environment, except in a trivial sense, so the robot does not have to adapt its behaviour by learning. Assuming the robot is optimally designed, its goal function will be identical to the cost function that is characteristic of the American kitchen. In this example, the cost function specifies the costs and benefits in terms of some measure of efficiency. The optimally designed robot is perfectly adapted to the American kitchen and will always carry out its duties in the most efficient manner.

Suppose, now, that the robot is transferred to a French kitchen and that the cost function characteristic of a French kitchen is different from that of an American kitchen. The robot will continue to behave in concordance with the notional costs and benefits embodied in its own goal function. It will still be an optimising machine, but it will not be behaving optimally from the point of view of the French cost function. In French eyes it would not appear to be an efficient machine, and it would not do well in the French market.

To a certain extent the robot could learn to adapt to the new environmental circumstances. It could learn to alter the constraints on its behaviour, so as to perform better in terms of its own goal function. An interesting question is — could the robot learn to alter its own goal function to make it more like the cost function of its new environment? An animal which could do this would greatly increase its overall fitness. However, we have to remember that all learning must be based on feedback from the consequences of behaviour that can be evaluated in terms of a set of criteria. In ordinary learning these criteria are provided by the goal function. Learned modification of the goal function could not, of course, be based on information about the cost function, unless we are prepared to allow that the animal understands the evolutionary function of its own behaviour. In other words, the goal function is a fixed property of the robot which cannot be modified by learning, except where the learning is entirely preprogrammed. In animals some learning is evolutionarily preprogrammed in the sense that the juvenile is predisposed to learn certain types of things, such as the nature of its habitat, its parents, their language. Such learning could involve a contingent change in the goal function (McFarland and Houston, 1981). Thus a very sophisticated robot could embody a rule such that when in a French kitchen it automatically switched to a preordained goal function.

Ignoring this finesse, we can see that, when operating in the environment for which it is designed, the robot can maximise efficiency by sequencing its behaviour in an optimal manner, within the limits set by the constraints inherent in the situation. In an alien environment we can expect the robot to adapt to a small extent but its behaviour will fall short of perfect because of the constraints on its behaviour and because of the discrepancy between its goal function and the cost function characteristic of the situation.

These are circumstances that normally face an animal in its natural environment. There are always constraints upon its behaviour which necessitate a certain amount of budgeting of time and energy. The environment nearly always differs from that for which the animal evolved, because of the evolutionary lag (natural selection takes time to catch up with environmental changes) and competition (which displaces the animal from its preferred habitat). In addition, the evolutionary stable strategy may result in a sub-optimal solution to a particular problem (Dawkins, 1980).

Suppose we now ask how the robot is internally organised. The most obvious simple organisation would be for the robot to have different programmes for different chores. It would then have a set of criteria for deciding which program to implement at any particular time. The decision-making process would rely on information about the robot's internal state, including the state of its fuel reserves, its memory of tasks recently accomplished, etc; and on information about its environment, including the untidiness of rooms, the time of day, etc. The decision-rules would involve such factors as the urgency of different tasks, their fuel costs, etc. The rules would also have to incorporate some optimisation principle. For example, suppose the robot rated each task on the basis of two independent indices: an index of task urgency and an index of fuel costs. We have to remember that fuel costs per unit time spent on a task will tend to be reduced as the total time spent is increased. This is because there will inevitably be a cost of changing between tasks. Thus, on the one hand it is better not to leave tasks unattended for too long (the urgency factor), while on the other hand, it is more fuel-efficient to change between tasks as little as possible (the fuel-cost factor). As in most decision-making problems there has to be some trade-off among opposed alternatives. The outcome of the trade-off depends upon the decision-rules, and the optimality criteria they embody.

Having decided which task to engage in, the robot starts work. It is here that we might suppose the robot's behaviour to be goal-directed. According to this view, the robot would have an explicit internal representation of the goal-to-be-achieved and would monitor its progress by reference to this goal. Such a model can work satisfactorily if we consider only one task at a time. In real life, however, the robot is considering many tasks simultaneously. To handle this the model has to consider some form of competition and choice among alternative goals, but it is here that goal-directed theory starts to run into trouble.

The problem becomes apparent when we consider what is to make the robot stop a particular task and start another. One scenario, with which the goal-directed approach has no difficulty, is that the robot changes to a new task if another goal suddenly becomes more important than the goal it is currently pursuing. When the baby spills ink on the carpet, the robot immediately recognises this as an urgent task, drops whatever it is doing and deals with the emergency. In the normal course of events, however, we have to ask whether we want our robot (1) to finish one task before starting another (this is difficult to engineer because it requires a lock-out mechanism which may prevent the robot from responding to emergencies); (2) to change to a new task when the importance of the current task drops (as a consequence of the robot's behaviour) below the level of an alternative goal (this means that tasks will rarely be completed); (3) to change to a new task when the balance of considerations, including the cost of changing to another task, favours the change. A sophisticated version of this arrangement employs a complex set of trade-off rules. Their implementation makes the goal-representation redundant, because it has little or no controlling role to play (see McFarland, 1989, for a more detailed discussion). Goal-directed behaviour is defined (above) in a way that requires the goal-representation to be instrumental in guiding the behaviour. If the behaviour is determined entirely by trade-off considerations, then the goal-representation cannot be guiding the behaviour. Therefore, the behaviour is not goal-directed. I shall argue (below) that, in talking robots, the goal-representation does have a role to play, but it is not a behaviour-guiding role.

A robot designed to make decisions entirely on the basis of trade-off principles will always be more efficient than a robot designed otherwise. The designer cannot avoid the issue, because the robot has to be able to change from one task to another. Psychologists and philosophers have avoided the issue in the past, because they tended to concentrate on one task at a time. Their models were the equivalent of one-task robots. Optimality theory tells us that the best design is to continuously trade-off among all important criteria. The effect of this design when implemented in a robot will be easily recognisable. The robot will sometimes concentrate on one task until it is finished, but at other times it will interleave tasks. The recent applications of optimality thinking to animal behaviour indicate that this is what animals do. Thus pigeons which are both hungry and thirsty, and placed in a position where they can work for food or for water, do not complete one task before starting the other. They interleave the two in a manner that can be accounted for in terms of optimisation (Sibly and McFarland, 1976). Foraging sticklebacks change their pattern of predation when there is danger from predators. They achieve an optimal trade-off between attention to prey and predators (Milinski and Heller, 1978; Heller and Milinski, 1979). Similarly, great tits change their pattern of foraging when their territory is threatened by intruders. They increase their vigilance at the expense of their food intake rate (Ydenberg and Houston, 1986).

My claim is that the behaviour of individual animals (and people) is guided, not by any goal-representation, but by myopic hill-climbing behaviour. An illustration of how this can work is given by Sibly and McFarland (1976). Each animal evaluates the situation for itself in accordance with its goal function (i.e. the goal function sets a value-scale on each relevant variable). This evaluation process forms the hill, which the animal then proceeds to climb, maximising height subject to the prevailing constraints. Any change in the situation changes the nature of the hill (i.e. a re-evaluation takes place).

Hill-climbing by gradient-maximising is a means of achieving goals that does not involve any goal-representation. An argument sometimes levelled against the hill-climbing model is that it works only for short-term goals, because it is not capable of going down a small hill in order to climb a larger hill. This criticism is valid in a landscape in which there are many hills. In our landscape, however, *there is only one hill*. We are dealing with systems designed by natural selection, in which the overall objective is to maximise inclusive fitness. Natural selection is itself a goal-achieving process with a single objective. It is true that in the genetic landscape there is more than one hill, and that individuals within a population may be subject to selective forces relevant to different hills. This argument is not relevant here, because we are interested in individuals. It is the individual's goal function that determines the nature of the hill. Goal functions are notional cost functions (see above), and it may be the case that there is bimodal variation among both the cost and goal functions relevant to the members of a population. This does not alter the fact that the goal function of an individual is immutable, and will have been designed as if there were a single hill in the genetic landscape.

The animal, or robot, surveys the options available at each point in time. These change according to the external circumstances and the animal's internal state. The options present themselves already evaluated in various ways. In the case of our robot, the evaluations will be preprogrammed. In the case of an animal, they will be partly preprogrammed and partly learned. What is evaluated is not the precise situation, but the operating range of the relevant variables. For example, an important variable in a robot is the state of the fuel reserves. Very likely (for reasons discussed by McFarland and Houston, 1981, p. 111), the value attached to the fuel reserves will be the square of the deficit. In weighing the options the robot will take account of this value, as well as the value attached to the variable indicating the proximity of the fuel source. Thus the priority given to the refueling option in competition with other behavioural options will depend jointly on the state of the reserves and the availability of fuel. Exactly how these two factors combine (i.e. the combination rule of McFarland and Houston, 1981) is a matter of design.

## The talking robot

Suppose we imagine two robots sharing the household chores. To do this effectively, they would have to communicate with each other. Let us suppose that they were designed to communicate in the English language. What would they have to say to each other?

Much would depend on whether the robots were designed to compete or co-operate. If one robot had full information of the internal state of the other, it could behave as though the other's state were part of its own state, and could organise its behaviour accordingly (assuming the two goal functions were the same). This would be the ideal situation for cooperating robots, but not for competing robots. As in animal behaviour (Dawkins and Krebs, 1978), it is in the interests of competing robots to control the information about internal state that is made available to others. Honesty is not always the best policy. It is in the interest of the individual robot to save time and energy by allowing the other robot to carry the greater burden of the household chores. As in the case of the single robot, we can expect there to be a trade-off between the benefits of keeping the house clean (to prevent competitive invasion from another species of robot) and the benefits of economising (thus costing less than a rival of the same species). 'What are you going to do next?' says robot A to robot B. An honest robot might reply 'My top priority, as determined by my internal state and my perception of the kitchen, is to do the washing up. My second priority is to make the beds, and my third priority is to clean the kitchen floor. However, because of the cost of going upstairs, I will probably do the washing up, and then clean the kitchen floor before making the beds.' A less honest robot might reply 'I intend to do the washing up'. If this were a complete lie, then robot A would soon learn that B was not to be believed, and B's utterances would become devalued. If the washing up were indeed B's top priority, then it might be better to say 'I intend to do the washing up' than to be completely honest. If B did not complete the washing up, and was challenged by A, B could say that the statement of intention was genuine, but that B had subsequently realised that some other job should be done instead. In fact, B may have known all along that the washing up would not remain B's top priority for long. The question of honesty in animal communication has received considerable attention (e.g. Dawkins, 1982; Mitchell and Thompson, 1986; Rohwer and Rohwer, 1978; Trivers, 1985; de Waal, 1982; 1986). It is clear that, from an evolutionary point of view, there are situations in which animals are designed to deceive others, and so gain sexual, social, or political advantage. Indeed, it has been suggested that self-deception, hiding the truth from the conscious mind the better to hide it from others, has evolved in humans to fulfil these functions (Trivers, 1985). As I have argued elsewhere (McFarland, 1989), this line of reasoning has a number of implications for our concepts of motivation and goal-directed behaviour in animals. For the present, I will confine myself to the following observations: The honest robot would be at a disadvantage in the robot community. It would be less efficient than its competitors, and would be discriminated against in the market place. It would be less efficient because other, less honest, robots would manipulate it into making bad decisions, in the apparent spirit of cooperation. The transparently dishonest robot would be discriminated against by other robots, who would soon learn (or their designers would learn) to recognise a cad in the community. They would be unable to co-operate with others, and so would be less competitive in the marketplace. The somewhat dishonest robot would sell well in the marketplace.

My point is that the teleological mode of communication is somewhat dishonest. It can summarise what the actor is likely to do, but leaves room for manoeuvre. Thus a robot that says 'I intend to clean the floor next' is not revealing its true state. The statement may be true at the time, but the robot knows that when the time comes it will have to refuel. Moreover, if cleaning the floor ceases to be the most advantageous task, the robot can easily make an excuse for not doing it. 'I intended to clean the floor, but ...' Thus, I am suggesting that the honest robot is exploited, the dishonest robot is avoided, and the teleological robot is the most successful at co-operating with other robots.

What about the intentional behaviour in humans? I maintain that the standard model (of an explicit (mental) representation of the goal-to-be-achieved that controls behaviour in pursuit of the goal) is flawed for the following reasons: (1) Behavioural evidence for such explicit representations is not possible (because of the uniqueness problem). (2) Physiological evidence does not exist, and probably never will. (3) Such a model cannot work for complex behaviour (the trade-off argument). (4) The behaviour that the model is supposed to account for can be explained in other ways (e.g. by a rule-governed, hill-climbing model). How then, do I account for the fact that the behaviour of other people (and maybe some animals and machines) seems to us to be intentional? I suggest that our linguistic behaviour (and some of our thinking) is organised along teleological lines for good evolutionary reasons (the honesty argument). Thus we communicate in teleological terms, partly as a shorthand and partly as a cover for our true motives. Our own behaviour seems to be intentional, because we are designed to be self-deceiving, the better to hide the truth from others. We may genuinely believe our actions to be intentional, but this belief should not be used as evidence in a scientific investigation.

**Suggestions for further reading.**

D.J. McFarland, *Animal Behaviour* (London: Longman and Menlo Park, California: Benjamin/Cummings Publishing Co. Inc., 1985). This is an animal behaviour textbook covering a wide range of topics including decision-making, language and cognition in animals. It is suitable as background reading for those not familiar with animal behaviour, but it only touches on the topic of intentional behaviour.
R.L. Trivers, *Social Evolution* (Menlo Park, California: Benjamin/Cummings Publishing Co. Inc., 1985). This is an excellent introduction to evolutionary theory as applied to animal behaviour.
F. de Waal, *Chimpanzee Politics: Power and Sex among Apes* (N.Y.: Harper and Row, 1982). This book provides an insight into the complex world of primate social relationships.

CHAPTER 5

# INTENTIONS AND CAUSES

## Alan Montefiore

Are there beings, entities, organisms or whatever that form intentions and effectively follow them up and, if so, is their behaviour in this respect also subject to 'normal' causal explanation? That 'we' — that is to say human beings in general — think of, describe and explain a great many of our activities in terms of the goals which we take ourselves or others to be or to have been pursuing is hardly a matter of dispute. But nor is it disputable that in many such cases other types of explanation can be provided showing those which may have been given in terms of goals pursued and of means chosen in furtherance of that pursuit to be at best irrelevant and at worst positively misleading.

Some, indeed, hold, that as a matter of good scientific heuristic principle *all* behaviour, including everything that may ever be done or even said by human beings, is to be regarded as explicable in essentially causal terms, and that if explanations in terms of intentions or the purposive pursuit of goals are not always to be dismissed as fundamentally irrelevant, that is only because of the extreme complexity of the causal factors involved. Reference to apparent intentions and purposiveness is likely to remain, they may concede, a necessary practical convenience for the sake of ready prediction, working 'explanation' or even 'ordinary' description and understanding. Others — including probably a majority of contemporary philosophers — would argue that whatever the possibilities or practicalities of causal explanation of this form of behaviour or that, those of explanation in terms of intention or purpose remain neither threatened nor enhanced. For, so they would argue, each is in principle wholly compatible with the other; if the first is of naturally greater interest to the scientific study of animal (including human) behaviour, the latter remains of necessarily greater concern to historians, lawyers, educationalists, pastors, politicians and, indeed people in general in the everyday, non-scientific pursuit of their lives.

Any really full discussion of this immensely complicated entanglement of issues would evidently involve extended preliminary consideration of the nature of causal (and other directly associated or comparable types of) explanation as such: of the proper delineation and analysis of such teleological concepts as those of intention, purpose, motive and goal: and only then of the relations between the diverse varieties of the one and the diverse varieties of the other. Since such discussion would inevitably be led to range over many of the central areas not only of relatively recent philosophical debate but, indeed, of the whole Western philosophical tradition since some time towards its beginnings, it is clear that the discussion to be attempted in this paper cannot aspire to anything remotely approaching fullness. Much will have to be taken for granted; many points that are in fact the subject of important controversy and disagreement will have to be assumed as given; subtle variations of analysis will have to be reduced to relatively crude generalisation. For all this, however inevitable it may be, apology is certainly needed. But apology, however sincere and however often repeated, cannot further remedy the situation. Let this opening apology therefore suffice for all the simplifications that are to follow.

The thesis for which I hope here to sketch out the strategy of an argument may be provisionally summed up as follows:

*First*: It is strictly inconceivable that proof should ever be provided of the total dispensability of concepts of effective intentionality. This is not because human beings have somehow been so programmed by the processes of evolutionary selection as to be unable to do otherwise than make use of these concepts; still less is it a matter of 'mere' practical convenience, however great that convenience might be. It is, rather, that a concept of intentionality must be embodied, or be at work, in the explicitation of the meaningfulness of any piece of discourse whatsoever — including, most notably, any claim to offer a proof of the dispensability of all such concepts.

*Secondly*: The concepts of intentionality and intentional behaviour are indissociable from any adequate analysis of meaning (and hence of any adequate analysis of the nature and significance of what one may call primary linguistic behaviour) because of the way in which they are tied to that of a capacity for adapting or interpreting behaviour in or as response to the demands of a norm or rule. This in turn is linked to a certain concept of a subject — a subject capable of assuming first, second or third-person roles in discourse, and with the intrinsic capacity of individuating itself through its own self-integration through time: that is to say, as an individual to be thought of as identical with itself throughout a past which it assumes to have been its own, a present which in some not fully Cartesian sense it must nevertheless deem to be undeniably its own and a possible future to which, paradigmatically, it must presume itself to be directed. Thus,

*Thirdly*: We have here a concept of intentionality through which events occurring at a given moment of time are to be thought of as being in part determined through a reference to what may be the case at a possible future moment, (future, that is to say, with respect to that given present); and this future state of affairs is, by the same token, to be thought of as not yet completely determined through any reference to that presently existing present (and its past) that does not include reference to the relevant forward-looking intention, an intention whose own fulfilment, moreover, cannot yet be taken as certain. Such a concept of intentionality captures in its own way what, in one way or another, has always formed the (no doubt 'natural') content of conceptions of finality, namely that of a determination of events by reference not to their past but to their future.

*Fourthly*: The concept of intentionality that has thus its roots in the very foundations of meaningful thought and language is also tied to powers of reflexivity and a certain capacity for self-consciousness, as well as

*Fifthly*: To certain notions of commitment and responsibility. In all these ways,

*Sixthly*: The conceptual (or 'logical') structure of this, as I would argue, fundamental concept of intentionality is different from those of efficient causation and of statistically based probability, in particular in so far as the temporal structuring of these different concepts is concerned.

*Seventhly and finally*: We have to return, however perplexedly, to the question of the relation between these two perspectives, stances or standpoints, the intentional on the one hand and the causal and/or statistical on the other. I shall try, however briefly and inadequately, to indicate some posssible grounds for the intuition that Humean compatibilisms, of whatever degree of sophistication, must always fall short of full satisfaction — and that we may perhaps in the end have to fall back on some version of what it may still be appropriate to call a Kantian dualism, even if, so far as its theoretical intelligibility be concerned, we may, like Kant himself, have to settle for little more than some comprehension of its otherwise paradoxical incomprehensibility.

First, then, there would seem to be something so directly *self*-defeating in any attempt to prove the meaninglessness of all discourse whatsoever that any elaborate attempt to defeat it from outside, as it were, may well be considered otiose. One might *perhaps* set out to prove that a 'proper' — that is, a properly 'scientific' — understanding of behaviour must always be able in principle to dispense with any sort of reference to intentions or to intentionality, including even the understanding of those forms of linguistic behaviour that result in the production of such forms of discourse as appear to consist in the presentation of such 'proofs'. Indeeed, as I presently understand it, that someone might embark on such an attempt is directly and fully demonstrated by one of the other contributions to the present volume. But what could one make of an argument that explicitly accepted that one of the logically implied consequences of its own acceptability would be its own thoroughgoing meaninglessness (together with that of all the elements of which it was composed)?

The conceptually graspable meaningfulness of one's own argument is a surely necessary presupposition of its presentability *as* argument, whether to oneself or to others. But then, it must surely equally follow that, if one could show a reference to intentionality to be necessarily implicit in the very concept of (discursive or conceptual) meaningfulness, then to present one's own argument as being in principle wholly intelligible in exclusively non-intentional terms must be as self-defeating as to present it as being itself devoid of conceptual meaning. (But notice the importance of the word 'wholly' in the preceding sentence. As will become clear later on, I do not, indeed cannot, deny that there must always be perspectives of non-intentional explicability from which any observable sequence of behaviour may be seen as explicable — fully explicable, indeed, so long as one remains within the limits of that perspective, even though the perspective itself may have to be seen as only a partial one.)

What is it, then, for a sequence of behaviour, or its at least temporarily enduring product, to be, or to be interpretable as being, an instance of meaningful discourse? We do not, of course, have to presume the producer of such a sequence to be himself/herself/itself explicitly self-conscious of his own behaviour as meaningful at the moment of its production. Nor do we have to presume every producer of meaningful discourse to be already in possession of anything like an articulatable concept of meaning. Very small children, for example, must surely be recognisable as participants in meaningful communication long before they are in any position to conceptualise it as such. But — and this is no doubt one of the central insights of speech act theory — they are only to be recognised as so participating to the extent that they are taken as intending to produce certain results in or through the sounds or gestures that they produce. (If it be objected that 'intending to produce certain results' is far too instrumental an expression in such a context, we may perhaps substitute 'intending to do or to achieve something further in or through their gestures or utterances').

Very often, of course, fond parents are suspected of taking the sound or gesture productions of their infant offspring as communicationally meaningful (and hence intentional) long before there can be any clear justification for regarding them as anything other than the in principle wholly explicable effects of antecedent efficient causes, (to be understood, no doubt, in terms of processes internal to the organism in interaction with its surrounding environment). In fact there is almost certainly no clear line to be drawn between this stage and the succeeding one of awakening participation in the discourse that forms such a crucial part of the surrounding environment. *In principle*, indeed, it must always make sense to look for causally determining antecedents of macroscopically identifiable events, those that consist in the production of noises or gestures as much as any other; that is to say that *no* assumption as to the meaningfulness of such noises and gestures, however strongly it may be justified, can ever aspire to the status of what (within the limits of a given conceptual perspective) may be called purely observational knowledge. But this assumption of communicational meaningfulness is nevertheless frequently indispensable — always indispensable, in fact, to those who cannot but take themselves to be engaged in discourse themselves; and it does indeed carry, as a necessary part of itself, the more specific presumption that the noises, gestures or marks produced by any participant in discourse as symbols or bearers of meaning, that is as the vehicles of his discourse, are so produced under the governance, however flexible or imperfect, of some linguistic norm. (This should not, of course, be taken as suggesting that there may not also be contexts in which noises, marks or gestures may be produced under the governance of norms that are not in any obvious sense linguistic.)

What, in turn, is it to produce a mark or a noise under the general governance of an appropriate linguistic norm? There are at least three types of case which it is important here to distinguish. There is, first, that where what occurs does so as part of a complex pattern of causally related states of affairs and events, where neither the occurrences themselves nor the causal conditions of their production are attributable to any recognisably intentional, let alone conscious, agency, but where there may seem to be plausible reasons of theoretical convenience for speaking of certain features of the overall complex of phenomena *as if* they constituted a language or code. For example, one may speak thus of the 'genetic code'. But this way of speaking carries with it no suggestion that any of the phenomena concerned actually occur in response to any normative expectations or demands (rather than to essentially non-normative antecedent causal pressures or triggers).

Secondly, there are those cases where we know perfectly well that the rules which determine the ordered sequences or relationships of the relevant phenomena derive from their deliberate devising and instantiation within (for example) the appropriate hardware or software by conscious human agents. In some such cases, no doubt, the ordered rule-conforming behaviour of the phenomena may eventually run far beyond anything that the original devisers of the rules could themselves have worked out and shown to be meaningful in advance. So long, however, as we know that there are, or may be, or may have been human agents to whom responsibility may be attributed for the devising of such rule-following machines (with their sometimes very sophisticated ability to interact with their environment in all sorts of self-adjusting and self-monitoring ways), we can have no compelling reason to attribute any sense of normative expectation or commitment to the machines themselves. On the contrary, these are cases where we can very well understand and admit the force of all those arguments designed to show that such goal-directive concepts as 'intention' are in principle entirely dispensable as unnecessary to the formulation of any conclusively full explanation of why the observable behaviour is what it is. (I should note, however, in passing that I do not myself think that the possibility of constructing 'machines', whether electronic or whatever, whose inner complexity such as to serve as the basis for properly conscious behaviour, can be ruled out on purely a priori grounds; but in any such case, I take it, there would have to be grounds for construing at least some of their behaviour as being, at least in part, 'autonomously intentional'.)

Thirdly, however, there are the cases of those participants in discourse who, as they strive to work out what to say to themselves or to others, or to understand what they hear said to them or take to be going on by way of discourse around them, have to decide on the production of their own marks or noises, and to assess the relevance or significance of those that are produced by others, in terms of their appropriateness or inappropriateness to the presumed demands of the situation. That is to say that in the use or interpretation of any mark or noise as a symbol or marker of, say, some sort of classification one must in principle be able to make sense of a distinction between 'getting it right' and 'getting it wrong'. In other words, for a sequence of behaviour to be interpretable as being an instance of meaningful discourse one must suppose that in the context in question the use of one mark or noise rather than another would make, or would have made, a difference not merely in so far as it would have constituted a different *de facto* feature of that context, and not merely in terms of the different causal consequences that may in fact have flowed from its production, but in terms of the relative success or failure of whatever one may have been trying (or have judged others to have been trying) to do.

It is important at this stage to recall and to continue to bear in mind certain points that have already been made. From a 'strictly observational standpoint', and hence from that of all studies conducted on the basis of 'strictly observational' data, however they may be obtained, it is neither possible nor, in a sense, necessary to provide conclusive identification of behaviour as goal-directive rather than as causally determinate. When men (or dolphins, or computers, for that matter) produce ordered sequences of noises, one does not *have* to treat them as instances of language production; one may in principle always seek both to describe and to explain them in terms of their physically observable characteristics and of their physical antecedents and context — and any puzzles that there may be as to the nature and origin of those antecedents and context may, no doubt, raise in their turn the same alternative sets of questions again. Of course, if one is going to *define* the goal-directive as some sub-class of efficiently causal behaviour, that will be another matter. But if, on the other hand, one is indeed going to treat the production of these sequences as instantiating linguistic behaviour and as being fully intelligible only when seen in this light, or if, in particular, one is approaching the matter from the first-person standpoint of one who is trying to work out what he or she is going to say, to write or to think, no such neutrality in regard to the goal-directiveness or non-goal-directiveness of their behaviour is available as a self-intelligible option. I cannot, as I reflect upon the content of my own on-going thought or discourse, represent it to myself as other than meaningful, or other than being directed towards the achievement of meaning, with all that that further implies.

It is true, of course, that no-one normally spends more than a very small portion of their time in direct reflection upon the nature of their own ability to think or upon their exercise of that ability. But to have the capacity for language is to have at least the potential for reflection on that capacity; the user of language is at least potentially capable of a self-aware self-recognition as such. Or, if there is felt to be something intellectually embarrassing about any such apparently straightforward reference to self-awareness, we may say rather that any 'full' participant in discourse must be capable of that self-awareness which consists in its own understanding that the marks and noises which it may produce are produced as symbols or bearers of meaning and in its own at least partial understanding of the meaning that they bear. (By 'full' I here mean nothing more mysterious — nor rigorously precise — than paradigmatically acceptable as a standard member of the relevant speech community.)

Why should the capacity for language necessarily carry with it this potential for reflection upon itself? In the history of philosophy Descartes is, of course, celebrated among those who have taken the capacity for reflexive self-awareness to be among the leading characteristics of consciousness itself. Curiously, it seems to me that, while Descartes was right at any rate so far as conceptualised and conceptualising consciousness is concerned, it is for very unCartesian or even anti-Cartesian reasons. They have their roots in what in one version may be seen as Wittgensteinian-type arguments as to the impossibility of a purely private language or a purely unilateral following of rules or observance of norms. To learn to use a mark or a noise as a symbol or bearer of meaning is, indeed, to learn to use it in accordance with some (however flexible) norm determining the appropriateness or inappropriateness of its usage according to context. But, (i) norms cannot in principle apply to in essentially unique occurrences; if the production of a mark or noise is to be normatively appropriate to a particular occasion or context, one must be able to conceive of its reiterated production as being in principle similarly appropriate to other relevantly similar occasions or contexts. (This is not, of course, intended as hypothesis or stipulation as to the actual conceptual powers of the particular producer of the mark or noise so much as to what, under appropriate conditions, the relevant participant in discourse must be capable of recognising or acknowledging.) And, (ii) it is impossible to conceive of an act as being under the governance of a norm if it is not possible at least to conceive of some way of encountering or establishing a check on whether the norm has been respected or not.

This latter requirement does not, of course, mean that a check must be in practice available for every occasion of meaningful utterance. It does mean, however, that it must be possible in principle to conceive of occasions on which and ways in which it might be available. But *this*, according to the Wittgensteinian-type thesis (which, for immediate purposes, I must take in effect for granted, even if in as full confidence as may be that in some version or another it can be convincingly made out), means in further crucial turn that the meaningfulness of any given speaker's or even thinker's own 'internal' discourse must in the last resort depend on or presuppose his being able in principle to conceptualise the possibility of encountering another speaker of his language, another participant in his discourse, and that of recognizing him as such. And *this* means that he must have at his disposal, within the resources of his language, the conceptual means of distinguishing between his own first person position in discourse and the positions, whether second person or third, of those others whom he might in principle encounter and who might, through such encounter, provide him with this indispensable possibility of a check.

The, no doubt intrinsically unsurprising, upshot of this line of argument is, then, that any 'full' participant in discourse, any 'standard' producer of conceptually articulated or structured thought, must have at his or her disposal the resources of the three personal pronouns or their functional equivalents, and must therefore be capable (as always in principle) of using the first person pronoun to present or to represent himself both to himself and to others. Furthermore, in as much as he is thus committed to the in principle justifiable use of both second and third person pronouns for the address and/or identification of potential partners in discourse, he is *ipso facto* committed to the presumption of the possible existence of *other* first person, and hence potentially reflexive and potentially intentional, perspectives upon the world as well as his own. For whoever may be the proper reference of a second or third person pronoun as a presumed fellow participant in discourse must by the same token be presumed to be capable of converting any such reference into his own first person account of the matter.

We have by this stage of the argument covered most of the first two points of the programme announced at the outset as well as most of the substance of the fourth. That is to say that we have followed the outline of an argument designed to show how the concept of intentionality that must be embodied in any explication of the meaningfulness of meaningful discourse is tied to that of a capacity for adapting one's behaviour in response to the demands of a norm or rule: how these two concepts, taken together, are further linked to that of a subject capable of assuming first, second and third person roles according to the nature of the discursive situation in which it finds itself: and, as foreshadowed in the fourth point, how and why an intentional, conceptualising subject of this sort must be presumed capable of reflexive self-awareness or understanding of itself as the producer of its own discourse. (This does *not*, incidentally, mean that, as the producer of its own discourse, it must be presumed to be the sovereign or exclusive source or master of its own meanings, or to have incorrigible or infallible knowledge of its own intentions.) We have still, however, to take up explicitly the crucial references to temporality to be found in what remains of the second point and, taken further, in the third.

Why, then, are we committed to understanding ourselves and whoever else we may presume to be our partners (and necessary counter-checkers) in discourse to conceiving ourselves and them as subjects 'with the intrinsic capacity of integrating themselves through time'? That we have to presume our potential partners in discourse to be subjects like unto ourselves is a point that has already been taken; if, as potential partners, we take them to stand in either second or third person relations to ourselves, it follows from the rules of the constitutive interconvertibility of personal pronouns that we must take them to stand in first person relations to themselves. But what about our mutual self-integration through time?

To adapt one's behaviour to a norm is, as we have already noted, to do more than merely produce a once and for all, self-contained event, looking neither backwards nor forwards to the events of any other possible moment; 'norms cannot in principle apply to in principle unique occurences'. If I seek to adapt my behaviour to a norm, I do so on the necessary presupposition that similar behaviour would be similarly appropriate on other similar occasions. In particular, if I intend my production of a mark or noise as that of a symbol or bearer of meaning, I have to aim at or intend some linguistic consistency in my linguistic production overall; (typically the relevant norm will already exist in broad outline at least, but in certain exceptional cases I may in effect be promulgating it for the first time). In like fashion I am bound to look for a corresponding consistency in the linguistic behaviour of any apparent participant in discourse that I might come across. But it must be a self-evident assumption of any attempt at or assessment of consistent behaviour that the behaving subject must be taken to be, as one says, identical with itself throughout the time of the different occasions of its behaviour. If I take my noise or mark to be produced in would-be accordance with a rule, I must take myself to be possessed of such continuity of identity across time as to be at any rate in principle capable of observing, or of having observed, the same rule on some other past or future occasion — past and future occasions to which I implicitly refer as being among my own possibilities when I refer my own present action to a norm.

In other words, in participating in the production and reproduction of meaning I (re-present) myself — both to myself and to all other actual or possible participants — as a subject of discourse, one with his own past and possible future, a past which was itself once a possible future, and a subject whose past, present and future, belonging each all to each other, together characterise him in his own distinctive particularity, distinct from you or the next man or woman or anyone else. (I am here ignoring possible Parfitian complications of maybe conceivable fission and fusion and of ancestor and successor selves, not because they present no interest or challenge, but because I do not believe that in seeking to meet their challenge one would need substantially to modify the main thrust of the present argument.)

But there is more to my relations with my own past and possible future than the necessity, in which I find myself caught up, of presuming myself to have emerged from 'my own' past and to be directed towards 'my own' future. As I hesitate between the next production of one sound (one mark) or another, as I seek to conceptualise, to classify, to re-cognise my present experience, as I struggle to build up my discourse, relating word to word and sentence to sentence, I know that in each move that I make I can get it more or less right or wrong, achieve greater or lesser success. I know this in as much as I must know these alternative possibilities to be together constitutive of the very sense of this, my normative endeavour. What I do now, the mark that I make, the word that I utter, the sentence that I inscribe, is determined by my awareness of the possible result at which, however uncertainly, I aim. And in my awareness of that possible future result, the as yet uncertain outcome of my present uncertain choice, I cannot but think of the possible outcome of my efforts as being, in part at least, dependent precisely on those efforts and on that choice — a choice that arises, certainly, out of that past to which it bears its own distinctive normative reference, but which, in its effort to respect, sustain or perhaps to modify the relevant norms, must as yet still remain open to an outcome of *either* failure *or* success.

In other words, in aiming at or intending the achievement of some future state of affairs — in the case here under consideration, in my own on-going guidance of myself according to some linguistic norm — I necessarily take the occurrence or non-occurrence of that future state to be at least in part dependent on the existence of my present intention and on my success or failure in seeing it through to its goal. To argue, as some seem tempted to argue, that this necessary assumption may nevertheless be nothing more than a necessary illusion is implicitly to argue that the assumption of the meaningfulness of our own discourse may likewise be nothing more than a necessary illusion. But this, as we have remarked above, would be a singularly self-defeating way of representing the (presumably meaningless) meaning of one's very own argument.

This future or forward-looking reference of intentional action, this determination of what I may do now by reference to my representation of what is, or may be to come is, of course, in one way or another characteristic of nearly all traditional characterisations of goal-directive behaviour.

My fifth claim was that this concept of intentionality, indispensable in the contribution that it makes to the explication of meaningfulness itself, is further tied not only to the concepts of reflexivity and self-consciousness, but also to those of commitment and responsibility. The ideas lying behind this claim are in essence simple enough. If, in producing a mark, a noise or a gesture, my intention is to produce it as a bearer of meaning, that is to say to produce it under the broad governance of some linguistic norm, then in so doing I must, (other things being equal, of course), effectively be committing myself to repeating the production of appropriately similar marks, noises or gestures in appropriate future contexts on appropriate future occasions.

Moreover, if some version of the anti-private language argument is indeed correct, then I must in principle be looking to similar consistencies of commitment from all my possible interlocutors, all my potential fellow-participants in discourse. I can only take their responses to my own attempts at meaningfulness to be functioning as the necessary checks in so far as I assume *their* production of marks, noises and gestures to be likewise under the governance of the relevantly appropriate linguistic norms. In the 'manifold' of our responses to each other we are, then, taken together, reciprocally responsible to ourselves and each other for the establishment and upkeep of the practices and structures of meaning within which our productions of mark, noise and gesture acquire and hold their status as symbols. (Nowhere is this clearer than in the situation of basic language teaching and learning to and by very small children.) In this area of human behaviour at least we may say that total irresponsibility is not even a possible option, since total lack of responsibility in the observance of linguistic norms would lead to a total loss of grip on meaning, and would thus fall out of the field of assessment of responsibility and irresponsibility altogether. This argument should not, of course, be understood as suggesting that I must, or even could coherently, regard myself as totally responsible for all my own meanings. I have, however, to regard myself as having my own part of responsibility for them. That is, I am responsible for myself and before (or to) others for my own status as participant in a common universe of meaningful discourse.

Sixthly, the concept of intentionality that is thus integral to those of meaning and meaningfulness is fundamental in that concepts (and intentions) of meaning are in effect presupposed by all other concepts and all other intentions (or ascriptions of intention) whatsoever. That the temporal or quasi-temporal structuring of such intentional concepts is different from those of mechanistic or efficient causation is, of course, some sort of commonplace. It is imposssible to characterise anyone as having a normative intention — i.e. the intention, implicit if not necessarily explicit, of doing whatever one is seeking to do with an eye on keeping in touch with the relevant norms — without referring in one way or another to some moment or moments of time future in relation to that at which the person in question is taken to have conceived or nourished the intention. More generally, even though it has to be acknowledged that in a great many cases it can in fact make no sense to look either for an objectively measurable or for a subjectively detectable temporal gap between the forming of an intention and the undertaking of the action or activity which is its object, to characterise someone as having an intention, or his action as being intentional, is already to refer, through that very characterisation, to that event or events whose occurrence is, if his intention is fulfilled, to be explained in part at least by reference to it. (In any case, cases in which there is thus no detectable temporal gap between the forming of an intention and the undertaking of some fulfilment-directed behaviour cannot constitute the norm; to show this it would only be necessary to refer once again to the relevant details of the situation of basic language acquisition.) Moreover, as we have already seen in part, it is among the presuppositions embedded in the conceptual structure of intentional discourse that, (i) the possession of an intention may not necessarily be followed by any action designed to secure its fulfilment — nor, of course, that it is necessarily probable that such action, if undertaken, be successful; (ii) the possession of an intention must nevertheless on some appropriate if indeterminate number of occasions be followed by action designed to secure its fulfilment, (for if it was not, then the criteria for the very ascription, including even the self-ascription, of an intention will not have been satisfied); and, (iii) the possession and activating of the intention is normally assumed to be, if not sufficient, at any rate necessary to the occurrence of the relevant course of action. (The literature includes some elaborate discussion of certain possible bizarre cases in which the existence of an intention may have to be accepted as having been neither necessary nor sufficient for the occurrence of the event intended, even though it may in fact have occurred. But the very peculiarity of such cases is in its own way effective illustration of how different is the contrasting norm.)

One might, certainly, find it natural to express this last point by saying that it is a presupposition of the discourse of intentional action that the existence and activation of an intention must be taken (normally at any rate) to play some necessary causal role in bringing about the course of events in question. However, this could be a very misleading way of putting the matter if it led one to overlook the fact that discourse of purely efficient causality is structured very differently. A familiar way of characterising this structure is to say that in any case where C is alleged to be the cause of E, it must in principle be possible to find some appropriate (so-called 'intrinsic') characterisation of C through which no reference whatsoever is made to E or to the time of E's occurrence. The point here is, no doubt, to stress the logical contingency of the causal relationship; not only might anything lead to anything else, but there can in alleged principle be no purely logical or conceptual assurance that any particular range of phenomena should exhibit any causal regularity whatsoever.

However, one does not have to go so far as to accept a Kantian account of causal structures as constituting a necessary presupposition of the objectivity of any experience in order to see that something must be wrong with this excessively Humean account of the matter. A total lack of discernible regularity in experience would produce a total inability to bring it into any classifiable (i.e. conceptualisable) order; or to put it the other way round, the classification of any item of experience as an object of some given sort carries with it the assumption that that object will, at least within a certain range of already familiar circumstances of active or passive interaction with other objects in its environment, continue to behave within a certain range of normally predictable ways. In stricter, more systematically Newtonian terms, we know, of course, that from a complete state description of a closed universe at any time 't' we could in principle deduce equally complete state descriptions of it for any other time whatsoever, whether 't + n' or 't − n'. It is here that lies the rub — not in the fact that descriptions of final or goal-directive causes make ineliminable reference to the future while those of efficient or mechanical causes make no future reference at all, for there is, strictly speaking, no such fact; it lies rather in the notable differences between the forms which these references take. The laws of efficient causation are time-reversible — not in the sense that causal(-cum-statistical) physics does not allow of the superimposition of a temporal arrow giving a one-way temporal direction to the order of events, but in the sense that whatever the powers of prediction and retrodiction, they are symmetrical to each other; the 'laws' of goal-directive explanation do not allow of such temporal symmetry. It may very properly be objected to this claim that the temporal arrow provided by the second law of thermodynamics points towards a final state of entropic disorder from whose description no retrodiction is theoretically possible to whatever the particular state of relative order from which it was a wholly predictable degeneration. At this level of characteristically thermodynamical description and explanation this objection holds. (It would not, presumably, hold at a level at which theoretical account was taken of the individual energy states of the individual molecules.) However, the point to notice here is that while explanations in terms of intentions and of causes (or of such probabilities as 'govern' the occurrences of quantum events) are explanations in terms of certain principles of shaping or ordering of the onward course of events, the second law of thermodynamics is by contrast a principle of *dis*order.

The primary concern of my argument so far has been to show that a concept of intentionality has to be presupposed as indispensable to any analysis of meaning and meaningful discourse; and that any argument designed to show that we do not have to take account in our explanations of human behaviour of the existence of such discourse, refutes itself by its own self-presentation as argument. I have not here so far made any attempt to debate the further question of whether the same or analogous forms of intentionality may plausibly, or even intelligibly, be attributed to beings or entities incapable of guiding themselves according to such rules. The line of argument that I have sought to establish has, rather, laid great stress on the notion of the subject that seems to be presupposed by any reference to conceptually meaningful (meaning-producing and/or meaning-participatory) behaviour and, first and foremost perhaps, by 'one's own' first person participation in it. This is a notion of a subject capable of recognizing the demands and applications of norms to its own performances, capable of that anticipation of its own future that must be implicit in any such recognition, capable too of a certain power of reflexive self-awareness (i.e. awareness of itself as the subject of its own discourse or as participant in that of another presumed to be capable of a similar first person reflexivity). It is a subject, in short, that is to be presumed and that necessarily presumes itself as capable of integrating itself through time and of integrating time itself through its own temporal self-integration. (Maybe this is another way of approaching that mysterious Kantian insight as expressed in the Schematism of the Categories in his reference to our own generation of time 'in the apprehension of the intuition'; or the Husserlian attempt to account for the nature of our inner time-consciousness in terms of retention and protention.)

In this present discussion, then, I have been led to root the primary sense (or, at the very least, *a* primary sense) of intentionality in the presuppositions of discursive self-awareness. In my contribution (Montefiore, 1971) to the Aristotelian Society's symposium on 'Final Causes' I laid central stress on the notion of possessing a certain conception of the future. To what extent may these two versions of the matter be taken as amounting to the same thing? This must depend on how one construes the reference to possession of a conception of some future state of affairs. My present inclination is to say that if one construes it as the capacity to represent some future state of affairs to oneself, they may indeed be taken as amounting to the same thing, but that if one does so take them, one must be careful to add an emphatic underlining of the phrase 'to oneself'; and it may also be well to stress the possibility of taking the term 'represent' as meaning 'to make present to consciousness something that is not, strictly speaking, of the present moment at all'. (Though the present re-presentation is, of course, 'strictly' present.)

Taken on its own, however, the notion of a representation, or at any rate the term 'representation', is one that I have come somewhat to distrust as serving too easily to cover up and render acceptable precisely that which needs to be seen as most problematic. For what constitutes a representation, whether explicit or 'tacit', a representation as such? There seems to be a tendency to take it as being whatever identifiable device (explicit representation) or overall arrangement of structure and interaction of parts (tacit representation) enables or ensures that an organism or a machine will arrive at — or at least tend towards — a state that observers may plausibly construe as a goal or end. But a goal from whose point of view? If the working of the device in question, or of the overall structural arrangement of the organism or machine, together, with the manner of its interactions with its surrounding environment, is capable of being depicted in thorough-going causal terms, then the 'representation' so-called can just as well be understood as that feature of the organism or machine whose working will (in interaction with its ongoing environment) as a matter of normal causal fact lead to the achievement or maintenance of whatever state of affairs is taken to be the goal. But we do not, in that case, have to suppose that this is a goal *for* the organism or machine itself, or that the so-called representation actually makes anything 'present to it' in advance; we may say, if we like, that its behaviour is goal-directed or goal-oriented without in any way implying that it is, so to speak, goal-self-directed.

Of course, we may — just as we may not — find it convenient, heuristically helpful or whatever to take, in any given case of experimental investigation or observation, what Dennett calls the intentional stance, and to treat the phenomena with which we have to deal *as if* whatever machines or organisms are in question contained representations of the future that were representations *for them* — that is, *as if* they had conceptions of what we take to be their goals and had intentions towards them. But it is only if and when we suppose that to treat them thus as subjects in their own right is in some way indispensable to an adequate characterisation of their behaviour, and indeed of what they themselves are, that we give ourselves any serious ground for holding that the conceptions of goals that we attribute to them — the representations of ends that we take as being effectively representations *for them* — must 'really' contribute to the initiation and control of the behaviour that is indeed calculated to lead to the goals in question.

It may be worth noting in passing that in the standard English translation of Kant's *Critique of Pure Reason* the word 'representation' is used to translate the German *vorstellung*, and that this in its previous turn had been used to translate the word 'idea' as it ubiquitously appeared in such writers as Locke, Berkeley and Hume (among, of course, many others). 'Ideas', for Locke, were 'whatever is before the mind', that is whatever is an item of (potentially self-conscious) awareness; and the notion of 'being before' is evidently well captured by *vorstellung*. Given the complicated Kantian doctrine of three-fold synthesis, with its strong emphasis on temporality and the necessary work of the productive and reproductive imagination, 'representation' seems an aptly appropriate term to use when the whole discussion goes back into English. *Vorstellungen* are no longer to be thought of as immediately recognisable icons, but rather as those contents of awareness which have to be capable of *re*-presentation (to the mind) if they are to be recognisable (or conceptualisable) at all. One thing that is constant throughout all this is, of course, the reference to the reflexively self-aware subject as the possessor or locus of the mind to which, or before which, ideas or representations must be presumed to be set.

Either way, then, the argument seems to lead back to a certain conception of consciousness — that of a reflexive or potentially self-conscious subject — as constitutive of a perspective from which concepts of effective intentionality must present themselves as indispensable to the articulation, description and explanation of (at the very least) that wide range of behaviour which may in one way or another be involved in the production of speech acts or in participation in discourse. It is not, of course, any accident that these references to reflexivity and to language have been interrelated in this way — to reflexivity, to language and, indeed, to normativity. There may or may not seem to be good reason to attribute some analogous forms of intentionality to creatures apparently incapable of language or of conceptualisation, but it is only from the standpoint of those for whom language is the indisputable vehicle of their own self-awareness that the (self-)attribution of intentionality in unrenounceable.

It may seem, perhaps, that to cast the main argument in this way is in effect to restrict the attributability of intentions to language-using creatures alone — human beings and, possibly, a few rather dubious hangers-on such as dolphins, chimpanzees, gorillas and the like. Maybe. But this seems to me, at present at least, to be a matter of great uncertainty and complexity. So let us see whether one may not approach it by a somewhat roundabout route.

Let us turn, then, to start with, to the rightly inescapable challenge, which we should in any case seek to anticipate, that even a successful demonstration of the indispensability of an assumption does not show that assumption to be true. Alright, I may be told; maybe it really is the case that we have no coherent choice but to take ourselves as capable of contributing to the onward determination of events through our own intentions. The fact remains that this indispensable assumption, this assumption which may indeed be inextricably bound up with our own understanding of the meaningfulness of our own discourse, may nevertheless amount to no more than an illusion; it may be the case that the appearance to our conscious minds of what we construe to be our own representations of future goals and of paths of action towards them may make no effective contribution to the control of the events that actually take place. And if all this is so, it may still be the case that in reality even our production of the sounds and marks of discourse may be explicable in essentially causal (and perhaps statistical) terms in some broad but at any rate broadly acceptable sense of those words.

Let us indeed suppose — and so far as the present state of knowledge is concerned, it can be no more than committed supposition — that such explications may in fact be provided. If the assumption of intentionality is still indispensable from a perspective which it is equally impossible for any thinking subject coherently to renounce (and even the scientist most deeply committed to causal determinism is himself an indisputably thinking subject), what possible basis can there be for declaring either one of these apparently incompatible but equally unrenounceable schemata of description and explanation to be closer to reality than the other? We have, moreover, to take into account the fact that the organisation of the data of observation and experimentation into the categories and structures of causally determinate, statistically indeterminate or mathematically optimising theories all lean heavily upon all the presuppositions that together go into that of the meaningfulness of that very organisation. From this point of view, it might seem, one might just as well claim a priority for the intentional view of reality as for the causal-cum-statistical view, whose own meaningfulness is thus parasitic upon it. From each point of view, the temptation, even the pressure, is there to regard the *other* as the product, in the end, of a certain inescapable illusion, or as being at the very least of subordinate status.

What might be the upshot of a set of arguments such as these? It seems to me that there are, broadly speaking, two families of possibilities. We find ourselves, in the very act of conscious reflection upon the matter, within an unrenounceable perspective of intentionality with all that that implies for our temporality (trans-temporality?... meta-temporality?...) as subjects; we seem, at the moment at least, to be equally committed to a perspective of causal-cum-statistical explicability-in-principle of whatever phenomena may be open to observation and experimental investigation, including, of course, all those phenomena whose occurrence we ourselves may initiate from the standpoint of our own intentionality, when they are viewed, as they must also be capable of being viewed, from the standpoint of observation. Given all this, we may, (i) have to reconcile ourselves as best we may to a not further reducible 'complementarity' of what we have to recognise as two mutually distinct perspectives — and this despite their equally indisputable interdependence: or, (ii) we may have to seek some way of representing the causal perspective as being somehow dependent upon or derivative from that of meaningful intentionality rather than the other way round.

If we do conclude that we have to reconcile ourselves to a not further reducible acceptance of two mutually distinct perspectives, we must nevertheless recognize in their complementarity no mere compatibility of the apparently comfortable sort that is on offer from Hume (and, indeed, from many of his predecessors and successors, sometimes in formidably sophisticated versions). Specifically, the complementarity that we should have to settle for would involve more problem and paradox than might be resolved through any account of the relations between teleology and causality, between reasons and causes, as being 'simply' those of alternative forms of description under which may be brought what may nevertheless be identified — 'in itself', as it were — as being straightforwardly one and the same state of affairs or event. For how *can* one and the same state of affairs be characterisable in two different ways that are mutually *in*compatible as to their temporal structure — that is to say, as being *both* fully determined in the time and place and manner of its occurrence by its relations to other states of affairs or events of the past *and* yet in part still open to further determination by its own intentional (or intensional) relation to the future? Or rather, for this is perhaps not the most accurate way of putting the matter, given that it is not the existence of my present intentional representation that is still open to further determination, how can I, as I find myself taking and taken in by my own intentional stance, regard what is to come as being *both* fully determined by everything that has gone before *and* yet as still open to further determination by what I may or may not decide to do on the basis of my own representations of various still partially indeterminate outcomes? The 'complementarity' here is of that peculiarly Kantian sort of which we may, in comprehending its necessity, comprehend at the same time, as he says, its very incomprehensibility.

The problem or paradox that seems to be thus ineliminable from our situation on this first possible way of viewing the matter is bound up with the fact that we appear to have open to us no intelligible reference to a third point of view from which to bring into one overall focus both the previous two. It may be that this lack of a third, unifying standpoint has to be recognised as a built-in limit to any theoretical comprehension that we (human beings) may, even in principle, ever hope to attain, but that we may in a sense, and in so far as we may succeed in remaining in tune with our own rationality, hope to achieve our own ever to be resought after unity in the reflective practice of our own lives. (I must, for example, recognise the impossibility in principle of ever giving a final, fully satisfactory theoretical unity to the diverse sets of arguments that I am attempting to build together in this chapter, though I may — indeed must — hope to glimpse such a unity in the practical experience of trying to work them all out.)

On this view, however, and however we may seek, within the constraints of a theoretically necessary imperfection, to articulate the presuppositions of our own reflective practice, we remain (again necessarily) unable to provide any theoretically adequate account of how one might conceptualise the occurrence of rationally inspired intervention in an already fully ongoing sequence of causally determined events. For myself, I should be inclined to argue that if we are really going to put ourselves into a Kantian perspective, then we must try and take Kant's own constantly reiterated commitment to his doctrine of Transcendental Idealism as seriously as both commitment and doctrine surely demand. In that case, so it seems to me, any implicit reference to a third point of view from which both causal and intentional viewpoints might themselves be thought of as holding together in a somehow after all intelligible unity, would have to be taken as a reference to a viewpoint that was in some sense prior to and yet generative of time itself. (Again we seem to be referred back to that mysterious passage in the Schematism and perhaps, in Strawson's words, to the bounds of sense itself; for if thought of such a viewpoint is to be represented as a transcendentally necessary presupposition of the not coherently totally deniable unity 'in the end' of theory and practice, it is not a thought to which any further thinkable content can be given.)

Any possible following up or out of such 'Kantian' clues as these, however, must clearly belong to another story. Here it remains only to add a briefly speculative word about the second of the two possibilities that were evoked four paragraphs ago. This, it would seem to me, might or perhaps must lie in some theoretical formulation of a dynamic interconnection between (what it might seem plausible to characterise as) different actual or possible spatio-temporal frameworks, the interconnections being mediated by what might plausibly be characterised as finding representation within such an overall theoretical formulation as acts of intentional self-direction.

If such a theoretical development were possible, it seems clear enough that whatever might find expression within one framework as subjectively 'self-recognisable' representation is almost bound to find reciprocal expression within some appropriately associated framework as physically characterisable structure or event; no doubt, too, such structures or events would comprise certain crucial neural aspects or, perhaps, aspects of some different intrinsic nature but structurally analogous to them. It *may* be that such structures, events and associated states of affairs may be found to characterise or to take place in the brains of dolphins, chimpanzees, gorillas and, indeed, in more or less rudimentary form, in those of a whole host of other creatures in contexts of the production of patterns of behaviour that it would, on other grounds, be plausible (or 'natural') to construe as intentional; and if that were so, it might provide good reason for attributing to creatures other than man a whole graduated range of proto-capacities for, perhaps, some more or less proto-intentional behaviour. But here too, of course, I am moving fast towards my outer limits of coherently intelligible speculation.

Indeed, it would be as well to make them the outer limits of this chapter as well — all the more so, perhaps, as it may not after all be so clear that what I have sketched in such exiguous outline as two distinct possibilities may not in the end turn out to be two merely initially different versions of what might equally well be taken as being one and the same.

CHAPTER 6

# INTENTIONAL ACTION AND PHYSIOLOGY

*Denis Noble*

In this chapter my purpose is not to formulate a specific theory of intentional action, still less to provide it with a physiological basis. I wish rather to do some ground clearing. My aim is to show why physiological explanations, as we currently conceive them, are incapable of accounting for intentional behaviour. I hope also to show why certain kinds of psychological theory are deficient. In the course of the discussion I shall try to answer the following questions:

1. Are intentions legitimate causes of neural events? My answer to this question will be no.
2. Does the existence of intentional behaviour require certain neuronal structures to exist? The answer here will be yes.
3. Could a computer display intentional behaviour? Here also I think the answer must in principle be yes.
4. If a purely physiological theory is deficient, how would this be apparent to the experimental scientist? The answer here is that it would be apparent in a rapidly growing number of unexplained contingent conditions.
5. Is intentional action consistent with biological evolution? On this my answer will be yes.

## Are intentions causes of neuronal action?

Intentions clearly can be mistaken for causes. Thus it may appear to be a correct reply to the question 'What made you drop the glass?' to say 'I intended to do so.' Note though that the answer is rather odd and it is certainly not sufficient. Depending on the context we may want to say more about the origins and nature of our intentions (for example, that 'I dropped the glass in order to make a noise'). But these will, significantly, not be physiological events. Moreover, if the question really is interpreted to refer to what, physically, caused me to drop the glass then it would be better to preface the answer with 'nothing' on the grounds that we can discuss the origins of an intentional action (its reasons and justification) but cannot, if the act is to be described correctly as intentional, admit physical compulsion. It would then be even better to expand the reply to 'nothing that is not already taken into account by the fact that I intended to do it'. This would allow for the fact that, on the view developed in this chapter, there is no causal inadequacy in intentional action, which must therefore have antecedents just as non-intentional movements do. But, because we normally look for a straightforward physical cause of an accident we are naturally prone to think that the fact that the same muscular movements could be intended means that the intention simply substitutes for the physical causation when an event is not accidental.

This is an error and it has been pervasive in the history of neurophysiological thought on the relations between mental and neural events. Even though the philosophical position taken by most modern neurophysiologists does not generally involve this error, the idea nevertheless persists. Sometimes it is merely implicit, as in the answer 'I intended to do so' discussed above. But it can also be quite explicit. Eccles (1986), for example, has recently discussed the way in which 'mental events' cause neural events and postulates the existence of a 'liaison brain' to carry the causal chain from intentions to neuronal action. This idea is based on a simple misunderstanding.

It may help to clarify the nature of the misunderstanding to first take a less emotive example of a similar error. A computer programmer has written a Pascal program, part of which reads:

```
x := 1;
REPEAT
    y := x;
    x := fncon(y);
UNTIL Abs(x − y) < epsilon;
Write('Finished');
```

This piece of program calculates a series of values of $x$ starting with 1 and for which each value is a function (*fncon* — here undefined) of the previous value. The program reports that the computation is finished when the difference between two successive values of $x$ is less than a parameter called *epsilon*. The program is run on one machine and after a few seconds the screen displays the message *Finished*. What caused the machine to do this? One is inclined to say 'the program'. That view would be reinforced by finding that the same thing happens, though after a different period of time, on a second machine. But suppose we find that on a third machine the message does not appear. The REPEAT-UNTIL loop simply continues indefinitely. That could happen if the value of *epsilon* is determined earlier in the program by inspecting the machine itself, for example by finding out what is the smallest number that the machine can distinguish from zero. It is possible that, on some machines, this would generate a value of *epsilon* that is never reached in our computation (which might eventually oscillate around a series of values all just greater than *epsilon*.) We might then hesitate and say that the machine was responsible for the appearance or non-appearance of the message.

We could, of course, modify our program-orientated explanation by saying that the instruction *Write('Finished')* caused the appearance of the screen display. On the last computer this line of the program was never reached, so the event didn't happen. But this is clearly as empty an explanation as saying that the glass dropped because my hand stopped holding it. Note also that this is not the same as the explanation 'I dropped it'. The 'I' in this sentence carries vastly more explanatory significance than 'my hand' just as a complete program provides a more satisfactory explanation than a single instruction.

It is easy to construct such 'trick' programs that require reference both to the program and to the machine in order to construct a satisfactory explanation for what happens when the program is run. I will have several uses for such a program in this discussion. The first is to illustrate the relation between machine events and program statements. In this case, in constructing an explanation that refers both to the program and to the machine we may be inclined either to insert a machine event 'into' the program explanation or make a program statement be a 'cause' of a machine event. I want to argue that both moves are confusing and only appear valid if we have the wrong conception of a program. That arises, I think, because we may be taken in by the fact that both the program and the machine events are arranged in a sequential order. In the case of the machine events, the order is sequential in time. In the case of the program, though, this is not necessarily or even generally the case. Only sometimes, in very simple programs, will the program statement order correspond with the order of events in time when the program is run. And even then, it would be wrong to think of the program order as a causal chain of events. Only occasionally can one statement (e.g. an IF–THEN type of statement) be plausibly regarded as the 'cause' of another. The program is rather an ordered sequence of instructions. It only controls a sequence of events in time through the processes of compilation and running.

Moreover, even in the case of an IF–THEN clause the fact that the truth of the IF statement leads to the THEN statement being obeyed is a matter of logical necessity not of physical causation. That is so even though it is *also* true to say that the machine events that occur when the program is run do form a sufficient causal sequence. This fact lies at the heart of a central puzzle. It leads us to ask questions like 'What *really* makes the computer do what it is doing when it runs a program?' The machine analyst will tend to say that, of course, the machine states are always sufficient to answer the question. That approach can best be countered by realising that the number of different machine state sequences that may occur is astronomically large. And most of them are totally meaningless in program terms. Our problem therefore is not *whether* there is a definite causal sequence but why this one occurs rather than billions of others. The answer, of course, is that by programming we select out those sequences that express particular logical relations. I use the phrase 'select out' here deliberately since that is also what natural selection has done in 'selecting out' intentional beings. There is nothing physically different about the sequences of neural and other physical events that occur during intentional action. The difference lies rather in the fact that they satisfy the conditions for expressing the logic of our intentional behaviour, whereas innumerable other physical sequences do not.

We would appear therefore to have two options for attempting to explain the screen display 'finished'. The first would be to study the machine states between first starting the program and the appearance of the screen display. We would, certainly, end up with an account in causal terms for why the screen display occurred. But, it would hardly be an explanation, for the account will be overloaded with unexplained contingent conditions; unexplained because, without consulting the program, we would not understand why the machine spent so long doing so many things before generating the screen display. Of course, anyone familiar with what computers *might* be doing will quickly jump to the conclusion that some sort of program loop is involved and start looking for the machine events that correspond to this. But notice that that intuition depends on the prior idea of a loop — which is a program concept.

The second approach would be to study the program and the value of *epsilon* and then to predict from our knowledge of mathematics whether the screen display will or will not occur. We would do that by studying the convergence of the series formed by successive applications of the function *Fncon* to itself. Nowhere in this explanation would we refer to any machine events, though, in using a particular value of *epsilon*, we would be using a program parameter dependent on a machine property. Moreover, we would certainly not need to look for a 'liaison machine' (*pace* Eccles' 'liaison brain') to see how the convergent properties of our series determined the appearance of the screen display. That is because these convergence properties are not events in the way in which the screen display, and the machine events leading up to it, are events. The convergent property does not exist in the same time scale. If it can be said to exist in time at all, its expression exists when the program displaying it is loaded and running. Many other properties of programs are not events in just the same way. Yet their existence and nature determine which machine events will occur. In this chapter, I will call these properties *program states*.

I wish to argue that an intention is much more like a program state than it is like a physical causal event. That is not to say that an intention, like a program state, cannot be said to be expressed at a particular time. Clearly, we can acquire and abandon intentions, and our intentions can evolve over time, so we must be capable of saying that we have them at some times and not at others. But the time scale involved here is more like that which is related to the loading and unloading of programs on computers than to the time scale of machine events. The holding of an intention is then better thought of as being analogous to having a particular program, with its program states, loaded than to a particular machine state that causes a screen display to appear. One way of appreciating the point about time scale that I am trying to make here is to note that this means that if I use the past tense and say that 'I intended to do X' I am indeed referring to a previous point in time but I am not referring to a particular event.

This also means that the appearance of the screen display has a quite different significance depending on whether it is regarded simply as one machine event terminating a sequence of other machine events or whether it is regarded as an indicator of a program state. This difference is analogous to the distinction between the movement of my fingers when dropping a glass accidentally and intentionally. The difference does not lie in the observed movements, but rather lies elsewhere in the significance of the event in a context in which the time scale of neuronal action is not relevant. Of course, there *might* be a difference at this level between accidental and intended movements (otherwise actors would not have to acquire the skill of making intended movements look like accidental ones), and these differences might be used by an external observer to judge whether the act was intentional, but such differences are not essential.

A persistent machine analyst might argue that, in studying the program for a programmed state we could, via a knowledge of the compiler, and the system under which it operates, work out a series of causally connected machine states underlying the behaviour when the program is run. Moreover, we could then even dispose with the program and use a hardware representation of the relevant states. This is analogous to replacing software computation of mathematical functions with a hardware maths co-processor. But this would not remove the essential difficulty of *understanding* the sequence of machine states. In a similar way, I would argue that the evolution of intentional action does not require that there should exist actual equivalents of software programs for intentional behaviour. Nature may opt either for software or hardware — that choice itself will be subject to the usual evolutionary pressures. The argument here is independent of the form of representation of the program, or indeed whether a program can be said to exist in any very strong sense at all. This point is important. I am not arguing that we will necessarily find programs in the brain in the same way in which we can find programs in a computer memory. To see this point, imagine being unable to distinguish between the operating system (which itself is a program — though at a different level, and it may be invisible to most users of the computer) and the programs that run within it. Imagine also not being able to distinguish clearly between the operating system and some of the physical structure. This is why the example program I used earlier required reference both to the program and to the machine to explain the computer's behaviour.

Evolution has certainly made use of 'machine properties' such as speeds of muscle actions, durations of neuronal delays, inertia of the skeleton and other structures, etc., wherever possible rather than select unnecessary software. Finally, add the fact that many programs are running in a parallel rather than series fashion. The result might be more like the nervous system, for nature clearly did not have to produce a result that conforms to the conceptual scheme we currently use to bring hierarchical order to our analyses of computer action.

Moreover, intentional action does not exclude a great degree of automaticity. The guitar player who learns to play Tarrega's tremolo masterpiece *Recuerdos de la Alhambra* may well end up with the control of the tremolo movements 'etched in', perhaps in some form of cerebellar circuitry, but the intentional nature of his playing depends in no way on whether that is so. His ability to implement his intention depends on whether his tremolo is rapid enough (the music in this case is meaningless if played too slowly) and that *may* depend on whether the representation has become a kind of hardware wiring in, but the intention can be there whether that is so or not. Even the struggling amateur for whom each tremolo movement is a matter of great deliberation may intend to play the piece.

To return to our original example, when I dropped the glass intentionally what in fact replaced the accidental cause? We could, of course, say that certain neuronal (machine) events were the cause. That would at least give a reply at the same level as that for an accidental event. The fact that that would be a very odd reply is because in ordinary analysis we recognise the point I am making, i.e. that when an event occurs within an intentional context a 'machine' description of what happened fails to make reference to the most significant facts. We may not even know where in the world to draw the boundary of the system we include in our explanation. By contrast, when my arm is accidentally knocked, we are not necessarily inclined to look further, for the events leading up to that event will be contingent in character with regard to the dropping of the glass. When I say that I intended to do something, I am signalling the fact that the antecedents are not merely contingent; they are on the contrary worth exploring as an explanation of my intention, just as the structure of a program would be worth exploring as an explanation of a particular program state expressed as some external events on the screen or printer. Of course, I might on a given occasion be wrong in signalling this state of affairs. I might be deluded into thinking that I had a particular intention when in fact I did not. I cannot, though, *always* be so deluded if I am to use intentional language correctly in the first place. I will argue later that a machine that is set up to fool us by referring to its intentions when the conditions for correctly doing so are not satisfied *could* be distinguished from a machine that does satisfy those conditions (though as I shall also argue, we might cease to call the latter a machine).

It is also important to emphasise that these delusions about our intentions must be rather special cases. For example, post-hypnotic suggestion might make me do something that I rationalise by saying that I intended to do it. And, in general, we may rationalise unconscious actions by referring to conscious intentions. We may even say something like 'I suppose I must have intended to do X.' But if all or even most intentional action was of this nature we would not be intentional beings and would not come to use intentional language just as, if we were always to lie we would not be rational beings. Lying can only have the effect it has if we do not always do it.

Even in these special cases like post-hypnotic suggestion there is room for doubt about the nature of the illusion. The reason for that is that it may be necessary for me genuinely to be put into the state in which I do indeed intend the post-hypnotic act for me to think that I intended it. There is a delusion here, but it is not necessarily in the false ascription of an intention. After all, in this chapter, I am not saying that intentional action has no antecedents. Quite the contrary. If the delusion does not consist in having a 'false' intention, it may rather lie in feeling that the intention is justified. On reflection I will of course find that it is not and it will then normally cease to be my intention.

### Does intentional behaviour require particular neuronal structure?

This question raises the possibility that intentional action may be independent of physiological structure, perhaps in the same way that programs are independent of computer structure. If so, what is the nature of that independence?

The first point to make is that, in a very obvious way, programs (or, at least, their implementation) are *not* independent of computer structure. Some languages (particularly highly structured languages like Pascal and Ada) are not capable of being implemented on all machines. Compiler writers are familiar with the compromises they must sometimes make to implement particular languages on some machines. In a very significant sense, therefore, to know that a particular program will run on a machine *does* imply important contingent facts about machine structure. Moreover, to appreciate this general point we do not have to be able to specify what exactly is implied. I would argue that in a similar way to ascribe intentional action to a body is to presume that certain physiological structure *must* exist even if in our present state of knowledge we are not capable of saying precisely what that structure is. There are two ways in which this 'must' can be interpreted and I intend both to be understood. The first sense is logical, the second is causal. The logical sense is that there must exist a certain repertoire of behaviour for it to be correct to ascribe intentions to a subject. That repertoire is known to us and would be what we would rely on if asked 'Can you really imagine X acting intentionally?' I am also saying that this repertoire must have a causal basis in a particular set of physiological structures and programs. This may be unknown to us and is certainly a matter for empirical discovery.

Incidentally, this fact provides the solution to an important problem in some philosophical concepts of a person. Thus Strawson in his account of persons (Strawson, 1959) uses the distinction between M (material) and P (person) predicates to define a person as something to which both M and P predicates are applicable. Williams (1973) in his well-known critique of Strawson shows this to be inadequate since it leaves us not knowing how to define P predicates without already knowing how to identify a person since all we are given about P predicates is that they do not apply to purely material bodies. The obvious way out of this problem is to say that there are certain predicates which must not only be applicable to persons, but must also be true. These would be precisely those predicates whose truth guarantees the applicability of P predicates in general. But this means that in order to apply P predicates at all we must already be making some claims to the truth of certain predicates. Here the sense of 'must' is simply logical. It refers to the repertoire of behaviour that we know must exist for it to be sensible to ascribe P predicates. As noted above, though, this repertoire must also have a causal basis, which we may not know and cannot therefore be the normal basis for justifying P predicate ascriptions.

This view leads to the conclusion that to be able correctly to ascribe intentions, a certain minimal set of predicates must be not only applicable but true. And since we believe that there must be causally necessary structural and functional features to make this repertoire physically possible intentional explanations cannot be completely independent of physiology.

There are nevertheless some senses in which it is true to say that the precise physiological mechanisms involved are not relevant. First, there may exist more than one way, at the hardware level, of satisfying the minimal set of conditions for the ascription of intentions. If computers can be said — now or in the future — to display intentional behaviour then I doubt whether it will matter whether the hardware is wet or dry. Second, conditions for the *ascription* of intentions to a subject do not guarantee the truth of any particular ascription, just as a computer satisfying the minimal conditions for Pascal to be used does not necessarily guarantee that Pascal is in fact installed on the machine.

Some may wonder why I hesitate to go so far as to say that it *cannot* matter whether the hardware is wet or dry. The reason is that I am actually forced to admit some residual doubt. It *could* just be that the only way to construct some of the features required involves water rather than silicon systems. Perhaps certain kinds of proteins that sit at oil-water interfaces, like the surface of nerve cells, are absolutely required for the complexity required in the space available (c.f. Dennett, 1987). This would be a rather dramatic form of dependence on structure and it would have far-reaching implications for the future construction of computers, which might have to become wet. Nature might just have found the only solution here.

## Could a computer display intentional behaviour?

If the central argument in this chapter is correct, i.e. that intentional action does not require any inadequacy of causal connections at the neuronal (machine) level and that there is no need to postulate the existence of a special mediating structure (such as the 'liaison brain' — see p. 82), then there can be no reason a priori to exclude the possibility that constructed machines could show intentional behaviour. Whether we would still call such machines computers, I don't know. I suspect that we might well wish to stop calling them machines. But what I think is clear is that, on my view, it cannot really matter whether these machines/objects/persons came into existence by natural selection or as human-created artefacts.

Of course, we can be certain that the complexity of structure required is way beyond that found in any existing computers. But it is worth noting that, at the present rate of growth of computer memory and of miniaturisation, a computer with the storage capacity of the human brain and about its size could be on target for construction at the beginning of the next century. We might, therefore, begin to construct intentional computers in, say, 25 years' time. I should, of course, hasten to add that the emphasis here is very much on the 'begin'. Sufficient memory in a small enough space is certainly necessary, but that alone will not solve the formidable problems in conceiving how to write the appropriate software.

Would such an achievement undermine the primacy of intentional explanation? It might seem so, for surely in this case there would be nothing to stop us pulling the bits apart and finding out how it works. Indeed, we wouldn't even need to do that, having built it ourselves.

Anyone who is seduced by this line of argument must still be unconvinced by the first two sections of this chapter. At the risk of some repetition I will recast some of the argument in terms of the behaviour of the hypothetical intentional computer.

If it really can produce human-like intentional behaviour then that will include actions whose significance is to be found only in considering them *as* actions, not just as particular movements, i.e. as having significance in a context that is rich enough to require, for example, the property of intentionality. I see no need here to address questions like 'how do we know such a machine actually does have the same subjective feelings that we have when we act intentionally?' It suffices for the present purposes that our descriptions of its behaviour would need to take account of the subtle differences by which intentionality is expressed. It will be this kind of property, in fact, that will make us hesitate in continuing to describe the object as a computer, and certainly hesitate in describing it as a machine. This would not be because we would be in any doubt about the question whether a machine description could be given (after all, if we built the object, we know what to do to describe its machine states), but rather that it would be impossible to account for the property of intentionality (and other properties of its mind) without referring to its ability to understand. For intentionality presupposes understanding. We must be able to express our intentions and say what we intended when questioned.

This is the point at which to comment on the reasons for this hesitation on terminology. My own would certainly not be that I strongly object myself to being called a machine — it is up to us to develop our language as we see fit and if we want the concept of a machine to include human beings I would not quarrel too much with that. What we would then need, though, is another vocabulary that captures the differences involved. My own view is that the word *machine* has so many connotations that are not appropriate for extension to intentional computers and human beings that we may well not want to extend its meaning in this way. After all, part of our present concept of a machine is precisely that it does not act intentionally.

The sceptical machine analyst might well, at this point, make the move made by some experimental psychologists, i.e. to doubt whether these mental ascriptions are valid, given their subjective nature. Variously they may argue either that we should do without them because we cannot make them objective or that they don't exist anyway. If the problem lies in the subjectivity, then I suggest studying some of the cases described in Oliver Sacks' recent book of neurological cases (Sacks, 1985). There is not much doubt that some neurological lesions can, tragically, indeed reduce human action to a series of events that form a mere Humean sequence (in the sense that they have little or no connection other than that they are the sequence of events that happened in time), one after the other with no evidence of intentional action of the kind that enables us to give a life history of the person concerned. But the very fact that we can so readily identify such behaviour as grossly abnormal and say what in the person's life history is missing shows us that the subjective quality is not a serious barrier. It simply means that to achieve objectivity we need a rich language with very subtle distinctions. Our intentional computer must also be rich enough in its behaviour to avoid being taken for such a case of neurological deficiency.

Even if the machine analyst overcomes his scepticism about mental ascriptions, he may still feel that because there is at least no doubt in the case of the intentional computer that a definite series of machine states occurs during intentional behaviour and that these obey the rules of the computer's construction, this is the description that must have primacy in explanatory power since it must be possible in principle to replace every intentional action analysis by a machine state description. And indeed, on my view, that must also be possible for human action.

Here it is worth recalling a similar debate that I had with Charles Taylor soon after the publication of his *Explanation of Behaviour*. In an article in *Analysis* (Noble, 1967) I pointed out an inadequacy in Taylor's antecedent conditions for teleological behaviour and that the case he wished to propose, where a difference existed at the level of teleological description but not at the non-teleological level, could not exist, and only appeared to do so because Taylor had omitted central nervous states in his causal sequence at the non-teleological level. Taylor (1967), in reply admitted this but then pointed out that his central argument could still be valid provided that one considered a whole set of such cases. It might then be that only at the teleological level did the set have a discernible pattern that could form the basis of an explanation. This position is very similar indeed to my argument here that a machine level account of intentional action would contain reference to too many purely contingent conditions. It remains a moot, but I would now argue a relatively trivial, point whether one considers the identification of such a situation to be a conceptual matter (as I argued — Noble, 1968) or as a special kind of empirical matter (as Taylor argued — see the discussion of this in Montefiore (1971) and Kenny (1969)). I now hold the view that this depends very much on the context in which the discussion arises and that, as with many central features of scientific theory, it is a matter of choice which parts one takes as conceptual (axiomatic) and which one regards as predictions that have empirical consequences. Laws can start off in science as empirical observation and then later become conceptual schemes, even after the original empirical observations have been refined to a point where the law is no longer accurate as a description.

But, with regard to the central point of the debate with Charles Taylor, I think we are now quite close to agreement, though we might put very different emphases on the way the point is formulated.

To return to the intentional computer, how would we know that it would not yield to a machine-level analysis? I have hinted at one criterion already, i.e. that in describing its mental history we would need to include the property of intentionality. This kind of criterion could be regarded as analogous to identifying a program state and it would apply only to the fully established computer.

Another type of criterion would apply to how the machine was set up in the first place. Here I can envisage two possible scenarios: the one developmental, the other instantaneous.

The developmental scenario would be one in which we build in the relevant features to make it possible for dispositional and intentional behaviour to occur and we then liberate the computer on the world rather like an infant. And then, like the infant, we let it develop and, in so doing, acquire its own dispositions and intentions. To be sure, some of these, like our own in consequence of our particular genetic make up, will be more likely to occur than others — the development cannot be completely machine-independent. But also, like our own dispositions and intentions, the development will be an individual case history and that will pose all the usual problems for a machine analysis of the resulting behaviour — our explanatory scheme would need continually to grow to take in ever-widening circles of interaction with the world, including those with other persons and intentional computers. And there would be no way, given the property of intentionality, in which our account could fail to refer to the kinds of actions that persons perform. It would become very odd indeed to use such reference in talking about events which influence our intentional computer (for example that it knows that X has fallen in love with Y) while refusing to use such descriptions when talking about the computer's own actions (suppose, for example, we want to say that the significance for it of the fact that X has fallen in love with Y is that it also loves Y and intends to act on that fact). This kind of matter is not just a matter of convenience — that we would find it tedious in the extreme to avoid using these references. It is also crucial to the question of explanation, for we would not understand what it was that we were explaining if we failed to make such references in our account. And ultimately we have to accept that explanations are to be understood as such by us.

The instantaneous scenario would be a much less likely one. What I have in mind here is that the computer builders not only construct the hardware and the relevant software tools that give the machine its range of possible behaviour but also, via much more specific software (and here it doesn't matter too much whether this is genuine software or etched-in hardware representation), give it a complete ready made set of dispositions and intentions. This would be more difficult because it would be incredibly tedious. In effect it would amount to giving the computer a large part, at least, of a life-time's complement of what at the machine level would be purely contingent data. Worse still, we ourselves, as constructors, could only make sense of such contingent data (which would amount to huge data banks) by making reference to the kind of disposition or intention we were endowing the machine with. What would otherwise be a senseless data bank lacking any more explanatory order than the series of zeros and ones of endless binary code would come to have order by reference to the very concepts that the machine analyst is keen to dispense with.

I said that the instantaneous scenario is unlikely. It is more probably impossible. At a conservative estimate, the human brain has around $10^{13}$ bits of stored information. This includes only the store represented by neuronal connections. If some memory is stored at the molecular level, the figure is even more astronomic. And evidence that this is actually used comes from the results of temporal lobe epilepsies or artificial stimulation where the memory recall is so detailed as to be consistent with the view that very large parts of our experience are stored *in toto*.

Even if our computer constructors knew how to do it, they would require a vast army of people working for a phenomenal period of time to 'key in' the relevant information. How much simpler to just release the thing on the world and let it develop! Not only simpler — it might be the only way to do it.

## How would the inadequacy of certain theories be apparent?

My discussion of the intentional computer already contains the essence of what I want to say here. A physiological analysis of intentional action at the level of neuronal circuits and memory stores must eventually make reference to the stored information that is used in forming the antecedent conditions for a particular intentional action. There are then two ways, at least, in which a theory of the action could be developed on the basis of such physiological observations. The first would be both tedious (for much the same reasons as 'keying in' the relevant information into an intentional computer would be tedious) and completely lacking in explanatory power (unless one wants simply to explain or show *that* there is a determinate set of neuronal events underlying the action. But I at least do not doubt that and would not find anything surprising in such a demonstration). The relevant data would remain a set of contingent conditions.

The alternative approach would be the more natural one, i.e. to seek to identify this data as corresponding to particular past actions. And to capture the required richness of features like intentionality, this kind of analysis would need to use descriptions of such actions that contain reference to distinctions between, say, the person's lover and 'the person who did X to him/her'. For we know that such distinctions matter. But, by then, we would surely abandon the claim that we had produced a purely physiological theory.

## Is intentional action consistent with biological evolution?

Behaviour, like structure, has evolved. It must therefore be subject to the process of Darwinian evolution. There must be a reproductive advantage in each evolved property or, at least, it must be genetically tied to a property that does have such an advantage and not cancel that advantage out. Moreover, evolution as a process is blind. For a vivid popular account of this see Richard Dawkins (1986). (I should say here that the conclusion referred to here is not Dawkins' conclusion. I think though that Dawkins' books, particularly *The Selfish Gene* have provoked some people to draw this conclusion. Dawkins himself though was careful to avoid this mistake — see, for example, the last chapter of *The Selfish Gene*.) There cannot be room for directionality, let alone intentions, in the evolutionary process. From this some draw the conclusion that our conviction that we act intentionally must be an illusion. On this view, we are deluded and that is so even if we cannot adequately account to ourselves (for reasons of consistency in using our language, or any conceivable variant of it) for that fact.

I agree with this line of argument up to, but not including, its conclusion. Of course, there cannot be room for intentions as a necessary part of the evolutionary process, just as, presumably there is no necessary room for consciousness. But we will perhaps be less impressed by this fact if we consider that in exactly the same way, there is no necessary room for *anything* as a feature in the evolutionary process. That includes all of the present human structure. If evolution had taken a different route following one of the early catastrophes that seem (on one theory of evolution) to have acted on the earth every few tens of millions of years (see e.g. Gould, 1985) then the basic structure on which we are built may never have come about. Creatures very fundamentally different would have evolved. Intentional and conscious action may never have occurred. Individual properties that have evolved are not, on this view, necessary. They are simply those properties that, in the particular history of life on our planet have turned out to have survival value at the time they occurred. But the process remains a particular story despite the existence of a general theory.

Now if amongst those properties there is intentional behaviour then such behaviour must have had — maybe still has — survival value. And if to produce that one requires individuals displaying the properties of consciousness, subjectivity, intentionality and so on, then so be it. To produce life as we know it required water. But the existence of water was not, nothing is, an aim of the evolutionary process.

This point seems so obvious when one sees it. Yet like some illusions it requires a certain perspective to see it properly and I have certainly met biologists and philosophers who feel that to admit that people really do act intentionally runs somehow counter to fundamental biological theory. It may help to acquire the required perspective if I sketch out a plausible scenario for the evolution of intentional behaviour. But in doing so, I do not wish to commit myself to saying that this is how it must have been.

First, we have to explain how a property that in its individual expression in particular acts may not be subject to evolutionary pressure (because it is hard to see any particular survival value in it), can nevertheless have evolved. The example I would choose to illustrate this would be the emergence of play behaviour. Clearly there is no difficulty in providing an evolutionary account of this. Play may be a safe way in which the young of a species can acquire the skills and knowledge required to make later actions 'for real' be more effective, e.g. in finding a mate, in reproducing, protecting the young, in minimising the energy cost of surviving, etc.

But it may not matter much what exactly the young (or old) get up to when they play. To look for an evolutionary advantage in each and every piece of play behaviour is not necessary. To stretch the point, if one of the young produces a Mozart concerto, another a Shakespeare play, we really do not have to find particular evolutionary advantage in this. There may not be any. The advantage may lie only in the skills that play behaviour in general develops.

In a similar way I would argue that while intentional behaviour in general may (I think must) be an evolutionary advantage, I see no reason to assume that a biological evolutionary analysis must shed much light on particular intentional behaviour.

I have deliberately overplayed the point being made here and for more sophisticated readers I had better qualify it. I have argued as though individual acts of play are, like the Brownian motion of some unicellular organisms, not necessarily advantageous in their individual characteristics even though the general class of behaviour certainly is. Brownian motion is advantageous to the unicellular organism which in this way may bump into food — or food may bump into it — but each motion is random and cannot possibly be selected for. This view regards all actions resulting from the particular property as potentially (though not necessarily actually) equipotent. That is, however, not at all necessary to the case I am making. For example, a unicellular organism might add to its motion by developing cilia and it might, by building in chemical control, make this additional motion more efficient in enabling it to find food. All motions it may make are not then equipotent. It would nevertheless still be true to say that an advantage does not have to be found in each and every motion. All that is required is that the average effectiveness of the motions should be increased by the property that evolution can select for. In a similar way, I would not want to argue that all forms of play behaviour are equipotent. Clearly they are not and the evolution of play behaviour no doubt has acted on this difference and made the average potency greater. That is not to say that particular intentional action may not have survival and reproductive advantages. If most intentional actions did not then we can be sure that intentional behaviour would not have evolved. And it may yet be the death of us if, for example, intentional action succeeds in initiating a nuclear holocaust. Strictly speaking, evolution as a process is blind to all this. It must certainly be blind to a nuclear holocaust, in the sense that it cannot anticipate its possibility and then try to avoid it. That though does not make the intentional action that may produce it any less real to us.

## Conclusion

Finally, I want to return to the question of time scale. Earlier in this chapter I drew attention to the lack of a strict matching between the time scale of machine events and the order of a program. That seems to me to apply *a fortiori* to the correspondence between neuronal events and mental ascriptions. It would not merely be exceedingly cumbersome, at the neuronal level, to answer a question like 'When did I start to intend X and when did that intention become the intention to do Y?', it may not even be a meaningful question on the time scale on which we record neuronal events. This point is akin to Wittgenstein's remark that we cannot think half a thought, and it also means that questions like 'do brain events *precede* an intention?' — see e.g. Libet *et al* (1983) — are not as easily interpreted as the subtitle of Libet *et al*'s paper (*The unconscious initiation of a freely voluntary act*) would imply. After all, even intentional acts must have antecedents on my view (see p. 82).

It is important to note that the difficulty is not merely that the neural events would be too fine grained to enable us to 'see' the intention change. It is also because, at the neuronal level, we might not be able to say that there was the intention to do X without making reference to accounts of states which, like program states, do not have existence in a way that can be measured in time by recording particular machine or neuronal events. It may even be misleading to refer to these as states for that is already to talk about something we normally locate in time. Remember my analogy with a program state. The analogy was based on the example of a convergence property which as a mathematical property certainly does not exist 'in time' though it can of course be expressed, as intentions are, by particular events in time. The word 'property' may therefore be better than state.

The analysis would then be quite incomplete without an understanding at the level either of program states or mental activity. And that includes the possibility that some of the states may acquire their explanatory significance by making reference forward to future events. It is, of course, characteristic of intentional behaviour that it does this. In a program representation of the behaviour the forward referencing might be replaced by nests of IF–THEN–ELSE or CASE statements. But as high level structured programmers are well aware, the significance particularly of some of the cleverer uses of such statements in programs can be elusive unless one is given the clue that the aim is to achieve X, i.e. that one understands the programmer's intention. And the fact that it was his 'intention' here is significant. This kind of understanding has a property akin to that which occurs when looking at some illusions that can be 'seen' in at least two incompatible ways. Once we know the aim of a program we 'see' it in that light and a lot of otherwise obscure programming will click into place in our explanatory scheme. The way we structure the program will, in good programming, be determined in part by that understanding. If that is true of computer programs, then it is even more likely to be true of understanding the behaviour of a person. And that is so despite the fact that I admit that, if we try to ignore the fact that we, as the subjects trying to achieve the understanding, are persons, there may well be accounts that from such a non-person standpoint are perfectly complete but which make no reference to things like intentions.

I am unclear though what it would mean to call such accounts explanations. Even the word 'account' might be too strong. For us, the phenomenon of explanation presupposes understanding, which requires that we be persons, are conscious, can have intentions etc. And there would be no demand for explanations if this were not true. I think this is the problem that lies at the root of very many philosophical puzzles in the concept of a person. It certainly underlies the incoherence of any theory that tries to account for our behaviour without making reference to intentions, for such an account, if successful, would remove the subject of understanding, and so remove the *raison d'être* of the problem. For us, that is not just impossible, it is inconceivable.

**Suggestions for further reading.** The background to the arguments that formed the original basis for the positions outlined in this chapter will be found in the debate following the publication of Charles Taylor's *The Explanation of Behaviour*. The published form of this debate is to be found in Kenny (1969), Montefiore (1971), Taylor (1967) and Noble (1967, 1968). A second theme that has contributed to my position is to be found in Strawson's *Individuals* (particularly the chapter on the concept of a person) and Williams' critique of Strawson in *Problems of the Self*.

Some of the arguments concerning the physical basis of intentional action will be found in Dennett's *The Intentional Stance*, particularly the chapter on 'Fast Thinking'. Curiously, perhaps, my position owes little of an overt nature to the writings of scientific authors, though I find myself in agreement with much of François Jacob's *Logique du Vivant* and Jean-Didier Vincent's *Biologie des Passions* (Editions Odile Jacob, Seuil, 1986). Vincent's book has an unusual feel for the subtlety of the problems encountered in giving a biological basis for affective behaviour. Unlike Jacob's book, it has not yet been translated into English, but it deserves to be. Finally, J.Z. Young has written a little book *Philosophy and the Brain* (OUP, 1987) that includes the very little we know of electrical changes accompanying intentional behaviour.

CHAPTER 7*

# COGNITIVE ETHOLOGY: HUNTING FOR BARGAINS OR A WILD GOOSE CHASE?

*Daniel C. Dennett*

**Strategies of simplification**

The field of Artificial Intelligence has produced so many new concepts — or at least vivid and more structured versions of old concepts — that it would be surprising if none of them turned out to be of value to students of animal behaviour. Which will be most valuable? I will resist the temptation to engage in either prophecy or salesmanship; instead of attempting to answer the question: 'How might Artificial Intelligence inform the study of animal behaviour?' I will concentrate on the obverse: 'How might the study of animal behaviour inform research in Artificial Intelligence?'

I take it we all agree that in the end we want to be able to describe and explain the design and operation of animal nervous systems at many different levels, from the neurochemical to the psychological and even the phenomenological (where appropriate!), and we want to understand how and why these designs have evolved, and how and why they are modulated in the individual organisms. AI research, like all other varieties of research on this huge topic, must make drastic oversimplifications in order to make even apparent progress. There are many strategies of simplification, of which these five, while ubiquitous in all areas of mind/brain research, are particularly popular in AI:

---

*I am grateful to C. M. Heyes and K. Akins for helpful suggestions on my handling of the topics in this chapter.

1. Ignore both learning and development; attempt to model the 'mature competence' first, postponing questions about how it could arise.
2. Isolate a particular subcomponent or sub-subcomponent, ignoring almost all problems about how it might be attached to the larger system.
3. Limit the domain of operation of the modelled system or subsystem to a tiny corner of the real domain — try to solve a 'toy problem', hoping that subsequent scaling-up will be a straightforward extrapolation.
4. Bridge various gaps in one's model with frankly unrealistic or even deliberately 'miraculous' stopgaps — 'oracles', or what I have called 'cognitive wheels' (Dennett, 1984b). (In the neurosciences, one posits what I have called 'wonder tissue' to bridge these gaps.)
5. Avoid the complexities of real-time, real-world co-ordination by ignoring robotics and specializing in what I call 'bedridden' systems: systems that address the sorts of problems that can be presented via a narrow 'verbal' channel, and whose solutions can be similarly narrowly conveyed to the world. (Dennett, 1980)

Many of the best-known achievements of AI have availed themselves of all five of these strategies of simplification: chess-playing programs, and natural language parsers and speech recognition systems, for instance. Some critics are hostile to any efforts in cognitive science enabled by these strategies, but there is no point in attempting to 'refute' them a priori. Since they are strategies, not doctrines or laws or principles, their tribunal is 'handsome is as handsome does'. The results to date are an inconclusive mixture. One theorist's deep but narrow insight is another's falsely lit detour; just which points of verisimilitude between model and modelled should count as telling partial confirmation and which as tricked up and misleading is often a matter of free-form dispute.

Instead of spending yet more time debating the wisdom of these strategies of simplification, one might just adopt some rival strategy or strategies, and let posterity decide which are the most fruitful. An obvious candidate, especially on this occasion, is to turn from the simulation of human cognition to the simulation of animal cognition. If human minds (or brains) are too complex, why not start with simpler minds — insect minds or bird brains?

'Why not try to do a whole starfish, for instance? It has no eyes or ears, only rudimentary pattern-discrimination capacities, few modes of action, few needs or intellectual accomplishments. That could be a warm-up exercise for something a bit more challenging: a turtle, perhaps, or a mole. A turtle must organise its world knowledge, such as it is, so that it can keep life and limb together by making real time decisions based on that knowledge, so while a turtle-simulation would not need a natural language parser, for instance, it would need just the sorts of efficient organisation and flexibility of control distribution you have to provide in the representation of world knowledge behind a natural language parsing system of a simulated human agent such as SHRDLU' (Winograd, 1972) — Dennett (1978).

So one reasonable motive for attempting AI modelling of animals is that it permits simplicity without unnatural truncation of systems — and you can get as much simplicity as you want by just descending the phylogenetic scale. If starfish are too hard, try *paramecia*. A simplifying *side*-step in this descent is to opt for the modelling of *imaginary* simple animals, living in simulated simple environments. Such thought experiments can be brought to half-life, so to speak, and halfway put to the test, thanks to the computer's capacity to keep track of, and resolutely follow up the implications of, the loose ends among one's assumptions. The three-wheeled Martian iguana I fantasised in 1978 has not, to my knowledge, been born in any computer, but several of its brethren have been created. Braitenberg (1984), coming from the neuroscientific end of the spectrum, has described a considerable menagerie of ever more complex 'vehicles' exhibiting increasingly 'psychological' competences, and coming from the opposite AI corner we have Rod Brooks' artificial insects, real robots that perform uncannily biological-seeming feats with extremely simple control circuits (Brooks, 1987).

Of course the farther you get from human beings the less likely your successes are to shed light on the puzzles of *our* cognitive economies, but by training our attention on the differences that emerge, as well as the invariances that persist, as one moves along the actual phylogenetic scale, we may harvest insights about fundamental design principles of nervous systems, and about the traditions and precedents of design that are the raw materials of subsequent design innovations.

There is nothing new about this strategy, except for the relative ease with which very intricate models can now be 'built' and 'flight-tested', thanks to computer modelling. Some will object that much of the best computer modelling of simple nervous systems has had nothing in common with AI — and is indeed often the work of people quite hostile to the methods, assumptions, and pretensions of the ideologues of AI. That is true, but I think it is a fact of diminishing interest. The gulf between neuroscientists trying to build realistic models of simple neural systems from the bottom up (e.g. Hawkins and Kandel, 1984) and 'pure' AI modelers who frankly ignore all biological constraints (e.g. Doyle 1979) is being filled in with just about every intermediate variety of modeller. The antagonisms that remain say more about the economics and sociology of science than about the issues.

One reason people in AI have been dissuaded from simulating animal cognition is that they would have to give up one of their favourite sources of inspiration: introspection and reflection about how *they* perform the cognitive operations they choose to model. I say 'inspiration' and not 'data' since only under the most structured and well-studied conditions do people in AI count a match between model and 'introspection' as corroboration of their model (Ericsson and Simon, 1984). But without the luxury of such self-modelling, or even the wealth of everyday lore we all accrue about human habits of thought, AI modellers are short on materials for the task of modelling animal cognition. It is here, of course, where the study of animal behaviour might come to the rescue.

## The intentional stance as a designer's strategy

All the AI efforts to simulate cognition, variously enriched by data from experimental studies of real creatures (and people) and by casual observation and introspection, are essentially *engineering* projects: attempts to design 'machinery' with particular 'psychological' talents. As engineering projects, their success depends heavily on the imaginative and organizational powers of the designers, who must juggle an ever increasing number of somewhat vague, somewhat conflicting sets of 'specs' — specifications — of the phenomena being modelled.

One way of imposing order — at least a temporary, tentative, order — on the interdependent tasks of *clarifying (and revising) the specs* and *designing a system that meets the specs* is to adopt the intentional stance. One adopts a strategy of treating the systems in question as *intentional systems*, approximations of rational agents, to whom one attributes beliefs, desires, and enough rationality to choose the actions that are likely to fulfill their desires given the truth of their beliefs. We all adopt the intentional stance towards our friends and relatives and other human beings, but one can also get results by adopting the stance when designing or diagnosing certain artefacts — typically computer systems — and when studying the behaviour of non-human animals.

My analysis and defence of adopting the intentional stance in the study of animal behaviour (Dennett, 1983) has been greeted by workers in the field with about equal measures of enthusiasm, dismissal, utter disinterest and sceptical curiosity. A particularly insightful curious sceptic is C. M. Heyes (forthcoming), who slyly wonders whether I have managed to drum up the enthusiasm by merely 'providing a concert party for the troops' — making ethologists feel better about their lonely and ill-understood campaigns in the bush — while failing utterly to make good on my promise to show how 'disciplined application of the intentional stance in cognitive ethology will yield descriptions of animal behaviour that are especially useful to the information processing theorist.'

This would seem to be the ideal forum for me to respond to Heyes' challenge, for while I am always willing to entertain, I do aspire to something more. Heyes quotes my central claim:

> The intentional stance, however, provides just the right interface between specialties: a 'black box' characterization of behavioural and cognitive competences observable in the field, but couched in language that (ideally) heavily constrains the design of machinery to put in the black box. (Dennett, 1983, p. 350)

and then goes on to ask 'but *how* might intentional accounts 'constrain' information processing theories?' In particular, since the ultimate destination of theory on my view is an utterly mechanistic account of the brain's activities, and since I insist that the most that the intentional stance yields is an idealised and instrumentalistic account, it seems to Heyes that the intentional stance is at best a digression and distraction from the task at hand. How can a frankly idealising model — which unrealistically describes (or prescribes) presumably optimal performance — actually constrain the development (from what I call the design stance) of a mechanistic and realistic model? To put it even more bluntly, how could instrumentalistic fictions help us figure out the mechanistic facts?

One can view the intentional stance as a limiting case of the design stance: one predicts by taking on just one assumption about the design of the system in question: whatever the design is, it is optimal. This assumption can be seen at work whenever, in the midst of the design stance proper, a designer or design investigator inserts a frank homunculus (an intentional system as subsystem) in order to bridge a gap of ignorance. The theorist says, in effect, 'I don't know how to design this subsystem yet, but I know what it's supposed to do, so let's just pretend there is a demon there who wants nothing more than to do that task and knows just how to do it.' One can then go on to design the surrounding system with the simplifying assumption that this component is 'perfect'. One asks oneself how the rest of the system must work, given that this component will not let down the side.

Occasionally such a design effort in AI proceeds by *literally* installing a human module *pro tempore* in order to explore design alternatives in the rest of the system. When the HWIM speech recognition system was being developed at Bolt Beranek and Newman (Woods and Makhoul, 1974), the role of the phonological analysis module, which was supposed to generate hypotheses about the likely phonemic analysis of segments of the acoustic input, was temporarily played by human phonologists looking at segments of spectrograms of utterances. Another human being, playing the role of the control module, could communicate with the phonology demon and the rest of the system, asking questions, and posing hypotheses for evaluation.

Once it was determined what the rest of the system had to 'know' in order to give the phonologist module the help it needed, that part of the system was designed (discharging, *inter alia*, the control demon) and then the phonologists themselves could be replaced by a machine: a subsystem that used the same input (spectrograms — but not visually encoded, of course) to generate the same sorts of queries and hypotheses. During the design testing phase the phonologists tried hard not to use all the extra knowledge they had — about likely words, grammatical constraints, etc. — since they were mimicking *stupid* homunculi, specialists who only knew and cared about acoustics and phonemes.

Until such time as an effort is made to replace the phonologist subsystem with a machine, one is committed to virtually none of the sorts of design assumptions *about the working of that subsystem* that are genuinely explanatory. But in the meantime one may make great progress on the design of the other subsystems it must interact with, and the design of the supersystem composed of all the subsystems.

The first purported chess playing automaton was a late eighteenth-century hoax: Baron Wolfgang von Kempelen's wooden mannikin, which did indeed pick up and move the chess pieces, thereby playing a decent game. It was years before the secret of its operation was revealed: a human midget chess master was hidden in the clockwork under the chess table, and could see the moves through the translucent squares — a literal homunculus (Raphael, 1976). Notice that the success or failure of the intentional stance as a predictor is so neutral with regard to design that it does not distinguish von Kempelen's midget-in-the-works design from, say, Berliner's Hitech, a current chess program of considerable power (Berliner and Ebeling, 1986). Both work; both work well; both must have a design that is a fair approximation of optimality, so long as what we mean by optimality at this point focuses narrowly on the task of playing chess and ignores all other design considerations (e.g. the care and feeding of the midget vs. the cost of electricity — but try to find a usable electrical outlet in the eighteenth century!). Whatever their internal differences, both systems are intentional systems in good standing, though one of them has a subsystem, a homunculus, that is itself as unproblematic an intentional system as one could find. Intentional system theory is almost literally a black box theory — but that hardly makes it behaviouristic in Skinner's sense (see Dennett, 1981).

On the contrary, intentional system theory is an attempt to provide what Chomsky, no behaviourist, calls a competence model, in contrast to a performance model. Before we ask ourselves how mechanisms are designed, we must get clear about what the mechanisms are supposed to (be able to) do. This strategic vision has been developed further by Marr (1982) in his methodological reflections on his work on vision. He distinguishes three levels of analysis. The highest level, which he misleadingly calls *computational*, is in fact not at all concerned with computational processes, but strictly (and more abstractly) with the question of what function the system in question is serving — or, more formally, with what function *in the mathematical sense* it must (somehow or other) 'compute'. At this computational level one attempts to specify formally and rigorously the system's proper competence

(Millikan, 1984, would call it the system's proper function). For instance, one fills in the details in the formula:

> 'given an element in the set of x's as input, it yields an element in the set of y's as output according to the following formal rules ...'

— while remaining silent or neutral about the implementation or performance details of whatever resides in the competent black box. Marr's second level down is the *algorithmic* level, which does specify the computational processes but remains as neutral as possible about the *hardware*, which is described at the bottom level.

Marr claims that until we get a clear and precise understanding of the activity of a system at its highest, 'computational' level, we cannot properly address detailed questions at the lower levels, or interpret such data as we may already have about processes implementing those lower levels. This echoes Chomsky's long insistence that the diachronic process of language-learning cannot be insightfully investigated until one is clear about the end-state mature competence towards which it is moving. Like Chomsky's point, it is better viewed as a strategic maxim than as an epistemological principle. After all, it is not impossible to stumble upon an insight into a larger picture while attempting to ask yourself what turn out to be subsidiary and somewhat myopically posed questions.

Marr's more telling strategic point is that if you have a seriously mistaken view about what the computational-level description of your system is (as all earlier theories of vision did, in his view), your attempts to theorise at lower levels will be confounded by spurious artefactual puzzles. What Marr underestimates, however, is the extent to which computational level (or intentional stance) descriptions can also mislead the theorist who forgets just how idealised they are (Ramachandran, 1985).

The intentional stance *postpones consideration of* some types of cost. It assumes that in the black box are *whatever cognitive resources are required* to perform the task or subtask intentionally described, without regard (for the time being) of how much these resources might cost, either in terms of current space, material and energy allocations, or in terms of 'research and development' — the costs to Mother Nature of getting to such a design from a pre-existing design. And so long as cost is no object, there is no reason not to overdesign the system, endowing it with a richer intentional competence than it usually needs, or can afford.

But it is precisely these costs that loom large in biology, and that justify the strategic recommendation that we should be bargain hunters when trying to uncover the design rationales of living systems: always look for a system that provides a mere approximation of the competence described from the intentional stance, a cheap substitute that works well enough most of the time.

When great tits do a surprisingly good job of approximating the optimal foraging strategy in Krebs' 'two-armed bandit' apparatus (Krebs, Kacelnik and Taylor, 1978), we do not make the mistake of installing a mathematician-homunculus in their brains to work out the strategy via a dynamic programming algorithm. As Krebs notes, we cast about for cheaper, more realistic machinery that would obtain similar results. When the honey bees' oleic acid trigger was uncovered, this deposed the public-health-officer-homunculus whose task it was to recognise bee corpses as health hazards and order the right measures.

But if such intentional systems are always destined to be replaced by cheap substitutes, what constraining power do the interim intentional stance descriptions actually have? Only this: they describe the ideal against which to recognise the bargain. They remind the theorist of the point of the bargain device, and why it may be such a good deal. For instance, the vertical symmetry detectors that are ubiquitous machinery in animal vision are baffling until we consider them, as Braitenberg (1984) recommends, as quick-and-dirty discriminators of the ecologically important datum that *some other organism is looking at me*. The intentional stance provides a tentative background against which the researcher can contrast the observed behaviour *as a competence* — in this case the competence to detect something in the environment *as* another organism facing head on, about which one might want to ask certain questions, such as: What is the prowess and cost-effectiveness of this machinery? — a question that cannot even be posed until one makes an assumption about what the machinery is for. If you consider it merely as a symmetry detector, you miss the rationale for its speedy triggering of orientation and flight-preparation subsystems, for instance. It is the intentional characterisation that can vividly capture the larger role of the machinery in the whole system.

To return to Heyes' question, with which we began, in what way does the intentional stance *constrain* the development of design hypotheses in information processing theories? It constrains in the same way arithmetic constrains the design of hand calculators. Arithmetic can also be viewed as an abstract, ideal, normative system (how one *ought* to add, subtract, multiply and divide), and then we can see that although individual hand calculators all 'strive' to meet this ideal, they all fall short in ways that can be explained by citing cost-effectiveness considerations. For instance, arithmetic tells us that 10 divided by 3 multiplied by 3 is 10, but hand calculators will tell you that it is 9.9999999, due to round-off or truncation error, a shortcoming the designers have decided to live with, even though such errors are extremely destructive under many conditions in larger systems that do not have the benefit of human observer/users (or very smart homunculi!) to notice and correct them.

Just as there are many different designs for hand calculators, all of which implement — with various different approximations and shortcomings — the Arithmetical System, so many different designs of the neural hardware might implement any particular intentional system — with different attendant fallings short. So an intentional stance characterisation does constrain design, but only partially. It is one constraint among others, but a particularly fruitful and central one: the one that reminds the designer or design-interpreter of *what the system is supposed to do*.

## Why vervet monkeys don't perform speech acts

Another way of looking at the intentional stance as a tactic to adopt in the field is to consider the likely fruits of *taking it as seriously as possible*. One says to oneself, in effect: 'Now if these animals *really* believed such-and-such and *really* desired such-and-such, they would have to believe (desire, intend, expect, fear) such-and-such as well. Do they?' It is the intentional stance's rationality assumption that generates ('a priori' as it were) the consequent to be tested. Such an exercise can help uncover particular aspects of falling-short, particular hidden cheap shortcuts in the design, and help explain otherwise baffling anomalies in an animal's behaviour. One uses the intentional stance to ask the question: What is it about the world in which this animal lives that makes *this* cheap substitute a good bargain? I will sketch an example of this drawn from my own very limited experience as an amateur ethologist (Dennett, 1988).

In June of 1984, I had a brief introduction to ethological field work, observing Seyfarth and Cheney observing the vervet monkeys in Kenya. In (Dennett, 1983) I had discussed the vervets and their fascinating proto-language, and had speculated on the likely fruits of using the intentional stance to get a better fix on the 'translation' of their utterance-types. In particular, I had proposed attempting to use what I called the Sherlock Holmes method: setting cognitive ruses and traps for the vervets, to get them to betray their knowledge and understanding in one-shot experiments.

Once I got in the field and saw first hand the obstacles to performing such experiments, I found some good news and some bad news. The bad news was that the Sherlock Holmes method, in its classical guise, has very limited appplicability to the vervet monkeys — and by extrapolation, to other 'lower' animals. The good news was that by adopting the intentional stance one can generate some plausible and indirectly testable hypotheses about why this should be so, and about the otherwise perplexing limitations of the cheap substitutes discovered in the vervets.

A vocalization that Seyfarth and Cheney were studying during my visit had been dubbed the Moving Into the Open (or MIO) grunt. Shortly before a monkey in a bush moves out into the open, it often gives a MIO grunt. Other monkeys in the bush will often repeat it — spectrographic analysis has not (yet) revealed a clear mark of difference between the initial grunt and this response. If no such echo is made, the original grunter will often stay in the bush for five or ten minutes and then repeat the MIO. Often, when the MIO is echoed by one or more other monkeys, the original grunter will thereupon move cautiously into the open.

But what does the MIO grunt mean? We listed the possible translations to see which we could eliminate or support on the basis of evidence already at hand. I started with what seemed to be the most straightforward and obvious possibility:

'I'm going.'
'I read you. You're going.'

But what would be the use of saying this? Vervets are in fact a taciturn lot, who keep silent most of the time, and are not given to anything that looks like passing the time of day by making obvious remarks. Then could it be a request for permission to leave?

'May I go, please?'
'Yes, you have my permission to go.'

This hypothesis could be knocked out if higher ranking vervets ever originated the MIO in the presence of their subordinates. In fact, higher ranking vervets do tend to move into the open first, so it doesn't seem that MIO is a request for permission. Could it be a command, then?

'Follow me!'
'Aye, aye, Cap'n.'

Not very plausible, Cheney thought. 'Why waste words with such an order when it would seem to *go without saying* in vervet society that low-ranking animals follow the lead of their superiors? For instance, you would think that there would be a vocalization meaning 'May I?' to be said by a monkey when approaching a dominant in hopes of grooming it. And you'd expect there to be two responses: 'You may' and 'You may not,' but there is no sign of any such vocalization. Apparently such interchanges would not be useful enough to be worth the effort. There are gestures and facial expressions which may serve this purpose, but no audible signals.' Perhaps, Cheney mused, the MIO grunt served simply to acknowledge and share the fear:

'I'm really scared.'
'Yes. Me too.'

Another interesting possibility was that the grunt helped with co-ordination of the group's movements:

'Ready for me to go?'
'Ready whenever you are.'

A monkey that gives the echo is apt to be the next to leave. Or perhaps even better:

'Coast clear?'
'Coast is clear. We're covering you.'

The behaviour so far observed is compatible with this reading, which would give the MIO grunt a robust purpose, orienting the monkeys to a task of co-operative vigilance. The responding monkeys do watch the leave-taker and look in the right directions to be keeping an eye out. 'Suppose then, that this is our best candidate hypothesis,' I said. 'Can we think of anything to look for that would particularly shed light on it?' Among males, competition overshadows co-operation more than among females. Would a male bother giving the MIO if its only company in a bush was another male? Seyfarth had a better idea: suppose a male originated the MIO grunt; would a rival male be devious enough to give a dangerously misleading MIO response when he saw that the originator was about to step into trouble? The likelihood of ever getting any good evidence of this is minuscule, for you would have to observe a case in which Originator didn't see and Responder did see a nearby predator *and* Responder saw that Originator didn't see the predator. (Otherwise Responder would just waste his credibility and incur the wrath and mistrust of Originator for no gain.) Such a coincidence of conditions must be extremely rare. This was an ideal opportunity, it seemed, for a Sherlock Holmes ploy.

Seyfarth suggested that perhaps we could spring a trap with something like a stuffed python that we could very slyly and surreptitiously reveal to just one of two males who seemed about to venture out of a bush. The technical problems would clearly be nasty, and at best it would be a long shot, but with luck we might just manage to lure a liar into our trap. But on further reflection, the technical problems looked virtually insurmountable. How would we establish that the 'liar' had actually seen (and been taken in by) the 'predator', and wasn't just innocently and sincerely reporting that the coast was clear? I found myself tempted (as often before in our discussions) to indulge in a fantasy: 'If only I were small enough to dress up in a vervet suit, or if only we could introduce a trained vervet, or a robot or puppet vervet who could...' and slowly it dawned on me that this recurring escape from reality had a point: there is really no substitute, in the radical translation business, for going in and *talking with the natives*. You can test more hypotheses in half an hour of attempted chitchat than you can in a month of observation and unobtrusive manipulation. But to take advantage of this you have to become obtrusive; you — or your puppet — have to enter into communicative encounters with the natives, if only in order to go around pointing to things and asking 'Gavagai?' in an attempt to figure out what 'Gavagai' means. Similarly, in your typical mystery story caper, some crucial part of the setting up of the 'Sherlock Holmes method' trap is — *must be* — accomplished by imparting some (mis)information verbally. Manoeuvering your subjects into the right frame of mind — and knowing you've succeeded — without the luxurious efficiency of words can prove to be arduous at best, and often next to impossible.

In particular, it is often next to impossible in the field to establish that particular monkeys have been shielded from a particular bit of information. And since many of the theoretically most interesting hypotheses depend on just such circumstances, it is often very tempting to think of moving the monkeys into a lab, where a monkey can be physically *removed* from the group and given opportunities to acquire information that the others don't have *and that the test monkey knows they don't have*. Just such experiments are being done, by Seyfarth and Cheney with a group of captive vervets in California, and by other researchers with chimpanzees. The early results are tantalising but equivocal (of course), and *perhaps* the lab environment, with its isolation booths, will be just the tool we need to open up the monkeys' minds, but my hunch is that being isolated in that way is such an unusual predicament for vervet monkeys that they will prove to be unprepared by evolution to take advantage of it.

The most important thing I think I learned from actually watching the vervets is that they live in a world in which secrets are virtually impossible. Unlike orangutans, who are solitary and get together only to mate and when mothers are rearing offspring, and unlike chimps, who have a fluid social organization in which individuals come and go, seeing each other fairly often but also venturing out on their own a large proportion of the time, vervets live in the open in close proximity to the other members of their groups, and have no solitary projects of any scope. So it is a rare occasion indeed when one vervet is in a position to learn something that it alone knows *and knows that it alone knows*. (The knowledge of the others' ignorance, and of the possibility of maintaining it, is critical. Even when one monkey is the first to see a predator or a rival group, and knows it, it is almost never in a position to be sure the others won't very soon make the same discovery.) But without such occasions in abundance, there is little to impart to others. Moreover, without frequent opportunities to *recognise* that one knows something that the others don't know, devious reasons for or against imparting information cannot even exist — let alone be recognised and acted upon. I can think of no way of describing this critical simplicity in the *Umwelt* of the vervets, this missing ingredient, that does not avail itself explicitly or implicitly of higher-order intentional idioms.

In sum, the vervets couldn't really make use of most of the features of a human language, for their world — or you might even say their lifestyle — is too simple. Their communicative needs are few but intense, and their communicative opportunities are limited. Like honeymooners who have not been out of each other's sight for days, they find themselves with not much to say to each other (or to decide to withhold). But if they couldn't make use of a fancy, human-like language, we can be quite sure that evolution hasn't provided them with one. Of course *if* evolution provided them with an elaborate language in which to communicate, the language itself would radically change their world, and permit them to create and pass secrets as profusely as we do. And then they could go on to use their language, as we use ours, in hundreds of diverting and marginally 'useful' ways. But without the original information-gradients needed to prime the evolutionary pump, such a language couldn't get established.

So we can be quite sure that the MIO grunt, for instance, is not crisply and properly translated by *any* familiar human interchange. It can't be a (pure, perfect) command or request or question or exclamation because it isn't part of a system that is elaborate enough to make room for such sophisticated distinctions. When you say 'Wanna go for a walk?' to your dog and he jumps up with a lively bark and expectant wag of the tail, this is not really a question and answer. There are only a few ways of 'replying' that are available to the dog. It can't do anything tantamount to saying 'I'd rather wait till sundown,' or 'Not if you're going to cross the highway,' or even 'No thanks.' Your utterance is a question *in English* but a sort of melted-together mixture of question, command, exclamation and mere *harbinger* (you've made some of those going-out-noises again) to your dog (Bennett, 1976, 1983). The vervets' MIO grunt is no doubt a similar mixture, but while that means we shouldn't get our hopes too high about learning Vervetese and finding out all about monkey life by having conversations with the vervets, it doesn't at all rule out the utility of these somewhat fanciful translation hypotheses as ways of interpreting — and uncovering — the actual informational roles or functions of these vocalizations. When you think of the MIO as 'Coast clear?' your attention is directed to a variety of testable hypotheses about further relationships and dependencies that ought to be discoverable if that is what MIO means — or even just 'sort of' means.

But is that all there is? Perhaps *this* is the 'concert party for the troops' Heyes supposes I am offering: I seem to end up saying that vervet monkeys don't *really* mean anything at all by their vocalizations. Am I also saying that vervet monkeys don't *really* believe anything? What *literally* can the intentional stance show us about animal belief — about what is going on in the minds of the animals being studied?

That question, I am saying, is misguided. The intentional stance attributions of belief, for all their caveats, are as literal as any attributions of belief — including self-attributions — can ever get. There are no deeper facts about the beliefs of animals — or about our own.* If you want to know the deep, objective *truth* about the contents of animal minds, then either you are curious about the actual design of their brains (at many levels of analysis), and the rationale of that design, or you just want to know the most predictive intentional stance characterization of the animal, with all its idealizations. If you think there is another, deeper sort of fact about animal minds, then the intentional stance won't help you to find it — but then nothing will, since if that is your curiosity, you are no longer doing the cognitive science of wild animals; you are on a wild goose chase.

---

* In disagreement with Griffin (1981, 1984), I think the more particular hope that cognitive ethology will shed light on animal *consciousness* is a red herring. The only concepts of consciousness that yield genuinely explanatory attributions are applicable only to creatures with a full-fledged natural language — human beings.

CHAPTER 8

# REPRESENTATION, FUNCTIONALISM, AND SIMPLE LIVING SYSTEMS

*Shawn Lockery*

## Introduction

Some people were quite relieved to see behaviourism fall from favour. Time and again in the history of science our commonsense view of the world has been stood on its head. Usually, after an initial period of intellectual vertigo, we adjust. Sometimes, however, the pronouncements of science hit too close to home. It is one thing to accept the paradoxes of relativity or the theory of natural selection, but to embrace the behaviourist's view that one's beliefs and desires are nothing but reflexive dispositions is quite another. Behaviourism thus led inexorably to a separation of the scientific and manifest image of ourselves and threatened to replace the human agent with a black box and the moral order with nothing. The joint advance of artificial intelligence and neuroscience has unseated the behaviourist and made it once again respectable to suppose that internal states cause behaviour. We now have working hypotheses concerning how a device or system or organism might internally represent and process information, and the biological wherewithal to put these hypotheses to the test.

But as we begin to get serious about internal representation and the nervous system, we are threatened with a new version of the rift between the scientific and commonsense account of ourselves. One can imagine many different ways the nervous system might represent information. In some versions of the story, information is contained in neural states that function in the production of behaviour just like beliefs and desires. In other versions, the information-bearing states in no way reflect the structure of beliefs and desires, or any other commonsense psychological states. Everyone in cognitive science agrees that the issue can only be settled by getting out the electrodes, so to speak, and that the stakes are high. If the states of the nervous system that cause behaviour do not exhibit the causal interactions characteristic of beliefs and desires, then the commonsense theory of human action is rendered false — every bit as false as the caloric theory of heat, phlogistic theory of combustion, and so on — and once again we are faced with a radical incommensurability between our manifest and our scientific self image, and the attending consequences.

With so much in the balance one is naturally anxious to get the physiological project underway. Unfortunately, there are currently some very impressive obstacles to studying the neuronal basis of mental states, or, so as not to beg the question, 'cognitive behaviour.' The best species for such an investigation are either off-limits on moral grounds, dauntingly complex or both. It thus becomes attractive to adopt what biologists call the model-systems approach to the problem: find a species that embodies a simpler and more tractable version of the same problem. One then relies on the fundamentally conservative nature of evolution, hoping that principles taken from simple systems will either prove immediately generalisable to 'higher' organisms, or at least yield important insights 'up' there. The difficulty with the model-systems approach in the study of mental representation is that the simpler a system or organism is, the less its behaviour resembles that of the systems to which common sense naturally attributes mental states. Thus one risks studying forms of representation that have no direct consequence for our understanding of mentality.

Much of what follows is therefore devoted to outlining principles by which we can assure ourselves that a potential model system is worthwhile. Since we shall be reaching a long way down the phylogenetic scale, much of the discussion will concern minimal conditions. In this spirit, Part I considers the minimal conditions a representational state must fulfill to qualify as an object of study in cognitive neurobiology. The minimal conditions on representational states are then put in terms of behavioural criteria for the selection of model systems. This is a necessary move because, although the issue whether a system actually has mental states is ultimately a question of physiology, one has first got to know where the issue can be raised nontrivially. Thus Part II considers special forms of classical conditioning which justify attribution of psychologically interesting representational states. Part III then surveys the scientific literature on classical conditioning in simple systems and ends with some speculative implications for the nature of mental representation.

## Part I

*What is a representational state?*

The notion of an internal representation of information is what sets the cognitive sciences apart from other psychologies. Internal representations are meant to be the currency of thought and the key to understanding intelligent behaviour. Thus, although representations of information are extremely widespread in biology, only some of them are cognitive material. The genetic code, for example, is an instance of representation *par excellence*, but not of cognitive representation. The cognitive sciences trade in information that arises from perceptual conditions, not from evolutionary history — and in information that guides the behaviour of the organism, not its ontogeny. From the cognitive scientific point of view, let us say that a state represents information — is a *representational state* — if it systematically co-varies with properties of the environment and in so doing contributes to the production of behaviour appropriate to that environment.

The simplest natural example of a representation, and also the most primordial, is sensation. To take a simple example, the membrane potential of a photoreceptor varies systematically with the intensity of light falling upon it; its internal state thus represents a fact about the environment: that there is such and such an amount of light coming from such and such a point in space. This form of representation is probably as old as life itself. Even single-celled organisms are equipped with sensory systems of various kinds. In bacteria, for example, the presence of both attractive and repellent substances is represented by the intracellular concentration of the methylated form of a particular protein. Attractants increase and repellents decrease the concentration of this material, leading ultimately to a change in the organism's swimming behaviour and positive or negative chemotaxis. Far away at the other end of the spectrum of representational sophistication are human common-sense psychological states. According to the principle of systematic co-variation, a full-blown human belief would count as a representational state, as long as the believer generally has true beliefs.

Between these two extremes lies a full range of representational states which vary in the properties they represent, the physical mechanisms which confer their representational capacity, the behaviours they cause, and the degree to which they approximate true mental states. The present task is to decide which species have representational states that approximate mental states.

This is not to say that the neurobiology of non-mental instances of representation is irrelevant to the question of what is the nature of mental representation. On the contrary, the most important lesson of the history of biology is that success on a complex problem comes to those who begin with a simple version of the same problem. Thus the study of genetic transmission by viruses was instrumental in making any progress at all on the more complex problem of inheritance in eukaryotic cells and the higher forms of life. There is obviously much to be gained in the way of discovering potential representational mechanisms by looking into the neurobiology of simple instances of representation. However, while it was obvious that genetic transmission in viruses and more complex forms of life were two versions of the same problem, this is manifestly not the case for our fledgling cognitive neuroscience. The early molecular geneticists knew that viruses were using the same material, the same representational medium, so to speak, as were the eukaryotic forms of life. The early cognitive scientists have, I suppose, the reassurance that cognitive animals all have a nervous system, but one has only to glance at a textbook of comparative neurobiology to realise that here the representational medium is far more heterogeneous than in genetics. It is by no means obvious that a snail would be representing information in the same way as a person, and therefore not obvious that snails are simplified model systems appropriate to the study of mental representation. The cognitive neurobiologist therefore is faced with the conceptually prior problem of demonstrating that his model system — if he can find one — is in fact a version of the more complex problem it is meant to help solve.

*When are representational states at issue?*

In addition to the homogeneity of the representing material, the early molecular geneticists had a second advantage. The simple and complex systems they studied were *obviously* engaged in the same project: ensuring that appropriate proteins were constructed at the right times or, what amounts to the same, that the correct phenotype was in every case produced. Thus the geneticist had recurrence of phenotype to suggest that genetic transmission was at issue, but what hint has the cognitive neurobiologist got that representational states are at issue? As in the genetic case, the answer is probably to be found in the nature of the system's output which, in terms of the subject matter of cognitive science, is behaviour. From a conceptual point of view, representational states are at issue when they are the cause of behaviour. Thus, the hint that representational states are at issue is the discovery of behavioural regularities that can be predicted — from first principles — only by adopting the behaving subject's point of view, that is, only by ignoring how the environment *is* in favour of how it *appears* to the organism.

Behaviourism is, of course, committed to predicting behaviour the other way around: by ignoring the subjective point of view and concentrating on objective properties of the environment. Thus, an obvious place to look for likely instances where representational states are at issue is where the behaviourist approach falters and a cognitive account of the same phenomenon succeeds. There are a good many instances of these, even in the realm of classical conditioning, the very heartland of behaviourism, and we will examine such cases in detail later on. First, however, it is important to be clear about what identifies an account of behaviour as adopting the subject's point of view, that is, of invoking representation as cause.

There are two major aspects to a subject's point of view: the first being what *objects* he takes to comprise the world; the second by what *descriptions* he knows them. An account of behaviour would suggest representation is at issue, then, if how the environment is described in the account makes a difference: if its true predictions become false when one alters the description of objects in the account. Similarly, though perhaps less obviously, representation is implicated if from a true account of behaviour one cannot conclude that the objects of representations mentioned by the account in fact exist. Philosophers will recognise here the well-known tests for *intentional* sentences. What I am suggesting is that representation is sure to be at issue when in predicting behaviour we really do rely upon a description of the environment from the subject's point of view, and that an objective test for predictions of this type is the presence of sentences of a special logical type: intentional sentences.

Plenty of sentences are not intentional. When one of these is true, there are a number of things we can conclude that we cannot conclude from an intentional sentence, however true it might be. Suppose the following non-intentional sentence is true:

Washington chopped down his father's favourite cherry tree.

Then it is also true that Washington chopped down his father's favourite *Prunus pennsylvanica*. Any description we substitute for 'his father's favourite cherry tree,' as long as it picks out the very same tree, results in another true sentence. Similarly, if the sentence is true, then we know for a fact that there was a person called Washington and there was a tree that was the favourite of the father of Washington. Contrast this sentence with the following that is also true:

John believes the morning star is on the horizon.

Notice that now substitution of another description of the morning star 'the evening star' does not necessarily preserve the truth of the sentence. We cannot conclude that John believes the evening star is on the horizon because we do not know whether John happens to be aware of the fact that the morning star and the evening star are identical, nor do we know that he would have made the connection had he been aware of the identity. This is a classic example of an intentional sentence detected by the test of 'substitution of co-referring expressions.' Suppose finally that the following sentence is true:

John believes that the god of love is in the sky.

However much credibility we are otherwise inclined to attribute to John, we cannot conclude that there is such a thing as the god of love. Notice that, in contrast, the related non-intentional sentence 'John sent a message to Venus' *does* guarantee the existence of Venus. This test, of so-called 'existential generalization', can also be used to detect an intentional sentence.

## When are representational states like mental states?

Many of the locutions common to everyday accounts of cognitive behaviour, 'thinks that p', 'wishes that p', 'learns that p' and so on, also produce intentional sentences. This suggests that, in addition to signalling the presence of representational states, the occurrence of intentional sentences always signals the presence of mental states. If this were true, we would have what we seek: a sure-fire means of locating species that have mental states. If prediction of its behaviour requires a theory that relies constitutively on intentional sentences, then its members have bona fide mental states and it is time to sharpen the electrodes. Unfortunately, the criterion of essential use of intentional sentences is still much too loose: there are plenty of intentional expressions one is very likely to find in explanations of an organism's behaviour that, though resoundingly intentional, do not attribute mental states.

An example well known to philosophers is an expression of the form 'x detects that p' (the philosophical literature has it as 'x registers that p', but the sense is the same). This is exactly the form of the sentence one would use to describe, in the information-laden terms required to explain any adaptive behaviour, the response of an organism's sensory receptors: the organism withdrew because its receptors detected that a shadow fell upon it (and shadows are positively correlated with approach of predictors, etc.). Notice that 'x detects that p' is an intentional formula: it fails both the test of substitution of co-referring expressions and existential generalisation. In regard to the substitution test, it does not necessarily follow from the fact that a photoreceptor detects the absence of light that it detects the absence, say, of Einstein's favourite form of energy (even though it is contingently true that light is Einstein's favourite energy). And as far as the existential test is concerned, photoreceptors, like all detectors, are capable of mistakes, in particular, of false alarms: of 'detecting' something that is not there. Thus, from the mere fact that a receptor appears to have seen something out there, the conclusion that it *is* out there is not warranted.

Just as in the examples above, we can recast 'x detects that p' in the related (though not synonymous) non-intentional form: the photoreceptor is activated by light. Notice that now the same substitution works just fine: if x really is activated by light, and light really is Einstein's favourite energy, then the photoreceptor really is activated by Einstein's favourite energy. Similarly, if the receptor truly is activated by light (just now), then there really is light out there (just now). This exercise points out the effect that a rather subtle shift in perspective can have on whether an explanation is intentional. As long as we are only interested in the blind mechanics of what goes on in a system, then our account is not intentional and representation is not at issue. But the moment we care about the larger picture, about how these mechanics are put to use, about how they serve the interests of the organism (how ever blind these may or may not be), then we have crossed the intentional threshold. This is precisely the difference between activation and detection: the former is pure mechanics, the latter implies use; activation is never intentional, detection always is.

This example shows clearly that using the occurrence of intentional language to detect the presence of mental states just will not work: one picks up too many false positives. Any organism posessed of even the most rudimentary sensory apparatus qualifies as a possessor of mental states and every animal is so equipped. This leads to a modern panpsychism of the most extreme variety. Literally anything with even a single reflex or taxis is granted mentality. One could probably make a good case for tropisms on the basis of asymmetric changes in internal state that lead to goal-directed growth. Thus the entire plant kingdom gains admission to the psychological club.

A number of philosophers have spent some time attempting to tighten up the criterion of intentionality. Dretske (1980), for example, has suggested that what sets truly mental states apart from their non-mental cousins (like 'detects that') has something to do with the *content* of states (the content of a state is what the state is about: 'p' in 'x detects that p' or 'x believes that p'). The content of mental states, he argues, is distinctive in that it is more 'fine-grained' than the content of states that are intentional (attributed by intentional sentences) but not quite mental. A receptor detecting the emission of light registers in addition everything that is, by the laws of nature, correlated with this fact. By contrast, much, much less is necessarily true of a person who *knows* that light is emitted; because the average person does not know *all* the laws of nature, he is not awarded the dividends in extra information conferred by all that is lawfully correlated with the emission of light. This tactic seems to take care of the obvious cases, telling fullblown human mental states from transducer outputs, but what happens when we move down the scale of psychological sophistication? Does a network of a half-dozen neurons, which clearly accomplishes more than simple detections, have mental states or is there still too much content? Just how much content is too much? Distinction between mental and non-mental states on a quantitative basis as advocated by Dretske ultimately becomes an arbitrary one in all but the most obvious cases, despite the fact that he does seem to be onto something here. There seems to be no principled answer to the question how much is too much, or just enough; this problem will recur.

Another philosopher to take up the content gambit is Fodor (1986). However, rather than employing the notion of fineness of grain, he focuses on the character of the content itself, the general types of stimulus properties to which the organism responds. His distinction between the mental and the non-mental follows from a distinction between two sorts of properties: *nomic* and *non-nomic*. Nomic properties are those in virtue of which an object falls under natural laws. Good examples of these are 'having mass', 'carrying a positive charge', 'being present at a concentration of five millimolar', and so on. Non-nomic properties are, as the name suggests, those which would never be named in statements of natural laws: 'being x miles from the Eiffel Tower', 'being a yellow Volkswagen', 'being a crumpled shirt', and so forth. The trademark of organisms with mental states is a predilection to respond to non-nomic properties. Human beings, the paradigmatic possessors of mental states, obviously are sensitive to properties that do not figure in the fundamental laws of science. Indeed, much of everyday human activity consists in behaviour directed toward things important in virtue of their crumpled shirtness, their yellow Volkswagenness, and so on. In contrast, any tropism, taxis, or reflex one can think of is controlled or triggered by standard nomic properties. Plants turn toward photon sources; protista follow concentration gradients; impact at the patella elicits the stretch reflex.

Although Fodor's appeal to nomic and non-nomic properties accurately reflects the deliverance of common sense in the obvious cases, it gives counterintuitive results in intermediate examples. This is important because the behaviour of species with promising physiology almost surely lies in the grey area between simple reflexivity and obvious mentality. To take an example of such an intermediate case, suppose one constructed a simple reflex: one triggered by the instantiation of one of Fodor's non-nomic properties, say, being a crumpled shirt. A complex pattern-recognition system would do for the input end. As for the output, make the system print 'Needs ironing!' Fodor states that such a system qualifies as having mental states, but this seems to be overly generous. The system we have constructed is really nothing but a reflex that is unusually discriminating in regard to its input. It is difficult to see how responding to just one kind of thing, however non-nomic its constitutive properties, ought to confer the exalted status of mentality. (The problem is not simply that the system is an artificial one. One can easily imagine natural examples of non-nomic reflexes that do no better: an escape response triggered by the property 'being the third stimulus in a row', for instance.)

The trouble with non-nomic reflexes, the reason why their representational states are not mental states, is a problem shared by all reflexes, nomic and non-nomic alike. One difficulty is simply that their intentional states do not accomplish enough. A reflex, or a whole system the behaviour of which is nothing more than a cluster of independent reflexes, does one and only one thing with each of its reflex-based representational states: it makes the response triggered by the appropriate stimulus. Another difficulty is that such representational states are the result of one and only one state of affairs. Paradigmatic mental states, in contrast, are the result of many states of affairs and have numerous consequences. Think of the number of possible routes to having any particular belief, say the belief that it is raining. A multitude of perceptual conditions will do: seeing wet pavement, hearing splatters on the roof, feeling a droplet on the head, and so on. Think also of the number of consequences of such a belief. Some are behavioural consequences such as dashing inside, donning protective gear, cancelling a picnic; others are logical consequences which result in the formation of new beliefs, such as the belief that the reservoirs are filling, that lightning might strike, that one is in for a drenching, and so on.

This point, that reflexes don't have mental states, can be put more succinctly once we have taken on board some additional philosophical apparatus: functionalism and the concept of the *functional role* of mental states. Suppose that you and I are quite similar people, outwardly at least. That is to say, from a behavioural point of view, we appear to have pretty much the same tastes, interests, and aspirations; we appear to have all the same prejudices and identical true beliefs. Thus, under similar circumstances we tend to notice the same things and say more or less the same things, even reach for the same things in the room. Like most people, you would probably be inclined to agree that often times I have the same pains, perceptions, desires, beliefs and so on, that you do. The only difference between us is that while you are a normal red-blooded human being, I am part prosthetic device: my brain is actually made of silicon. The question then is how we can have the same mental states. Since our physical constitutions are so different, the identity of our mental states cannot lie in the identity of our physical states. The one thing about a type of mental state that *can* be preserved, no matter what material or device harbours it, is the set of causal relations it bears to (1) perceptual conditions, (2) other mental states, and (3) actual behaviours, that is to say, its functional role. Functionalism, then, is the view that individual mental states are instances of the same type when, in their respective psychologies, their causal or functional relations run in parallel.

Historically, functionalism arose as a means of preserving the intuition, highlighted in the thought experiment above, that mental states can be enjoyed by any sufficiently sophisticated agent, regardless of its origin (natural or artificial), construction or, closer to home, its anatomy and physiology. The idea that two agents might have identical mental states but very different material instantiations of them is not necessarily so far-fetched as the preceding might lead one to think. For all we know, the neurological similarities between persons may end at the level of EEGs and PET scans: the firing patterns which underlie each person's belief that $\pi$ is irrational may differ in an arbitrary way from everyone else's, just as the physical states of the silicon brain's beliefs differ *arbitrarily* from the physical belief states of the human brain. It is even logically possible that such unsystematic variation could occur in a single individual across time. Functionalism emerges as an important conceptual advance since it enables one to insist that mental states are identical with physical states — and so ward off the spectre of dualism — while at the same time being generous to non-human agents who seem for all the world to have mental states. But it also reveals itself to be a necessary commitment of empirical inquiries employing the model-system strategy. A model system in neurobiology will, by definition, be a non-human nervous system. It is highly likely therefore that the physical correlates of mental states in the model will bear little or no *typological* resemblance to the physical correlates of human mentality. This means the only way to establish cross species correlations will be by appeal to similarity of causal role among stimulus conditions, other mental states, and actual behaviours, and that is the conceptual pith of functionalism.

To return to Fodor's non-nomic reflexes, what makes their representational states non-mental ones seems to be the fact that their respective functional roles are far too impoverished. The representational state inherent in a reflex is the result of just one stimulus condition, interacts with no other representational states, and causes only the designated reflexive movement. Part of the problem is strictly quantitative: the representational states at issue in reflexes just do not have a large enough repertoire of causal relations. This, of course, is simply a consequence of the nature of reflexive behaviour which, by definition, consists in a direct link between one stimulus and one response. If we wanted to plug the leak in Fodor's criterion, we might say that in addition to representing non-nomic properties, a representational state, if it is to be a mental state, must have a list of functional roles of such and such a size. But we have already seen that this quantitative tactic can only lead to the drawing of an arbitrary numerical threshold.

There is also a complementary qualitative problem with the non-nomic properties approach. Not only is it true that the non-nomic representational states do not do enough things, they also do not do the right kinds of things. In particular, they are distinctly unco-operative; they never join with other representational states to cause new behaviours or to engender new representational states. This is a rather oblique way of saying that they do not participate in a quintessential aspect of mentality: *inference*. Notice, in contrast, that bona fide mental states, like beliefs, do take part in inferences. They combine with other beliefs to cause behaviours as in this causal chain: because John believed that all men were mortal and that Socrates was a man he soon realized that Socrates was mortal. They also combine with other mental states — especially desires — to cause behaviours as in: John wished it would rain and believed that it rains every time he washes his car, so John went out and washed his car.

The idea that mental states are things that must have not just many but also *particular* causal relations suggests another way to set up the criterion whereby we could tell mental from the non-mental representational states. Dretske and Fodor both played the content card. Perhaps we would be better off betting on functional role. We might say, for instance, that a representational state achieves mental status when it has the right kind of function in an organism's internal handling of information. We could specify that having the right kind of function would include participation in inference-like behaviour, as in John's concern for

Socrates' fate; it might also include playing a role in a so-called practical syllogism, as in John's car-washing behaviour. Any representational states that, however intentional their descriptions, refused to co-operate with other representational states would be disqualified. This would, for example, effectively rule out all sensory receptors as having mental states, since receptors do nothing more than pass along the information. To be sure, the state of one or a set of receptors might still be part of a belief-state; the point is rather that representational states of receptors are not, unto themselves, mental.

The same can be said of stages of perception further into the nervous system than receptors. There are neurons in regions of the primate cerebral cortex concerned with vision which seem tuned to detect the presence of quite complex — even abstract — objects such as monkey faces and hands (Desimore et al., 1984). These neurons are quite plainly detectors of non-nomic properties, since being a face or a hand is a property unlikely ever to be enshrined in the laws of nature. However, from the foregoing, we would conclude that the firing of a hand-detector neuron does not constitute the belief that there is a hand there now. At least, not from what we know about this neuron so far. To qualify as a mental state, the state in which this neuron fires would have to be shown to interact appropriately with states representing other pieces of information, or with states representing the animal's desires or motivations. Right now, we simply do not know enough of the relevant circuitry to say one way or the other.

*How mental is just mental enough?*

There is a certain attraction to adopting types of function as the basis for the distinction between mental and non-mental representations. Dretske's approach from the point of view of fine-grained content has, as we saw, the disadvantage that it forces us to make an arbitrary quantitative distinction to answer the question how fine grained is just fine grained enough to count as mental. And if we try to tighten Fodor's criterion of non-nomic properties by stipulating that single-stimulus, single-response representational states do not make the grade, we will run up against the same problem. We will soon be asked how many functions — causal relations — must a state bear to count as a mental state? Once again, of course, the only way out is stipulation, and that does not wear well. It seems as if a difference in kind is just what we are after, especially a principled difference like the requirement for inference-like *type* of functionality. Why not then maintain that a representational state is a mental state if among its causal relations there is at least one which names another representational state as antecedent or consequent? This would pick out, for example, John's belief that Socrates was a man because it has one of these state-state causal relations: if John is in a state such that he believes Socrates is a man, and in a state such that he believes all men are mortal, then he will enter the state such that he believes Socrates is mortal. (Of course, the belief that Socrates is a man has many more functional relations.)

This might work, except that ultimately we will want to generalize from the neurobiology of borderline cases of mental states to real human ones which, like John's belief that Socrates is a man, have far more than one state-state causal relation. Critics will no doubt grant that we have with our electrodes told them something mildly interesting about belief and desire functional analogues, but surely they will want to know how analogous they are. Once again we are up against the quantitative question: how analogous is just analogous enough?

At this point the biologist can reply that, well, one has got to start somewhere. Admittedly, a primitive representational state with a single instance of participation in an inference is a very, very distant cousin to ordinary belief. But, after all, the issue here really is how to choose a *model* system: the organism that is going to be to the cognitive scientist what the virus was to the molecular geneticist. In the choice of model system, probably the single most important thing to get right is function: one has at least got to study entities — or parts of entities — that are doing roughly the same job. This was obvious in the case of inheritance. It is less obvious in the case of cognition. Representation is a good first try at answering the question, What is the constitutive function of cognitive systems? But it leaves the field wide open, as we have seen. Processing information is probably closer to the mark; to represent information is merely to possess it, but to process information is to put it to work. The hope here is that the conceptually simplest possible instance of information processing is the combination of one piece of information with another in an act of inference. If we could find a living system in which we have good reason — on behavioural grounds — to think that something like this is going on, and this system turned out to be simple enough to understand neurobiologically, then the results would be significant.

## Part II

We are now in a position to give the zoologist and the comparative psychologist our wish list. First, the desired model system must exhibit behaviours whose prediction requires adopting the subjective point of view, that is, the attribution of representational states. The intentional-sentence assay gives us this information. Second, the theory that predicts the organism's behaviour must attribute representational states with special kinds of functional roles: they must have one or more state-state causal relations, and the more the better. Finally, given that our electrodes are large and it is hard to hold more than several at once, we need a species with large neurons and a small brain. The demand for tractable neurophysiology stems from the biologist's implicit commitment to functionalism. To say anything about the physical nature of a mental state he must first convince us that the physical state he has analysed is in fact the one that corresponds to the mental state in question. The only way to do this, of course, is to demonstrate functional role isomorphism: to show that the functional role of the physiological state as it participates in the shifting pattern of physiological states parallels the role of the mental state in the mental life of the organism. Obviously, the biologist must understand the actual and possible causes and effects of the physical state with extreme thoroughness and precision. In vertebrate animals, physiological analysis at this level of detail has been possible only for aspects of the sensory and motor sides of the nervous system, and for a couple of reflexes (Byrne, 1987). In general, not enough of the intervening circuitry is known to specify potential mental-state analogues, let alone demonstrate their identity with known mental states. Given the comparative simplicity of some invertebrate nervous systems, one might expect more luck down there on the phylogenetic scale. However, there is a potentially severe behavioural problem: is any physiologically simple invertebrate sophisticated enough in behavioural terms to deserve attribution of mental-state analogues? To answer this question will require taking a look at the kinds of experiments that guarantee mentality is at issue.

## Classical conditioning from the subject's point of view

Classical conditioning might seem a rather optimistic place to go looking for tests of the presence of representational states, let alone mental states. Early behaviourist manifestos made it quite clear that internal states of organisms were unscientific objects (Jennings, 1906; Watson, 1913) and for the next fifty years or so, animal learning theorists conscientiously stripped their theories of intentional terms and the representational states they attribute. How successfully behaviourists proved that behaviour in general could be explained by external variables alone is a matter of debate (Dennett, 1978a), but progress was generally steady, at least within the confines of the Skinner box.

Difficulties first arose when certain variations on the basic classical conditioning theme produced behaviours that were extremely difficult to square with a traditional stimulus-response (SR) model of animal learning (Dickinson, 1980). The problem came in trying to predict from first principles which association between conditioned stimulus and reinforcer the animal would form when confronted with several equally valid alternatives. The conceptual resources of SR theory were limited to the idea of *stimulus contiguity*, which led to the rule that any stimulus that coincided in time with the reinforcing stimulus would be associated with it. As classical conditioning procedures grew in sophistication, the contiguity rule began to break down. These more sophisticated procedures — which came to be known as *selective association paradigms* — are worth examining in some detail, partly to better appreciate the difficulties they presented to SR theory, but also because they have a distinctly cognitive character and will figure importantly in the choice of model systems in cognitive neurobiology as this is developed below.

One of the earliest selective association paradigms to raise problems for the SR theorists was the so-called 'blocking' experiment (Kamin, 1969). The procedure is usually three-staged (Rescorla, 1971). Light and tone are the initially neutral or so-called conditioned stimuli (CSs), and shock the reinforcing or unconditioned stimulus (US). Such a procedure is illustrated in Table 1. In stage 1 group 'B' is presented with paired presentation of tone and shock until they have learned the tone–shock relation. In stage 2 they are presented with pairings of a compound stimulus and shock, where the compound consists of the original tone plus a flash of light. Finally, in stage 3, the amount

Table 1. Blocking and Super-Conditioning

| Group | Stage 1 | Stage 2 | Stage 3 | Learning index |
|---|---|---|---|---|
| (B1) | T–Sh | LT–Sh | Test L | 0.35 |
| (C1) | Sh alone | LT–Sh | Test L | 0.40 |
| (C2) | T/Sh(r) | LT–Sh | Test L | 0.40 |
| (SC) | T–No Sh | LT–Sh | Test L | 0.48 |

*Notes:* T = tone; L = light; Sh = shock; r = random. Learning, in this and following tables, is expressed as 0.5 − suppression ratio. Suppression ratio (see Dickinson, 1980) is defined as $A/(A+B)$, where A is the rate of production of an appetitive response during the test stimulus, and B the rate immediately prior to the test stimulus (After Dickinson, 1980, and Rescorla, 1971).

they have learned about the light–shock relationship is assessed by presentation of light alone. The SR theory, which can invoke only temporal contiguity of CS and US to predict the acquisition of stimulus-associations, makes incorrect predictions about the behaviour produced by blocking procedures. It predicts that the group B animals will learn as much about the light-shock relation as a control group C1 that received no pre-exposure to a tone–shock relation prior to being subjected to the compound and shock in stage 2. According to the SR theory, both groups should learn the same amount about the light–shock relation because both groups received the same number of light-shock pairings. In fact, however, group B animals learn little about light and shock, in contrast to group C1 which learns the usual amount. Learning about this relationship by group B is said to be 'blocked' by what is learned in stage 1.

There are a good many other conditioning procedures that are difficult for SR theory. One task closely related to blocking is so-called super-conditioning. The only difference between blocking and super-conditioning lies in the nature of the pre-exposure stage, where instead of a tone-shock relation, the animals are placed in a situation in which shock occurs, but never in the presence of the tone (Table 1, Group SC). They are, in effect, pre-exposed to a tone–no shock relation. The second stage is just as in blocking. The animals are given a compound stimulus of tone and light, followed by shock. For a second control group, C2, the pre-exposure stage is random or uncorrelated occurrences of tone and shock (Table 1). Finally, in a third stage, the amount that has been learned by each group about the light–shock relation is assessed. Once again, both groups have received the same number of light–shock pairings, so SR theory predicts that at the test stage, both groups will show the same amount of conditioning to the light. But in fact conditioning to the light is improved. The SC group learns more than control animals.

A final twist on the basic blocking design is post-trial surprise (e.g. Dickinson et al., 1976). Here, pre-exposure is once again to a tone–shock relation, however this time not one but two shocks follow the tone, separated by a brief delay (Table 2, Group B1). If animals are subsequently exposed to a tone–light compound followed by paired shocks, blocking occurs normally. That is, learning about the light–shock–shock relation is prevented by pre-exposure to the tone–shock–shock relation, as would be expected on the basis of the results of a normal blocking experiment.

Table 2. Post-Trial Surprise

| Group | Stage 1 | Stage 2 | Stage 3 | Learning index |
|---|---|---|---|---|
| (B1) | T–Sh–Sh | TL–Sh–Sh | Test L | 0.04 |
| (B2) | T–Sh | TL–Sh | Test L | 0.18 |
| (C1) | T–Sh–Sh | TL–Sh | Test L | 0.06 |
| (C2) | T–Sh | TL–Sh–Sh | Test L | 0.21 |

Notes: T = tone; L = light; Sh = shock (After Dickinson, 1980, and Dickinson et al., 1976).

However, in a post-trial surprise experiment, there is a group of animals for which the pre-exposure stage is followed by a slightly different second stage: for this group the second shock in stage 2 is omitted (Table 2, Group C1). Since a shock still occurs after the tone–light compound, one might expect that blocking would proceed normally. However, just the opposite is the case. Conditioning to the light returns as comparison of groups B1 and C1 shows. The reciprocal experiment, where the 'surprise' in stage 2 is the addition of a second shock is also effective. This can be seen in comparing the results of group B2, a normal single-shock blocking group, and group C2, which received an extra shock during stage 2. Thus, whether the surprising event is the addition of a stimulus or its omission, the result is the same: the blocking effect is reversed and learning occurs. This is a paradoxical result, even for some of the non-SR theories designed expressly to cope with the results of blocking and related experiments, but SR theory has a particularly difficult time. This is not surprising. Because SR theory cannot predict the occurrence of the blocking effect in the first place, it can hardly be expected to give an explanation for release from blocking. Moreover, SR theory is generally committed to relations between actual stimulus events and bodily movements. But here the significant event is the omission of a stimulus. Such an occurrence is, in the words of one troubled behaviourist, a 'non-occurrence' (Schoenfield, 1950), and non-occurrences are not the sort of events that the behaviourist is happy to admit into his theory.

We noted in Part I that the characteristic feature of behaviour caused by representational states is that it compels us to adopt the subject's point of view in order to predict behaviour successfully from first principles. Post-trial surprise training — especially in the case of stimulus omission — produces just this kind of behaviour. An omitted shock can only be an event — let alone a behaviourally significant one — against the background of expected shocks. That is, it can only be an event for a subject expecting shocks, and what is this but to adopt the subjective point of view? In light of the discussion in Part I concerning representation and intentional sentences, it is reassuring that we have here indeed lapsed into intentional usage. The sentence 'the animal expects that reinforcing events occur' is an intentional sentence by either the test of substitution of co-referring expressions or existential generalisation.

## Classical conditioning and representational states

Experiments like the ones described above (and many others) have provoked a new generation of theories of classical conditioning, which we shall examine shortly. All are expressed in intentional terms. This is good because it suggests that representational states are at issue. Better, the intentional terms in the theories denote *causes* of learning and behaviour, which means that representational states are essential to these accounts. Finally, the representational states posited by the theories generally have rather complex functional roles. In particular, it is common that the ability of an animal to enter a certain representational state is dependent on the presence — or absence — of other representational states.

That is, the functional roles of representational states often include causal relations not just with environmental conditions and behaviour, but between the internal representations themselves. Following the discussion of Part I, this means that the states attributed by the new theories of conditioning could be strongly analogous to mental states.

Insofar as this is true, it is time to take a closer look at these new theories. Do they really attribute representational states? And if so, do they attribute representational states that are good mental-state analogues? There is not space to consider all such accounts individually, but since they are generally rather similar, let us look at one such account that has been particularly influential: the one offered by Mackintosh (1975).

According to the Mackintosh theory, the amount an animal learns about a stimulus A as a potential signal for a reinforcing event is a function of how attentive the animal will be to A on the trial in question. The more attentive the animal is, the greater the likelihood that learning occurs. The degree of attentiveness to a particular occurrence of A in turn depends upon how reliable A-stimuli are as signals for reinforcing events. Attentiveness to A increases as A reliably and non-redundantly predicts a change in reinforcement, whereas attentiveness to A decreases where A is unreliable or redundant. Thus, in condensed form, the Mackintosh theory can be expressed in terms of several conditionals:

(i) If the animal does not expect that the reinforcing event occurs, and given stimulus A it regularly does occur, then attentiveness to A will increase.
(ii) Conversely, if the animal already expects that the reinforcing event occurs, and given A the reinforcing event regularly occurs, then attentiveness to A will decrease.
(iii) If, given A, the reinforcing event regularly occurs, and the animal is attentive to A, then the animal will learn that A predicts the reinforcing event.
(iv) If the animal learns that A predicts the reinforcing event, then, given A, the animal will respond as if the reinforcing event occurred (with a probability or amplitude proportional to the amount of learning that has occurred).

Following the principles developed in Part I, the Mackintosh theory attributes representational states if it refers to the cause of behaviour with intentional terms, that is, if the antecedents of the theory's conditionals are intentional sentences. The above expressions, 'expects that' and 'learns that', occur in the antecedents and clearly render the respective sentences intentional. For example, from the fact that the animal learns that A predicts the reinforcing event, it does not necessarily follow that the animal learns that A predicts the shock, even though, in the experiment as performed it was contingently true that the shock and the reinforcing event were identical. The same, of course, can be said of the sentences using the term 'expects'.

It is worth noting here that the question how — under what description, so to speak — an animal represents stimulus events is not just a philosophical fine point. One can in fact design experiments that determine, in a rough and ready way at least, the description under which an event is remembered or expected. One such procedure is the trans-reinforcer blocking experiment shown in Table 3. The issue in the study illustrated (Bakal, Johnson and Rescorla, 1974) was whether the reinforcing event was expected as a stimulus of a particular modality, or simply as an aversive event, with no reference to its sensory qualities.

Table 3. Trans-reinforcer Blocking

| Group | Stage 1 | Stage 2 | Test | Learning index |
|---|---|---|---|---|
| C |  | TL–Klaxon | L | 0.08 |
| K | T–Klaxon | TL–Klaxon | L | 0.26 |
| S | T–Shock | TL–Klaxon | L | 0.29 |

*Notes:* T = tone; L = light. (After Dickinson, 1980, and Bakal *et al.*, 1974).

The experimental design is like the blocking experiment already shown in Table 1, except that Stage 1 learning involves aversive reinforcing events of different stimulus modalities in different groups. Thus one set of animals, group K, was exposed to the association of a tone and a loud noise (a klaxon, which rats find aversive), while a second, group S, was given a tone-shock association. A control group received only Stage 2 training: a compound stimulus of light and tone followed by the klaxon. After stage 2 training, all groups were tested for the amount they had learned about the light–klaxon association presented in stage 2. As expected, control animals learned the light–klaxon association. In group K, a standard blocking group, learning about the light–klaxon association was prevented since the reinforcer was already well predicted by the tone. Group C is the interesting one. If the animals learned in Stage 1 that tone predicts shock as such, then blocking should not occur, since the klaxon, first delivered in stage 2 for this group, is a novel stimulus and would not be expected upon presentation of the tone. On the other hand, if the shock in Stage 1 is encoded only in general terms, as something — anything — aversive, then blocking should occur, because an aversive event was already expected. The results were clear: blocking occurred for groups K and C, showing unequivocally that the reinforcer was expected only as something aversive, and with no regard to its particular sensory qualities.

This amounts to an experimental application of the logical test of substitution of co-referring expressions. From the fact that the animal expects an aversive event we cannot conclude that the animal expects the aversive event under a different description, however contingently true this description might be. To do so leads to an unwarranted, and in this case false, prediction of behaviour.

This ought to be enough to demonstrate that representational state attributions occur in the Mackintosh account and to guarantee that representational states are at issue as far as similar theories of classical conditioning are concerned. However, it might be objected at this point that we are taking things too literally: the intentional sentences above simply borrow a little intuitive plausibility and comprehensibility from commonsense psychology. No animal learning theorist *really* supposes even for a moment that animals really expect things. After all, intentional usage is common in cases of behaviour that we have every reason to believe are not under the control of informational and motivational states. For example, we quite commonly use expressions such as antibodies 'recognize' foreign proteins, water 'seeks' its lowest level, petunias 'prefer' rich soil, and so on. In fact, the objection continues, the behaviour of any system having a minimum of two possible output states and the capacity to exchange one for the other can be given an intentional description: one simply names the exchange as the system's 'goal' and attributes the desire and know-how as required for the system to switch ouputs. In light of these examples, there is little stopping the sceptic from maintaining that current theories of classical conditioning use intentional terms in this figurative way.

To make matters worse, the Mackintosh account — and its relatives — can be restated in mathematical terms. This version of the theory is completely unencumbered by intentional expressions yet predicts behaviour perfectly well. But things are not as bad as they might seem. We have seen that according to functionalism, a mental state is identified ultimately by its functional role. As model systems theorists by hypothesis, we are, as pointed out in part I, committed to functionalism. This means that if the mathematical version of the Mackintosh theory of classical conditioning refers to states with functional roles just like those of the representational states in its non-mathematical formulation, then it refers to those same states after all. Does the mathematical account imply states with determinate functional roles? And are these the functional roles of recognisable representational states?

To answer this question it will be necessary to present the mathematical model in the Mackintosh account in sufficient detail to reveal the functional roles of states implied by it, if any are. The initial intuition which the model is designed to capture is that the amount of learning about a stimulus $A$ on a given trial is a function of the degree of attentiveness to $A$ at the time. The relation between attentiveness to $A$ and learning about $A$ is expressed by the formula

$$dV_A = B a_A |L - V_A| \qquad (1)$$

where $V_A$ is the *associative strength* of $A$ on that trial and $dV_A$ is the change in associative strength as a result of that trial. The associative strength of a stimulus, roughly speaking, is its capacity to elicit a conditioned response. The change in associative strength is thus a change in the capacity to elicit responses and so is an approximate index of behavioural plasticity or learning. The terms $B$ and $a_A$ are parameters governing the rate of learning. They stand for the effective salience of the stimuli involved. $B$ depends only on the intensity of the reinforcer, which is usually constant. The term $a_A$, on the other hand, varies with the animal's experience of $A$. If $A$ proves to be a better predictor of reinforcement than any other stimulus or cue, then the significance of $A$ goes up and $A$ becomes worthy of more attention. This is modelled as an increase in the value of $a_A$. Conversely, the significance of $A$ drops as other stimuli prove better predictors of reinforcement, and this is reflected in a decrease in the value of $a_A$. The term $L$ is the associative strength $A$ would have once conditioning to $A$ were complete. Thus, the term $|L - V_A|$ expresses the degree to which conditioning is complete on the trial in question.

The second intuition that the model is meant to formalise is that the degree of attentiveness to $A$, or the value of $a_A$, is a function of the value of $A$ as a predictor of the reinforcing event in comparison with other simultaneously occurring stimuli. Over the course of any series of reinforcing events, associative strength will accrue not just to $A$, but to any other stimuli regularly present just before the reinforcing event. These stimuli include any additional stimuli introduced by the experimenter, as well as stimuli provided by the context. Taken together, the extra stimuli plus the contextual stimuli can be said to have the combined associative strength, $V_X$. Under the terms of the model, good predictive stimuli are those for which conditioning is, or almost is complete. Poor predictors are those for which little conditioning has occurred. Thus, for good predictors, the difference between $L$ and the current associative strength $V$ is small, whereas for poor predictors the difference approaches $L$. Since the value of $a_A$ is, by definition, dependent upon relative degrees of predictiveness, it is found by comparing the degree of completeness of conditioning to $A$ and to all other stimuli $X$. Thus $a_A$ increases from its pre-trial value whenever $A$ is a better predictor of reinforcement than all other stimuli combined. That is

$$da_A > 0 \text{ when } |L - V_A| < |L - V_X| \tag{2}$$

Whereas, $a_A$ decreases from its pre-trial value when $A$ is a worse predictor of reinforcement:

$$da_A < 0 \text{ when } |L - V_A| \geq |L - V_X| \tag{3}$$

In addition to a pre-trial value, all potential predicting stimuli have a positive initial or pre-experimental $a$ value. Thus, the values of $V_A$ and $a_A$ on any given trial are determined by successive iteration of (1) in accordance with (2), and (3), the constraints on $da_A$.

This has been a superficial account of the Mackintosh model of conditioning. Nevertheless, it should at least be clear that the theory consists of several mathematical formulae and supporting sentences that provide the interpretation of them. As noted above, the model appears to predict conditioned behaviour without intentional terms. This raises the possibility that the Mackintosh theory as expressed in (i)–(iv) (p. 136) uses intentional terms in a merely figurative sense, in which case the theory does not make essential reference to representational states, and classical conditioning would not really be evidence of representational states at work. However, the absence in the mathematical account of the intentional terms of (i)–(iv) ('expects' and 'learns') does not imply the absence of intentional states. The clue lies in the sentences necessary to give meaning to the mathematical expressions; reference to intentional states is hidden in the interpretation of the mathematics.

To see this, let us try the following thought experiment. Suppose Mackintosh had not himself created the mathematical account to represent his classical conditioning theory but found it ready-made. Suppose in glancing at the *Journal of Arcane Cybernetics*, he happened upon **M**, a mathematical theory of stimulus contingency semantically equivalent to the one given above. Suppose further that, intrigued by a sense of *déjà vu*, and having nothing better to do, he decided to see whether there was any similarity between the states referred to by his theory and by **M**. **M**, of course, lacks any mention of expectation, attention, and learning. However, in giving sense to the mathematical terms $V_A$, $V_X$, $a_A$, $B$, and $L$, it clearly tells how the value of each term is altered by environmental conditions and the current values of other terms: it contains the semantic equivalents of (1)–(3). Finally, it explains how the output of the system is predicted by $V_A$. Mackintosh's puzzle then is to see whether certain mathematical expressions can be fitted into (i)–(iv) (p. 136) while preserving the truths of **M**, namely, that variables bear the said relations to stimulus conditions, each other, and to output. He will eventually discover that for one set of substitutions, all the pieces fall into place. In particular, if he lets $|L - V_A| < |L - V_X|$ stand for the state of not expecting the reinforcing event to occur, $da > 0$ for attentiveness to $A$, $L$ for maximum associative strength, and so on, then, without contradicting a single tenet of **M**, he discovers:

(i′) If the animal is in the state $|L - V_A| < |L - V_X|$, and given stimulus $A$ the reinforcing event regularly does occur, then $a_A$ will increase.

(ii′) Conversely, if the animal is in the state $|L - V_A| \geq |L - V_X|$, and given $A$ the reinforcing event regularly occurs, then $a_A$ will decrease.

(iii′) If, given $A$, the reinforcing event regularly occurs, and the animal is in the state $a_A > 0$, then $V_A$ will increase.

(iv′) If the animal is in the state $V_A > 0$, then, given $A$, the animal will respond as if to the reinforcing event with a probability or amplitude of response proportional to $V_A$.

Notice that (i)–(iv) (p. 136) and (i′)–(iv′) are identical, apart from the substitution of state-names from **M** for the intentional terms of (i)–(iv). This is proof that **M**–states have functional roles in the explanation of output — behaviour — which are identical to the functional roles of the intentional states of (i)–(iv). Now we can put our commitment to functionalism to work. Since we have already seen that an intentional state is defined by its functional role in the explanation of behaviour, we are forced to conclude that **M** refers to states identical to those referred to in (i)–(iv). Of course, **M** is just the mathematical formalisation of the original Mackintosh account of conditioning. Thus the Mackintosh account, however expressed, makes essential reference to intentional states and representational states are non-figuratively at issue in this, and related theories of classical conditioning and its modern permutations.

So much for representational states, but do we find analogues of mental states here as well? In covering some of the same territory, Lloyd (1987) has reported finding mental representations in reflexes exhibiting nothing more than simple classical conditioning. This view seems open to the same criticism as Fodor's non-nomic reflex. There is a strong sense in which a reflex that detects repeated stimulus pairings is nothing more than a pairing-receptor. Receptors, as we have seen, have representational states, but they are sorry mental analogues. Their functional roles are far too elementary, and the functional role of the state representing the contingency between conditioned stimulus and reinforcer is no better: it results from essentially one sort of environmental condition, has no effect on other representational states, and has but one behavioural effect, causing the conditioned response. Of course there is a strong odour of mentality about the representational state induced in simple classical conditioning since event contingency is just the sort of information that minds seek and use by nature, but there is no mind in a simple reflex because its repertoire of responses is too limited.

The suggestion that mental representations are at issue in simple classical conditioning is also weak on the grounds that it is unparsimonious. The stimulus substitution rule of SR theory is perfectly adequate to the task of predicting when simple conditioning will occur. In the absence of evidence to the contrary, there is no reason to relinquish stimulus contiguity in favour of internal representations.

Would a reflex that exhibited, in addition to classical conditioning, more complex forms of learning fare any better? Take the case of a blocking experiment. The first stage in blocking is simply a standard instance of classical conditioning in which the animal detects — and so represents — the information that the conditioned stimulus predicts the reinforcer. In the second stage, the first conditioned stimulus is put together with a second, and the entire compound is paired with the reinforcer. As we saw, learning that the second stimulus also predicts the reinforcer — which in objective terms it does — is blocked by the prior exposure to the first conditioned stimulus. It seems reasonable to say here that the representation of the first predictive relationship prevents the detection of the second. This means that the representation in question has at least one state-state relation in its functional role: that it blocks the *acquisition* of a representational state that refers to the contingencies involving the same reinforcing stimulus. In fact, the situation is probably somewhat better than this. According to the theory, the representation of the correlation between one stimulus and the reinforcer blocks the detection of *all other possible correlations* involving that reinforcing stimulus. This means that hidden in the general rule for a blocking experiment lies a host of other state-state relations.

Table 4. Second-Order Conditioning

| Stage 1 | Stage 2 | Test |
|---|---|---|
| $CS_1$ – shock | $CS_2 - CS_1$ | $CS_2$ |

*Notes:* $CS$ = Conditioned Stimulus

In virtue of the state-state relation inherent in the explanation of the blocking result, the representation of the information gained in the first stage of the experiment counts as a non-trivial analogue of a mental state. This means that a reflex that was susceptible to simple conditioning and blocking would be a worthwhile model system in which to seek the neural basis of *mental* representation.

The blocking example is less than ideal in that the mentality conferring state-state relation is between an *existing* state and the acquisition of possible ones, rather than a relation between two existing states. A psychologically more familiar form of evidence for a mental analogue's being at issue would be demonstration of inference-like behaviour: as if in stage 1 the animal learned that A predicts B, in stage 2 that B predicts C, and the test stage showed it had made the connection that A predicts C. This is formally similar to second-order classical conditioning, first studied by Pavlov, and illustrated in Table 4; the only difference being that the order of presentation of the two 'premises' is reversed.

In second-order conditioning we have the first example of two *existing* representational states combining to produce an effect on behaviour much as the two premises of a syllogism entail the conclusion. One could hardly ask for a more thought-like form of information processing than the computation of syllogisms. Thus the representations of information detected in stages 1 and 2 of a second-order conditioning experiment would seem to be positive candidates for the status of mental-state analogue.

It is worth returning to the question, how analogous is just analogous enough? Under the principles we have been trying to develop for selecting among possible model systems, once a reflex has crossed the qualitative threshold of having one state-state causal relation, the choice reverts to quantitative grounds: the more complex conditioning paradigms a reflex succeeds in, the more complex the functional roles of its representational states necessarily become, and the more like real mental states they are. Thus, other things being equal, a reflex that showed blocking, second-order conditioning, and super-conditioning would be better than one which showed only blocking and second-order conditioning, and so on. Of course, not all reflexes are created equal from a physiological point of view. Behavioural promise is tempered by the requirement for tractable neural circuitry, as we shall see.

With the conceptual ground cleared, there is nothing for it but to turn to the data. What is known about the ability of physiologically tractable reflexes to learn? And do we find any that seem likely to reveal the neural correlates of mental-state analogues?

## Part III

*Classical conditioning in invertebrates*

We have seen that the model systems approach is implicitly committed to functionalism. Within this context the task of demonstrating mental–physical correlations is clear: to find the neural correlate of a mental-state analogue is to describe a physiological state with a particular functional role in the shifting pattern of physical states within the nervous system. Given what it means to identify a neural correlate, some reflex preparations are more suited to physiological analysis than others. Explication of a state's functional role requires detailed knowledge of the pattern of connectivity among the set of neurons specific to a state and between sets of neurons. Information of this sort is necessary for explaining how a state comes to be, how it interacts with other states (actual and possible), and how it contributes to behaviour. At our present technical level, working out connectivity patterns is not insurmountable, even in vertebrates (Byrne, 1987; Thompson, 1986). Specification of state, on the other hand, currently exerts a much stronger constraint; in this regard, invertebrate preparations have some distinct advantages. Principle among these is the fact that invertebrate neurons of some species can be recognised as distinct individuals, making it far easier to define the set of neurons relevant to a particular state. A second important feature of many invertebrates is simply that their neurons are quite large. This means that they are readily recorded from and manipulated, both electrophysiologically and biochemically. Consequently it is much easier to observe their intrinsic properties and to discover the cellular mechanisms which confer on a neuron its particular functional role and representational capacity. On these terms, invertebrate preparations are generally more tractable. Ultimately we will want to solve the problem of mental representation in the cognitive aristocracy; the point here is that we might profit from first trying out our ideas among the cognitive rabble.

Classical conditioning is surprisingly widespread among invertebrates, but some conditionable invertebrates are not especially advantageous from a physiological point of view. Although the octopus and honey bee can readily be conditioned (Wells and Young, 1968; Menzel *et al.*, 1974), their neurons are numerous, small, and generally not identifiable; one might as well work on a rabbit. At the other extreme is the *paramecium*, which although apparently conditionable (Hennessey *et al.*, 1979) lacks a nervous system altogether. Between are a number of species which are conditionable and have tractable physiology (see Table 5).

Although the representational states underlying simple classical conditioning are of general interest, we have seen that much stronger mental analogues are found among the states implicated by selective association, second-order conditioning and other forms of complex classical conditioning. Asking for these forms of learning shortens the list considerably. Blocking has been demonstrated in *Limax* (Sahley et al., 1981) and *Aplysia* (Colwill, 1985); second-order conditioning only in *Limax* (Sahley et al., 1981) and bees (Menzel, 1983), which we have already ruled out. It would be surprising if higher forms of conditioning were impossible to produce in the rest of the list. The only published negative example to date is blocking in bees (Couvillon et al., 1983); the other species are evidently untried.

The physiological analysis of higher forms of classical conditioning is underway. In *Limax* the conditioned behaviour-exploratory locomotion in the vicinity of various food odours is a difficult one to analyse at the cellular level. The behavioural paradigm does not lend itself well to physiological experiments, which require restraint and, to expose the nervous system, partial disassembly of the animal: a so-called *semi-intact* preparation. Conditioning of the initiation of ingestive behaviour can be produced in semi-intact animals, but this is a different response for which there is as yet no evidence of complex conditioning. The report of blocking in the *Aplysia* siphon- and gill-withdrawal reflex is promising because the reflex can be studied in a semi-intact or fully isolated nervous system and the circuitry and mechanisms of associative learning are already well understood. Unfortunately, however, this study included complex contextual cues among the conditioned stimuli, and the neural substrates for this kind of sensory reception are poorly understood. Although complex forms of conditioning have not yet been investigated in *Aplysia* using well-understood sensory input, in principle these experiments are feasible and in progress (Hawkins, personal communication).

## *The neurophysiology of mental representation*

The plasticity of invertebrate behaviour in general, and in particular the demonstration in *Aplysia* and *Limax* of higher forms of classical conditioning, augurs well for cognitive neurobiology. At present we can say nothing definitive regarding the physiological nature of mental-state analogues since we must wait for physiological experiments to catch up to behavioural studies. On the other hand, we can make some rather concrete speculations, thanks to the fact that the *Aplysia* gill-withdrawal reflex has been

Table 5. Classical Conditioning in Selected Invertebrates

| Technical name | Common name | Behaviour |
| --- | --- | --- |
| *Limax maximus* | garden slug | odour preference (1) |
| *Pleurobranchaea* | — | food preference (2) |
| *Lymnaea stagnalis* | pond snail | appetitive response (3) |
| *Achatina fulica* | land snail | food preference (4) |
| *Hirudo medicinalis* | medicinal leech | shortening (5) |
|  |  | stepping (6) |
| *Hermissenda crassicornis* | — | decreased phototaxis (7) |
| *Aplysia californica* | sea hare | gill withdrawal (8) |
|  |  | conditioned fear (9) |
|  |  | feeding cessation (10) |

Notes: (1) Sahley and Ready, 1985; (2) Mpitsos and Davis, 1973; (3) Audesirk et al., 1982; (4) Croll and Chase, 1980; (5) Sahley and Ready, 1985 (6) Sahley and Ready, 1985; (7) Crow and Alkon, 1978; (8) Carew et al., 1981; (9) Walters et al., 1979; (10) Susswein and Schwartz, 1983.

so thoroughly analysed. The cellular mechanism of simple classical conditioning in this reflex is sufficiently understood that it has been possible to ask the theoretical question whether the known cellular mechanisms and neuronal circuitry are sufficient to produce various forms of complex conditioning (Hawkins and Kandel, 1984). Such an educated guess, bolstered by computer simulation of the circuitry, indicates that the reflex ought to be capable of second-order conditioning, and perhaps blocking as well (Gluck and Thompson, 1987; Hawkins, personal communication).

These are, of course, the results of speculation. However, at least in regard to second-order conditioning, the theoretical mechanism builds so closely on the actual mechanism of classical conditioning that there is not much room for manoeuvre: chances are good that if the reflex exhibits second-order effects, then the underlying mechanism will be as proposed. It thus becomes hard to resist the temptation to pretend for a moment that the gill-withdrawal reflex really does exhibit second-order conditioning in the way supposed by Hawkins and Kandel. What do the mental-state analogues look like? What properties endow them with their particular functional roles? And what sort of consequences would representations so structured have for various positions in philosophy of mind and cognitive science?

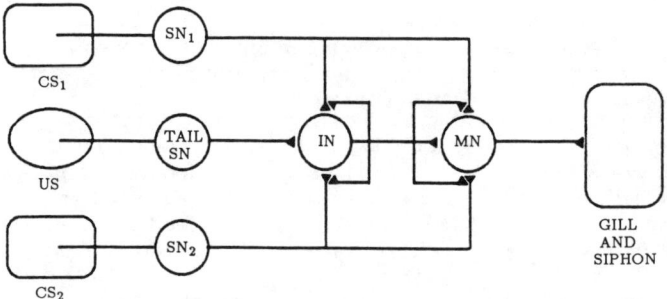

*Figure 1.* Minimum neuronal circuit for the *Aplysia* gill- and siphon-withdrawal reflex in second-order conditioning. Stimulation of the siphon or mantle skin (small box) causes contraction of the gill and siphon (large box) via sensory to motor-neuron synapses. Shock to the tail (oval) excites the facilitatory interneuron. Co-activation of a sensory neuron and the interneuron results in activity-dependent facilitation of sensory-neuron synapses. Abbreviations: CS, conditioned stimulus (mechanical stimulation of skin); US, unconditioned stimulus (tail shock); SN, sensory neuron; IN, facilitatory interneuron; MN, gill and siphon motor neuron (after Hawkins and Kandel, 1984).

Before we can consider the nature of representational states in second-order conditioning, we must first understand the mechanism of simple classical conditioning in the gill-withdrawal reflex. A diagram of the gill-withdrawal circuitry is shown in Figure 1.

In untrained animals mechanical stimulation of a sensory neuron causes a moderate gill response via the sensory to motor-neuron synapse. If sensory stimulation is paired repeatedly with shock to the tail, the strength of the sensory to motor-neuron synapse is increased, resulting in a much stronger gill withdrawal on subsequent test trials when the sensory neuron alone is stimulated. This effect has been traced to the nearly simultaneous occurrence of action potentials in the presynaptic terminal of the sensory neuron and the terminal of the facilitating interneuron, which responds when the animal is shocked. It is therefore regarded as an activity-dependent form of synaptic facilitation. Importantly, it is not confined to the sensory-neuron terminals but, under similar conditions, may occur at other synapses as well.

These other sites of activity-dependent facilitation endow the *Aplysia* nervous system with the potential for second-order conditioning. During paired sensory stimulation and shock, activity-dependent facilitation also occurs at an initially weak synapse between the sensory neuron and the interneuron, since the temporal arrangement of activity in the sensory and interneuron terminals here is the same as at the sensory to motor-neuron synapse. Second-order conditioning is a two-stage process involving not one but two conditioned stimuli (see Table 4 — p. 144), where each conditioned stimulus is the activation of an individual sensory neuron. In stage 1, paired stimulation of the first sensory neuron, $SN_1$, with shock causes facilitation of the sensory to motor-neuron synapse as above, and gill withdrawal to stimulation of $SN_1$ is strengthened, that is, first-order conditioning occurs as usual. At the same time, however, the sensory to interneuron synapse is also strengthened, so that, by the time the gill reflex is fully conditioned $SN_1$ can, by itself, fire the interneuron. This means that the conditioned sensory neuron can now take over the role of the shock in stimulating the interneuron. In stage 2, stimulation of a second sensory neuron, $SN_2$, is paired not with shock, but with stimulation of the first sensory neuron. This results in facilitation of $SN_2$'s sensory to motor-neuron synapse, even though this neuron has never been paired with shock, that is, second-order conditioning.

We now have enough information about the mechanisms of learning in the gill-withdrawal circuit to pick out the neuronal properties whose co-variance with stimulus conditions constitutes representation of the information presented during the various phases of conditioning. What we find is not especially mysterious: stimulus relationships are encoded in memory by the presence or absence of activity-dependent facilitation. An animal or reflex stores the information that a certain stimulus is well correlated with shock if and only if the synaptic terminals of the relevant sensory neuron have undergone activity-dependent facilitation. Thus, if $SN_1$ is paired with shock in stage 1, then facilitation of $SN_1$'s terminals represents the information that a conditioned stimulus to the field of innervation of $SN_1$ — call it $CS_1$ — predicts shock. By the same token, facilitation of $SN_2$'s terminals, which occurs during stage 2, represents the information that $CS_2$ predicts shock.

The co-variance between facilitation and the occurrence of stimulus pairing amounts to a strong suggestion that, for an arbitrary sensory neuron — $SN_i$ — the physical state 'having facilitated terminals' is identical with a certain mental-state analogue: 'having the information that $CS_i$ predicts shock.' We have seen that, according to functionalism, for mental and physical states to be identical, they must have identical functional roles within their respective descriptive contexts. So far we have merely shown that having facilitated terminals and having the information that $CS_i$ predicts shock have parallel relations to sensory input. A full functionalist identification requires assuring ourselves that relations to other states and behaviour also run in parallel. For the present discussion this is trivial. The only type of state-state relation we need to consider is the one promised by second-order conditioning: if the system has the information that $CS_i$ predicts shock, and registers the information that $CS_j$ predicts $CS_i$, then the system will enter the state bearing the information that $CS_j$ predicts shock. The question then is whether a parallel state-state relation obtains at the neurophysiological level. Is it true that if $SN_i$ has facilitated terminals, and $SN_j$ and $SN_i$ are co-activated, then $SN_j$'s terminals will be facilitated? Of course, this is just what happens, and there is also a trivial parallelism as far as output relations are concerned, since a facilitated sensory neuron causes a strong gill response, the mark of conditioned behaviour and of having the information that the shock is predicted by stimulation of that neuron.

Advocates of functionalism would be heartened by such a result, since it amounts to the first demonstration of the causal role isomorphism upon which they rely so heavily. Since causal role isomorphism warrants state-state identity, it seems we would also have the first demonstration of a mental state–physical state identity, at least insofar as the mental-state analogues here count as mental states. It is worth pointing out that we are not just talking about identities between mental and physical state *tokens*. On the contrary, since all members of the species share the above circuitry and the relevant instrinsic neuronal properties, states such as 'having the information that $CS_i$ predicts shock' will have neural correlates which form projectible types across individuals. Finally, philosophers will already have noticed that all this amounts to a *smooth intertheoretic reduction* (Churchland, 1986) between the account at the psychological level and the neurophysiological theory. The reduction here is, of course, limited to mental-state analogues possessed by *Aplysia* only, a so-called *domain specific* reduction (Churchland, 1986). Nevertheless, if the *Aplysia* nervous system turns out to operate in this way, then we will have the first bit of concrete evidence to weaken the claim — known as *eliminative materialism* — that successful neuroscience will replace our folkpsychological talk of mental states, because the very concept of a mental state is a physical will o' the wisp, like phlogiston, caloric, and witches (Churchland, 1981).

If eliminative materialism is the most pessimistic view of the fate of mental states in the face of scientific progress, the most optimistic view is the *language of thought* hypothesis (Fodor, 1975). This is the idea that to have a mental state is literally to possess a 'sentence in the head', written in a neurophysiological code, that expresses the content of the state. Thus for John to believe that the morning star is on the horizon is for John to have encoded in his brain a sentence of 'mentalese' which translates to English as 'The morning star is on the horizon.' At the heart of the theory, and the reason it is of interest here, is the attempt to explain logical relations between mental states in terms of causal relations between physical states. Because the language of thought is literally a physical code, different sentences have different physical properties, much the same way that sentences in written English have different shapes, or to use the computer metaphor, different lines of programming code result in different sets of voltages in the relevant memory registers. These physical differences confer on each sentence unique causal powers in the interplay between sentences: exactly those which mirror the logical relations between sentences.

Of course, this is just how a computer operates. All the language of thought theorists have done is simply to flesh out the familiar slogan that the brain is a computer. As one might imagine, the idea has generated a lot of controversy, especially in regard to its conceptual plausibility, but it remains the dominant paradigm in philosophical psychology. Whatever the outcome of the conceptual debates, there remains the problem of neurophysiological plausibility, and the hypothesis entails some rather demanding physiological assumptions. One of these is the concept of sentential encoding: the existence of functions that map properties of neurophysiological states to objects in a linguistic code. Another is that the neuronal properties that make a state correspond to a particular sentence in the language of thought are precisely the ones that endow a state with its unique causal-inferential role.

From what we know of how the gill-withdrawal network exhibits second-order conditioning, we have a chance to put these assumptions to the test, since in second-order conditioning we have the first instance of a relation between representational states that is formally inferential. A mapping relation between physical properties and units of the sentential code is not hard to set up. The identity of distinct conditioned stimuli is represented explicitly by the network: one sensory neuron being dedicated to each stimulus type (where stimuli are distinguished by bodily location). We can say then that there is a one-to-one mapping of stimulus type to sensory neuron. The property of having facilitated terminals seems to do the work of representing in memory something like the predicate 'predicts-shock', or 'hurts', or 'warrants-strong-withdrawal'; it therefore maps to one or another of these simple, non-relational predicates. Finally, the coactivation of two sensory neurons (as in stage 2), or of a sensory neuron and the facilitating interneuron (as in stage 1 or 2), seems to do for perception what having facilitated terminals does for memory: it represents the perception that two stimuli are closely related, perhaps as mutually predictive, perhaps as identical. For the sake of argument let us say it maps to the relational predicate 'is-identical-to'.

So much for the mapping assumption. We are now in a position to ask whether the physical properties that serve as linguistic tokens — symbols of the mental code — guarantee the appropriate causal-inferential role for individual mental-state analogues. Placing lines of mental code alongside their physical representations we obtain:

| Code | Physical State |
|---|---|
| $CS_i$ predicts-shock | $SN_i$ has facilitated terminals |
| $CS_j$ is-identical-to $CS_i$ | $SN_i$ and $SN_j$ are coactivated |
| $CS_j$ predicts-shock | $SN_j$ has facilitated terminals |

The question then is whether the *logical* relations between the sentences of mental code in the syllogism on the left are mirrored at the physiological level by *causal* relations among the physical states on the right. If $SN_i$ has facilitated terminals and $SN_i$ and $SN_j$ are coactivated, will $SN_j$'s terminals become facilitated? The answer is, of course, yes, since this is precisely how the gill circuitry is supposed to operate. This suggests that the physiological assumptions of the language of thought are not thoroughly incommensurate with what is known about an actual nervous system.

Obviously, the *Aplysia* gill-withdrawal circuit is an extremely primitive instantiation of the language of thought. The fact that the gill reflex has forty four differentially conditionable sensory neurons (Byrne et al., 1978) increases the number of possible representational states, but the syntactic simplicity of the system remains. It possesses only one kind of singular term ($CS_i$, $CS_j$, etc.), and two kinds of predicate, and though sentential it lacks a constitutive property of language: what linguists call generativity, the ability to create new sentences by embedding sentences within sentences, by using operators such as negation, and so on. Thus, before the model systems approach can have a significant bearing on the empirical prospects for the sentential theory of representation, we have to find a system with greater 'linguistic' competence. This may still be possible at the invertebrate level if studies of learning in simple systems reveal the existence of representational states the causal relations of which require a more enriched syntax at the psychological level. It is interesting in this regard that the mollusc *Limax* has recently been shown to exhibit inhibitory conditioning — acquisition of the information that a stimulus predicts the *absence* of a reinforcer — which would seem to warrant the inclusion of negation in the organism's representational syntax.

Lest the language of thought theorists take too much comfort in this simple example, it is worth pointing out that gill reflex can also be assimilated without much difficulty to a 'connectionist' model of information processing, which makes no appeal to sentential representation (for a discusion of such models see Rumelhart and McClelland, 1986). The sensory neurons can be seen as the layer of 'input units'. These all connect directly to a single 'output unit' (the motor neuron); in this analogy there are no hidden units. The connection strengths or 'weights' for each synaptic input are adjustable according to the principle of activity-dependent facilitation. Upon activation of any number of input units, the network's task is to develop a level of activation of the output unit that corresponds to the degree of 'danger' inherent in that particular pattern of sensory stimulation. When the output activation is insufficient, the experimenter delivers a shock. This corresponds to the 'teaching input' and preferentially increases the weights of active synapses. In naive animals, no stimuli are perceived as dangerous by the network and motor-neuron activation is low. During training, the synaptic weight of input units regularly paired with shock increases until the network can detect input patterns which signal shock. Second-order conditioning can also be incorporated in a connectionist interpretation. After reaching a certain level of performance, the system gains access to the teaching input (the facilitating interneuron). Stimuli that began to occur along with a pattern that signals shock would eventually be themselves incorporated into the pattern.

There are certainly other formalisms to which the gill-withdrawal reflex can be assimilated, in addition to the two discussed here, leaving one with the impression that the reflex can be anything to anyone. This is probably quite true and serves to underscore the observation that local physiological facts are not by themselves sufficient to settle the question what function a segment of the nervous system is performing. Presumably this project requires taking a much broader view of the nervous system: one that includes many other parts of the system and an assessment of how the system's behaviour is best explained at the psychological or information-processing level. Another lesson to be drawn from theoretical consideration of the *Aplysia* circuitry is that one can achieve undeniably cognitive functions from small numbers of neurons, each employing the most rudimentary and unmysterious representational mechanisms: variation in connection strength and 'labelled lines'. This probably is no surprise to theoreticians who have been studying the information-processing properties of small networks (Sutton and Barto, 1981), but here we have the first indication that actual neurons, using known intrinsic properties and patterns of connectivity, can achieve similar competences.

The most significant observation offered by analysis of *Aplysia* conditioning is that neurophysiological facts could contribute to the specification of the logical form of mental states. Notice in this regard that the most obvious account of the steps of learning and inference in second-order conditioning of the gill circuit is not supported by the neural mechanisms. One might have thought, from the operational form of a second-order conditioning experiment, that in stage 1 the animal learns that $CS_1$ predicts the $US$, in stage 2 that $CS_2$ predicts $CS_1$, and concludes that $CS_2$ predicts the $US$. However, the physiological analysis of the circuit has shown that in its memory the system can only represent relations between $CS'$s and the $US$. The circuit never has a lasting representation of the information that $CS_2$ predicts $CS_1$. Granted, the system can detect the co-occurrence of $CS_2$ and $CS_1$ and the simultaneous activation of the relevant sensory neurons represents this fact, but this representation disappears as soon as the stimulation is over. In this sense, attributing a mental-state analogue of the form 'believes that $CS_2$ predicts $CS_1$' is physiologically incorrect. This raises the interesting possibility that the physiological and psychological accounts of systems will tend to co-evolve: cognitive psychological studies working from *above* to define the tasks a system is performing, and neurophysiological studies working from *below* to sharpen the cognitive interpretation of the system's output.

## Conclusion

In the preceding sections I have argued that the complexity of the nervous system compels us to adopt the model-systems approach to the study of the nature of mental representation. Although representational states are widespread in the natural world, some representational states function more like mental states than others, and hence are more worthy of the physiologist's attention. Interesting mental-states could be identified as being at issue for a system or organism when it performed favourably under one or more forms of complex classical conditioning, the explanation of which, as we saw, compels the use of representational states with mentalistic functional roles in the explanation of behaviour.

The question then arose whether this special class of representational state — the mental-state analogue — could be found in a physiologically tractable model system. Several invertebrate reflexes passed the behavioural test for mental-state analogues being at issue, but too little was known about the neural mechanisms of learning in these cases. Although the relevant behavioural tests have not been applied to the *Aplysia* gill-withdrawal system, we saw that enough is known about the mechanisms of learning in this circuit to predict how it might produce second-order conditioning. This led, finally, to some provisional conclusions regarding standing issues in philosophical psychology regarding functionalism, psycho-physical reduction, eliminative materialism, and the nature of mental representations. Suppose that the *Aplysia* gill-withdrawal circuit does function as proposed. Further, suppose we found the same conclusions could be drawn from *every* invertebrate system we were able to investigate. What would this mean for the generality of these conclusions? What reason do we have to suspect that complex nervous systems represent information and put it to use in a similar way?

It seems that we have every reason to suspect that the opposite is the case: the structure and organisation of the vertebrate nervous system — let alone that of behaviourally sophisticated mammals — is extremely different from that of the invertebrates. On this basis, we should no more expect the representation in a rat that $CS_i$ predicts shock to resemble the functionally equivalent representation in *Aplysia* than we would the representation of, say, $2 + 2 = 4$ in a VAX computer to resemble the same addition on an abacus. However, recent evidence from the study of the neural mechanisms of associative (classical and operant) conditioning suggests that the representational states of vertebrate and invertebrate nervous systems can be more similar than suggested by the obvious anatomical discrepancies.

All studies to date indicate that learning is associated with a change in intrinsic properties of neurons. It does not appear to involve the establishment of new pathways, nor of new activity patterns (the reverberating circuit hypothesis), and this appears to be as true for vertebrates as invertebrates (Byrne, 1987; Carew and Sahley, 1986; Thompson, 1986). The fact that information is represented by changes intrinsic to individual neurons has important consequences for generalizing across the invertebrate–vertebrate divide. The intrinsic properties of neurons — their biochemical and biophysical properties — are surprisingly alike in vertebrates and invertebrates. Thus it is likely that vertebrate circuits will employ representational mechanisms similar to those identified in invertebrate model systems. There is already some evidence to support this prediction. The picture emerging from invertebrate learning studies is that learning is associated with a change in membrane conductance, which in turn affects a cell's ability to transmit information, either by altering its excitability (*Hermissenda* and Locust) or its synaptic efficacy (*Aplysia*). Although a variety of mechanisms could cause changes in membrane conductance, learning in these systems appears uniformly to involve conductance changes mediated by biochemical signals within the cell: so-called second-messenger systems. Preliminary evidence from vertebrate studies implicates both conductance changes and second messengers in associative learning. Eye-blink conditioning in the cat is associated with decreased conductance and increased excitability in motor neurons controlling the conditioned response, and this effect can be mimicked by intracellular injection of a common second messenger (cyclic GMP) in an activity dependent fashion (Woody et al., 1976; Woody, 1982). A similar training procedure increases the excitability of pyramidal neurons in the hippocampus — a structure strongly related to memory — and this change is associated with a decline in conductance (Berger et al. 1983; Disterhoft et al., 1986). In addition, long-term potentiation in the hippocampus, a kind of synaptic plasticity which resembles learning in many respects, requires $Ca^{2+}$ as a second messenger that ultimately results in increased excitability (Lynch and Baudry, 1984).

On balance, the basic invertebrate representational mechanisms — the neuronal properties which co-vary with sensory stimulation and training — may well be the same for vertebrates. Insofar as this is true, we can expect the co-variation to be *systematic* in vertebrates as well. This suggests that *types* of representational states will correspond with *types* of neurophysiological states, insofar as representation of sensory conditions is concerned. This is the kind of relation which underlies type-type psycho-physical identity. However, it is important to remember that the relation to sensory conditions is only part of a representational state's functional role, and to identify a representational state with a physical state we must show complete causal role isomorphism. A state's ability to affect behaviour must also be assessed, and the same is true for its relation to other representational states. Unlike the representation of stimulus and training information, which makes use of only instrinsic neuronal properties, the causal relations between representational states will undoubtedly be a function of patterns of connectivity, since what is involved is the effect of information stored at one place upon information stored at another. This suggests that network properties will influence state-state integration mechanisms, and at this stage of the analysis we may well expect the differences between vertebrate and invertebrate to be greater. Nevertheless, it is unlikely that this difference in mechanistic detail would undermine the demonstration of functional role isomorphism: if representation at the stimulus side of things is systematic, then so must be the mechanisms which operate on such representations.

However promising this might make the prospect for a cognitive neurobiology seem, we must not lose sight of the fact that associative learning, though fundamental, is not all there is to cognition. Obviously, there are a great many cognitive tasks for which there is no functional parallel among the physiologically tractable invertebrates. Here, of course, the model systems approach finds its natural limit.

**Suggestions for further reading.** For a brief, yet complete and readable, introduction to learning theory see Dickinson (1980). Mackintosh (1975) is the source for the representative account of classical conditioning used in the present chapter.

For a thoroughgoing review of progress on the physiological and biochemical basis of learning, see Byrne (1987). The *Aplysia* gill withdrawal reflex remains the conditionable system most completely understood. A review of that system and speculation on its ability to exhibit more complex forms of conditioning, is contained in Hawkins and Kandel (1984). The stunningly cognitive abilities of *Limax* were first reported in Sahley et al. (1981).

For an introduction to philosophy of mind, see P.M. Churchland (1984) and P.S. Churchland (1986). The latter also contains introductory material on the neurosciences.

The touchstone (and lightning rod) for theories of mental representation is Fodor (1975). The same author turns his gaze to the invertebrate world in Fodor (1986). For a more sympathetic look at representation in simple systems, try Dretske (1980). Cherniak (1986) is another attempt to set minimal conditions for cognitive behaviour.

CHAPTER 9

# REPRESENTATION AND EXPLANATION

*Kathy Wilkes*

## Introduction

The general topic up for discussion in this volume is the legitimacy of using certain 'mental' or 'psychological' terms in the explanation of goal-directed behaviour. But which ones? Here, I think, there is some unclarity. In its non-technical sense, 'intentionality' concerns the forming or having of intentions, representations of goals to be achieved. A technical use of the term, though — frequently spelled 'inten*s*ionality' — makes it cover a very much wider range of terms; not only intentions, but beliefs, desires, hopes, fears, expectations, thoughts; all those mental phenomena that are 'about' things and states of affairs (which may or may not exist or obtain); mental phenomena which have content.

Although there is room for disagreement (think of classical behaviourism) I have no doubt but that intensionality-with-an-s will prove ineliminable in the description and explanation of behaviour. After all, neuropsychologists freely use such terms when talking about the operations of, say, amygdala or hippocampus; computer scientists need intensionality to explain their computer programs. We find intensionally-laden phrases in abundance in these areas: consider 'expectancy generators', 'reward neurons', 'scanners', 'filters', 'comparators', 'detectors', and above all the term 'information' itself. Maybe the way in which computer science or neuroscience deploy intensional terms to cope with the 'aboutness', or 'directedness on a possibly non-existent object' is feeble and watered-down in comparison to the rich and subtle intensionality that — we think — human thought enjoys; but it is there all the same. However that may be, though, this chapter at least is concerned only with the narrower problem: with that subclass of intensional (with an *s*) terms that are intentions (with a *t*); or are 'representations of goals to be achieved'. (I shall take these two locutions — 'intentions', and 'representations of goals' — to be equivalent for our purposes, since both are being examined with respect to their common causal, and/or explanatory, role in the explanation of behaviour.)

This means, most fortunately, that we can sidestep much of the colossal (and insufficiently examined) question of just what 'representations' are, when they are postulated across the board in the brain and behavioural sciences; in perception, recognition, learning, memory. Of course the term 'representation' is going to be problematic: so were the Cartesian and Empiricist 'ideas', and 'representations' are but 'ideas' in modern dress — sounding more respectable because the word is longer (see in this connection Montefiore's comments in chapter 5, p. 75 about the German translation of the Cartesian and post-Cartesian 'ideas'.) Happily, the problem at stake here is more circumscribed: whether a representation, taken to represent (in whatever manner) a goal or an intention, is a necessary postulate in the explanation of behaviour that is, or seems to be, purposive.

Even when we thus restrict the problem, it is still hard to get agreement about where the disagreements lie. Just what is our ontological commitment, when we say that intentions or representations *are* needed? If they are indeed required for the explanation of behaviour, is this because they are *causes* of behaviour? Or might 'explanation' come apart from causation here? The chief difficulty is to specify the matters at issue in a precise form. But to see that we shall need to go the long way around. This chapter is, then, primarily an exercise in ground-clearing.

## 'Explicit', 'implicit', 'tacit'

I want first to make some *preliminary* comment on different sorts of representation. For we cannot answer the question 'are representations, or intentions, needed in the explanation of behaviour?' unless we have some agreement about what they are; different interpretations of what is to count as one will dictate very divergent answers. However, the discussion can only be preliminary at this point; as we shall see, any distinctions we may hope to draw between various kinds of representations will depend heavily on several further factors.

'Explicit' representations seem to be things worth individuating *per se* — and this is emphatically not the truism it may at first appear. There are lots of things which of themselves are not worth individuating; for example, the set of objects currently cluttering my desk. This set is a contingent, accidental, and boring confluence of individual items — various papers, a book or two, a cup and saucer, a cassette. This is not, of course, to say that no sets of things are worth individuating; for instance, it may well be worth identifying the contents of that bookshelf (= my complete edition of Proust). So 'a' representation might be a highly *complex* sort of thing; but it must have some systematicity if so; it must be something we want or need to (re)identify. A little later we shall say more about the nature of these wants and needs; they will vary from context to context.

Probably, second, we want to say that explicit representations 'exist'. This too sounds like a vacuous condition, but I think it is not — indeed, as we shall see, it may well prove false of explicit representations in some kinds of psychological explanation. However, if we want a realist interpretation of scientific psychology (we shall say more about this soon), then we will want some ontological commitment to the notions cited in the explanations; what *kind* of commitment this may be — in other words, what it means to say that representations or intentions exist — is a highly vexed business. But at this stage I am sketching with a very broad brush; for the moment we need only some intuitively-clear account of what might count as 'existence' for explicit representations. One such Dennett provides: '... information is represented *explicitly* in a system if and only if there actually exists in the functionally relevant system a physically structured object ...' (1982–3, p. 216). This, apparently unproblematically, makes the existence in question a function of its physical realisation, and seems to give us the sort of thing we need. Let us adopt it for the moment; we shall soon see, though, that it is less clear than it looks at first sight.

Examples might help. Intuition, which may be thoroughly fallible, invites us to cite as examples of explicit representations such things as the thought-in-words: 'I will assassinate Lincoln tomorrow', or the state of the sprinter who runs with his mind occupied by the mental image of breasting the tape — very literally having in mind the 'goal to be achieved'. Here we appear to be making some sort of ontological commitment to something that has at least temporal — and maybe, if we adopt Dennett's definition, physical and hence spatial — boundary conditions; an event or state, something reasonably discrete and distinguishable, 'worth individuating'.

We can hope for no sharp or clear line between representations that are 'explicit', and those that are not. Put another way, we need not hope for anything better than a blurry sliding scale between those instances where most people would be happy to say that we had 'a representation', or 'an intention', and those where we are less confident about the propriety of such ascriptions. For instance, if one intends some end — killing Lincoln, say — then in a sense one intends the various means to that end; one may be said to intend whatever the guiding intention implies. Thus, perhaps parasitically, Wilkes Booth ('also'?) intended to shoot Lincoln; to fire a gun; to pull the trigger; to crook his right index finger. We are, I think, much less certain about whether these are 'explicit' or not. We might call them 'implicit', in that they are *implied by* something that is (perhaps) explicit. But we have no clear intuitions about whether, or when, they are 'worth individuating', or what it means to say they 'exist'. The problems of individuating intentions are, unsurprisingly, exactly the same as those of individuating actions: both are articulated in the same means–ends, constituents–ends, hierarchy. (It is no less true than 'Wilkes Booth killed Lincoln' to say any of: 'he shot Lincoln'; 'he fired a gun'; 'he pulled a trigger'; 'he crooked his index finger'.) There comes a point, low down in the hierarchy, when we want to reject all talk of 'intentions'; it is, to put it mildly, odd to say that the concert pianist 'intended' to hit C-sharp when playing a fast prelude. (Note, though, that if he were for any reason prevented from hitting the note, he could of course say 'I was going to ...', or even 'I intended to ...'.) For parallel reasons it is *misleading* to say that what Wilkes Booth did was to crook his finger, even though it's unambiguously true.

We thus find a sliding scale from the apparently clear cases of explicit (or at least explicitly stated) intentions to those that seem 'merely' implicit; and evidently have a hefty theoretical problem in the specification of 'the' intention, or representation, that guides, governs, explains, modifies, or perhaps causes, purposive behaviour.

What of 'tacit' representations? Consider the following example. When walking along a road, it is curious how accurate one can be in predicting, even from some distance away, which foot (right or left) will hit a specific spot, or whether the spot will fall mid-stride. Somehow we have 'represented' in us our own current stride-length. A fancier example might be the dolphin that somehow represents the differential equations of hydrodynamics, *in that* its behaviour is reliably in accordance with them. A simpler example would be the pocket calculator that acts in accordance with principles of arithmetic. Tacit representations seem to be dispositions, abilities, know-how: where and what we can do depends upon the way we are, or — sometimes — on what we have learned.

The same abilities may be due to tacit, or explicit, representing. That is: we could in principle construct a robot-dolphin which had represented explicitly in it the differential equations of hydrodynamics. Some learned skills may at first require some degree of explicit representation — e.g. tying a bow tie — but then come rather to look like 'mere' know-how. How, then, do we know when we have tacit, and when explicit, representations? I do not think we can tell a priori. Perhaps we should appeal again to the (as yet vaguely phrased) conditions that what 'actually exists' to explain the capacity should be 'worth individuating'. To see the point here, consider an analogy to 'tacit representation' borrowed from a paper (unpublished) of Naomi Sheman:

> An advertisement claims that unbeknownst to most drivers (perhaps because the automobile manufacturers are in cahoots with the oil companies), there is a fuel-saving device in all cars, and for a mere $29.95 we will send you what you need to know in order to activate it. When you send in your money what you receive is a set of tips such as: avoid jack rabbit starts, use the highest possible gear, do not overuse the choke, disconnect your air conditioner, and so on. Now, it's true that if you follow such tips you and your car will be performing the function of conserving fuel, but it is worse than misleading — it is simply false — to claim that there is in the car a fuel-saving *device*. That is, there is no physical token — however complex — which corresponds to the functional description 'fuel-saver'.

No 'fuel-saving device' *exists* here. Yet cars have the capacity to economise on fuel, under certain conditions; and this is due to the way they are constructed.

Tacit representations are not really worth challenging. For talk of them seems to be shorthand for a set of statements describing features of the systems' structure and organisation; a way of talking about some of their abilities in certain conditions. I shall therefore assume that disagreement will arise nearer the 'explicit' end of the spectrum — while repeating that it might often be highly obscure which end of the spectrum we've got.

This section has at least indicated the *problems* in getting clear about what we should count as 'a representation'. We turn now to problems about what counts as explanation.

## Explanation

What is the purpose of an explanation? Trivially, it seeks to remove puzzlement. No doubt it does many other things as well; but that 'removing puzzlement' is one central aim is not, surely, in dispute. This simple fact at once reminds us that people can be puzzled by any number of features of any event, whether that event is behavioural or physical. More to the point, puzzlement in science may not cover the same range as the puzzlement of the layman (I shall say more about this shortly); more specifically, and within science, the puzzles of ethologists may not be those of psychologists, which may not be those of physiologists. Van Fraassen (1980, p. 127) makes this point tellingly with a simple example:

Why did Adam eat the apple?

The layman might want to know any number of things: why it was Adam who ate it (not Eve, or the snake); why he ate it (rather than kicking or painting it); why it was an apple he ate (rather than a banana or a mango). It is less clear how this particular event could be a subject for *scientific* investigation; but perhaps human consumption-behaviour, or weak-willed behaviour, would be possible candidates. Any number of similar examples could illustrate the central claim here. Our wants, interests, needs, and background knowledge will vary; they determine what we find it appropriate to pick on and identify.

A second point, perhaps less trivial. Explanation is not necessarily transitive. I am not saying that it is *in*transitive; just *non*-transitive. By this I mean that if $A$ is explained by appeal to $X$, $Y$, and $Z$, and if these three in turn are explained by $a$, $b$, $c$ ... $n$, it does not follow that $A$ can be explained by $a$, $b$, $c$, ... $n$. (Although sometimes it may be: hence I am not saying that explanation is *in*transitive.) A simple example suffices to show this. Consider two different gases of the same temperature. We can explain the sameness of temperature in terms of the fact that they have the same mean molecular kinetic energy. Suppose that we could explain in terms of atomic theory why each gas has that mean molecular kinetic energy. Intuitively, the sameness of temperature of the two gases would *not* be explained by the atomic level of description; for at this level we have lost the 'sameness' which is what we were seeking to explain in the first place. An omniscient mind, perhaps, would find the atomic level account a satisfactory explanation for the fact that the two gases have the same temperature. But only for an omniscient being could explanation ever be fully transitive; and such a being would only understand how the descriptions on the atomic level ensured the sameness of temperature if he understood how each ensured the sameness of mean molecular kinetic energy — how it explained the temperature *by* explaining the molecular movement. In short, the 'molecular' level is not dispensable.

Hence not all 'reductions' are 'explanations' — although the very notion of 'reduction' is used very loosely, and carries different connotations in different hands. Some macro phenomena, such as (to take Putnam's familiar example) a peg-board with round holes and a set of square pegs, are in one clear sense 'no more than' what their description in terms of the atomic lattices that make up board and pegs provides us; so, given that some use 'reduce' in this broad sense, we can 'reduce' the board and pegs to their description in terms of atomic lattices. But it would clearly be dotty to attempt to explain, at the atomic level, why the square pegs won't fit the round holes. In general, '$X$es are nothing but $Y$s' does not entail that $X$es can be explained in terms of $Y$s.

Incidentally, this shows what is right about, and what is wrong with, the much-vaunted argument that psychological phenomena are 'multiply realizable' in the neural hardware. It is often going to be a mistake to look for 'type-type correlations or identities' between phenomena described at a macro-level, and phenomena described at a micro-level; equally, it is usually a mistake to suppose that the micro-descriptions 'explain' the macro phenomena. If someone makes these mistakes and tries to correlate or identify dispositions like intentions or beliefs with 'micro' phenomena like neural synapses, or tries to explain the former in terms of the latter, then of course he is likely to lose *both* the explanatory benefit, *and* will be impressed by the multiplicity of ways in which intentions or goal representations — just like gas temperatures — can be 'realised'.

Third: not all explanations are causal explanations. This is obvious once the pragmatic nature of explanation is taken seriously; if one job of explanation is to remove puzzlement, then evidently people can be puzzled by well-nigh anything, and removing their puzzlement sometimes requires reference to causes, at other times does not. Some wholly adequate explanations are simply redescriptions: 'Why did he put out his arm?' — 'He's signalling a right turn; his indicator is broken'. At other times one may simply pick out a feature of the phenomenon to be explained: 'because he doesn't understand English', 'because it's a magpie', 'because he doesn't know his violin is out of tune'. Some explanations are descriptions of how a system works — which of course involve reference to causal mechanisms, but need not be classically 'causal explanations' — and would not cite 'a' cause. Others appeal to features of the contextual background: 'because it's raining', 'because the banks close at 3.30 p.m.' Indeed, every phenomenon occurs against a whole slew of background factors. Rarely if ever are the events we call 'causes' necessary conditions, still less sufficient ones; by and large (and very roughly) the things we call causes tend to be those factors which we see as intruding on various standing conditions. Thus we say that it is the insertion of money that causes the cigarette packet to drop out of the machine — not so much the fact that the machine was filled last week, or the causal mechanism of the machine itself, 'causally necessary' as both these factors are. But what counts for some as a 'standing condition' may strike others as a 'cause'; it all depends on what you expect and know already. In sum, explanation is 'making intelligible'; *sometimes* this is best done by citing 'the cause', sometimes by citing a causally necessary background condition, sometimes by redescription, sometimes by reclassification; sometimes by redescribing, or highlighting bits of, the background against which the event is to be seen.

The fourth point I want to make is more contentious, as Dennett's 'second-round' comments (chapter 13) show; I defend it further in chapter 11. I have suggested already that the explanatory interests of scientists and laymen often (I would say usually) diverge. The import of this for our present problem is considerable. Science seeks to 'carve nature at the joints'; to search for 'natural kinds' and to explain their characteristic or systematic properties in as general a way as possible. Thus, although the sciences are concerned with gravitational forces, electron spin, or tectonic plates, they are not concerned with curtains, editions of

*Macbeth,* or puddles — which are sometimes matters of concern for the layman. Now: what is distinctive about natural kinds is their systematicity. For instance, typical natural kinds are grouped and explained by laws (whether universal or statistical does not matter here), by symmetry principles, or by statements alleging similarities of structure or organisation. What distinguishes the layman's preoccupations and explanations is, by contrast, their very lack of systematicity: he is interested, for instance, in what *George* will do when he discovers that his youngest son has become a skinhead, not what parents — or fathers — tend to do in such circumstances; and for him 'laws', generalisations, or symmetry principles are well-nigh irrelevant.

When we apply these observations to purposive behaviour, we are evidently confronted by the need to find the description under which purposive behaviour should be put by the appropriate sciences; that is, to seek the most systematically-fruitful way of carving up such behaviour into 'natural kind' *explananda*. Behaviour does not come wrapped-up like Cadbury's chocolate bars, which are segmented and thereby invite division into eight pieces; although we hope and believe that there is structure, 'nature loves to hide'; God is subtle even if not malicious — not everything that attracts our attention is a suitable topic for systematic study. We have to discover, in the behavioural sciences as much as in physics, how to individuate and describe the flux before us. Put another way, we want a description of behaviour analogous to 'gold mass', rather than one like 'Susie's brooch'. One of the symptoms of, and reasons for, the underdeveloped state of the behavioural sciences is the colossal difficulty of identifying these (natural kind) descriptions: of characterizing the appropriate *explananda* and *explanantia*. The point is of fundamental importance. The neuroscientist, that is, can cheerfully agree that no description in his terms will explain why Flora flounced out of a party only ten minutes after she had arrived; such an event, as described, is not an appropriate *explanandum* for him. But he might wish to contribute to the explanation, now or one day, of such phenomena as reactive depression, anterograde amnesia, face-recognition, habituation, short-term memory for strings of digits, the mobbing behaviour of chaffinches, or maze-learning in goldfish, rat, or chimpanzee.

*Explananda* that are not natural kinds — which are not, in other words, amenable to *systematic* explanation — are subjects for common sense rather than for a science. Here the behavioural flux can, within limits, be divided according to the interests of the observers. This, if anywhere, is the natural home for explanations in terms of intentions, beliefs, desires. Hence one strand of our initial topic is already answered: yes, citing intentions has been found indispensable in commonsense psychology in the explanation of behaviour. (But as we have already seen, this does not entail that intentions explain behaviour *by causing* it; explanations can be adequate without citing causes.) There is little point in praising, or criticising, the prevalence of intention-talk in commonsense psychology; it's not going to change much, whatever is said about it. And no more it should. Consider that we still routinely say 'the sun's rising', or that someone is 'possessed'; note that the French are having little success in eliminating 'Franglais', nor English purists in eliminating the 'misuse' of 'hopefully', or the assimilation of 'disinterested' to 'uninterested'; even those hostile to Freudian theory may find it appropriate to describe someone as 'Oedipal' — although this may only be a trendy way of saying that he's fond of his mother. Everyday parlance has a jackdaw mentality — it picks up anything that strikes it as useful, amusing, economical.

Moreover, note that it is almost entirely irrelevant what (if any) neurophysiological processes underlie the psychological dispositions or processes which we cite in such explanations — these have no bearing on what interests us. After all, ancient Greek psychological explanation is intelligible and clear, even though most of the dramatists whose writing we still read with pleasure thought that the organ of sentience and sapience was the heart rather than the brain. We can read to children stories about Pinocchio, or ice-maidens, without worrying about the inadequacy of the physical hardware of the agents. Even if (*per* almost *impossibile*) we were to find some hideously complex set of cerebral processes which correlated with some of the states we ascribe to an agent, these will tell us nothing we, *qua* laymen, want or need to know about why Flora flounced out of her party. For exactly the same reasons we do not want to investigate the microstructure of the cricket ball that breaks the window; that won't inform us about why our window shattered. It's quite enough that we know it's a small hard object, proceeding at speed. Moreover, just as there is no *systematic* correlation between fences and their physical constitution (some are wooden, some iron, some steel, others made of wire, some plastic; they come in assorted shapes, lengths, structures, and patterns; and so forth), so there may be no systematic correlations between descriptions of intentions and of cerebral processes. Objects picked out by common sense, since they are not necessarily (indeed not often) natural kinds, won't usually have any systematic reductive correlations with any microstructural descriptions.

When commonsense intentional explanation is at issue, then, it will be true, albeit not very exciting, to agree that intentions enter into the explanation of behaviour, and to deny that there will be any 'reduction to', or 'explanation in terms of' neural states. But we don't need or miss it. Moreover, our ontological commitment to these *explanantia* is left wholly unspecified. (We shall return to this point in a different context.)

In the sciences, though, we want psychological terms to pick out systematic *explananda*. However, if they are to be systematically explained, then they had better be natural kind terms: characteristic and pervasive regularities. In other words, we must have some reason for believing that we have, or are approximating towards, a taxonomy of behaviours and of psychological states which carve the domains of the behavioural sciences at their joints. At the moment there is little agreement on such a taxonomy. Debate rages about whether (for instance) 'learning', 'memory', 'consciousness', 'recognition' have sufficient unity to be sensibly treated as natural kinds: phenomena which tolerate systematic explanation. Some of the papers in this volume can be regarded as discussing whether 'intention' or 'goal representation' are terms appropriate for scientific theory, whether as *explananda* themselves or as *explanantia* for purposive behaviour. Further, as we have seen, there is simply no reason whatsoever to presuppose that if they are to be systematically explained themselves by the neurosciences, then such explanation will come directly from the nerve-cell level of description. The distance between these two levels of description is surely greater than is that between the temperature of a gas and its atomic level of description. 'Jumping' levels is unlikely to clarify anyone's puzzlement — *even if* intentions, or representations, can ultimately be described as 'no more than' sets of processes in amongst nerve cells. Peg boards are 'nothing but' atomic lattices, programs in ADA are 'no more than' machine code operations: we get no assistance from such jumps.

We shall return to exploit some of these points later. For the moment we should take a closer look at the ontological and referential implications that the postulate of 'intentions', or 'goal representations', may carry. We have already touched on this; now it is time to go into greater detail.

## Realism

Realism about theoretical terms in science is typically characterized in terms both of reference, and of truth. Terms for theoretical entities (e.g., electrons) are putatively referring; and the laws of the theory involving them are putatively true. These two — reference and truth — generally go together, simply because the truth in question is taken to be truth 'by correspondence with the facts'; and so one reason why theoretical statements are thought to be true is because the terms used in them are thought to correspond to real entities, processes, or states.

The viability of realism in general, and the many variant kinds of realism, need not detain us. We are here concerned simply with the plausibility of realism with respect to intentions and goal representations. Postulates such as these are fishy in a way in which most theoretical entities in the physical sciences are not (and, of course, vice versa: realism in psychology is not bothered by anything like the 'Copenhagen or not?' dispute in quantum mechanics). As we have seen, it is vastly unclear what it *means* to say that 'there are such things as' intentions, or goal representations. Yet if they are to be worth citing as 'causes' in the explanation of behaviour, then, evidently, they must exist. If they have a role in explanation, but not as *causes* of behaviour, then the matter is less clear. So this question must somehow be answered.

I return at this point to Dennett's characterisation of explicit representations. Here is his full definition:

> Let us say that information is represented *explicitly* in a system if and only if there actually exists in the functionally relevant place in the system a physically structured object, a *formula* or *string* or *tokening* of some members of a system (or 'language') of elements for which there is a semantics or interpretation and a provision (a mechanism of some sort) for reading or parsing the formula (1982-3, p. 216).

Now this looks like the sort of thing the realist wants to accept. Few would deny that such a discovery would licence existential commitment to representations: the realism is to be grounded in a 'physically structured object', and such objects seem unproblematically real, and the sorts of things that can contribute to causal explanations. But the matter is not as clear as we might hope. At the moment we are, inevitably, handwaving about the nature of the 'physically structured object' and its accompanying parsing mechanism. Must this object in turn be something 'worth identifying' — discrete and identifiable? And should we look for, or expect, systematic (type-type) correlations between 'it' — whatever 'it' proves to be — and the representations it realises? Consider: all ornaments are composed of some physical elements. But the way in which atoms and molecules constitute ornaments is not something amenable to scientific investigation; and *for that very reason* 'ornament' is not an *explanandum* for physics.

We have a most intriguing problem. There seem to be various possibilities: (a) At some level of neuroscientific description there are systematic correlations between representations on the one hand and identifiable 'physically structured objects' on the other. If so, then we unproblematically have both realism and the potential for explaining the former, to some degree at least, in terms of the latter. (b) There are *loose* correlations between the two — representations may be variously instantiated by 'physically structured objects'. If so, then we still have realism, but far weaker explanatory power. (c) There are no systematic correlations to be found at all between representations of a certain type and 'physically structured objects' of a certain type.

This last possibility — that representations are related in only a radically token-token way to descriptions of brain processes — obviously abolishes any explanatory power that neuroscience might have with respect to representations. But more than that: it might put into question the viability of representations as appropriate scientific *explananda* or *explanantia*. If representations cannot be explained systematically by states of the brain, what is the scientific justification for postulating them in the first place? One reply, of course, is to say that psychology is 'autonomous': representations serve to explain behaviour, and that's justification enough for postulating them; they can't in turn be explained systematically (= scientifically) by neuroscience, but that just shows that psychology must proceed independently of neuroscience. This, of course, is a reply with immense implications for both sciences, which we cannot explore here; but it has its own problems. We have seen that explanation of action in terms of representations or intentions need not be causal explanation. (It might be, but then again it might not.) Realism is now put back into question; for if there are no reliable and regular correlations between representations and 'physically structured objects', and if representations don't necessarily *cause* actions, how do we know that there are such things? Even if a scientific psychology needs the postulate of representations to explain behaviour, it might construe them instrumentalistically. How, lacking systematic correlations, could we recognise 'a' physically structured object? Are they not beginning to look more like the 'fuel saving device' in Sheman's example? In which case, of course, they would start to look more like *tacit* representations, and — given the characterisation of realism above — only dubiously 'real'.

For now we swing to the other extreme. Suppose 'intentions', or 'goal representations', are like fuel-saving devices. Then, although one might be cheerfully admitting that the brain and its operations are ultimately responsible for purposive activity (just as features of the car explain how fuel can be conserved), and might even claim that this 'responsibility' is systematic and law-governed (so that psychology need not be 'autonomous' of neuroscience), representations *per se* would play no central part in explanation; and any systematic relationship between psychology and neuroscience (if indeed there is one) would relate quite different sorts of phenomena.

To avert unnecessary misunderstanding, let me repeat in one parenthetical paragraph that there is no problem here at all for commonsense psychology. This can cheerfully claim 'autonomy' from neuroscience, as we have noted already. So, to recap strands from the earlier discussion: it can safely say that it wants and needs to postulate intentions, and successfully explains everyday behaviour in terms of them. Equally, it needn't bother about whether these intentions are explicit and real, or tacit and hence not really 'there' in any strong sense. In other words, when we ascribe intentions to an agent, we are not *usually* (although sometimes we may be) committing ourselves to the existence of a physical correlate *to that very intention*. Certainly the man in the street would not think of his ascriptions as false, if he were informed that there are no specific sets of neurophysiological events with which the psychological states he cites could be identified. Put another way, commonsense psychology does not seem to me to need to be construed realistically at all points, and most of our ascriptions of propositional attitudes (intentions, beliefs, desires) are generally not so construed. The admitted fact that in everyday life we explain behaviour by appeal to intentions and their ilk does not entail realism about them. For we can agree (a) that intentions (etc.) serve to explain behaviour; we can agree (b) that behaviour is caused; but we need not conflate the two and say that (c) intentions explain behaviour *by* causing it — a conclusion that would give us realism. (c) may, or may not, be true, independently of the acceptability of (a) and (b). (Try substituting 'make intelligible' for 'explain' in (a), and then the failure of (c) to follow from (a) and (b) emerges more clearly.) These considerations for a measure of non-realism in commonsense psychology would certainly need to be spelled out more fully if the main subject were not the behavioural *sciences*. Since commonsense psychology is not something where 'laws' and 'psycho-physical correlations' are at issue anyway (compare Flora above) we can leave this here (and see my 1984 and 1986).

Now: there may be tenable positions in between these extremes of physically-grounded realism and the quasi-instrumentalism of tacit representation. We find in several sciences that there are many theoretical terms that refer to entities half-way between straightforward, unitary, and unproblematic 'existents', and the non-existence of 'fuel-savers'. The most familiar example is that of the gene, where there is no one-to-one relation between genes as functionally specified and any biochemical structural mechanism. The biochemical surround is invariably crucial to explaining the role of the gene; thus to explain phenotypic traits one needs to describe a complex set of conditions and mechanisms in which DNA segments figure prominently but not exclusively. In this case it is misleading both to assert, and to deny, that 'there are such things as genes', because of the danger of over-interpreting either the existential claim, or its denial.

'Intentions' and 'goal representations' may thus be scientifically irrelevant, like ornaments; or they may be more like electrons, more like fuel-savers, or somewhere in between, like genes. Settling the question of realism with respect to intentions, or goal representations, is thus *largely* an empirical matter (although not entirely, as we shall see). Therefore it must remain unsettled for a very long time, simply because of our lack of knowledge of brain structure and function.

Here, I think, the computer analogy for the mind can be dangerous. The computer has several 'levels', starting from the machine code, then the assembly language ... all the way up to BASIC or ALGOL. We know all about these levels; so realism with respect to computer states is relatively easy to comprehend and determine. We can distinguish between the (probably) non-realist ascription to a chess-playing computer, 'it wants to use the knights' fork', and ascriptions referring to states specified by the program. (But remember how unwise it would be to try to 'jump levels' and *explain* instructions in a high-level program with, say, machine code operations: explanation isn't transitive. We must expect a step-by-step reductive and explanatory sequence. If we don't, we'll be fooled into thinking that psychological posits are *all* like ornaments: multiply realisable, and hence not suitable for systematic study.)

In psychology and neuroscience, though — by contrast to computer science — we have practically no idea what, and where, the relevant 'levels' between (at one extreme) the macro-states postulated by the behavioural sciences, and (at the other extreme) the individual synaptic connections described by neurophysiology, are. We lack an agreed neuropsychological taxonomy 'in the middle'; and, as noted already, psychology at the 'macro' level still has little consensus about its taxonomy of *explananda*. The top 'level' is very loosely characterised as yet; and the levels beneath that are still largely matters of mystery. Thus we do not know whether 'intentions', or 'goal representations', have a suitably-systematic relation to anything on the next level down (whatever that might be); equally, we do not know what sorts of phenomena Dennett's 'physically structured objects' will be. It is no accident that confidence about 'representations' of other sorts — i.e. not goal representations — derives from much more detailed, or simpler, functions: such as the explorations of the structural basis in the visual cortex for representing moving edges, colour contrasts, or texture-gradients, or Lockery's investigation of processing in very simple systems. Here we find work that proceeds simultaneously on closely-related, and relatively well-plotted, 'levels'.

Our neuroscientific knowledge is at present far from allowing us to establish the truth of the postulate of representations. Elsewhere in this volume both McFarland and Noble doubt that it ever will. Yet it is difficult to understand what it can mean to say that 'representation' refers to something, or that statements citing intentions can be *true* (or false) if we abdicate from a step-by-step attempt to fill out the hierarchy of levels that correlate systematically the macro level of 'representations' with, ultimately, the cellular or biochemical level of description.

## Scientific values

If empirical data can't as yet help much, what else could? One handle on this question is to compare theories that do postulate intentions or goal representations with those that do not, and look to see which are the more promising. The trouble here is the familiar one that all theories are underdetermined by the data, a problem made worse by the underdeveloped state of the theories in question. Further, there are several 'good-making features' of theories, and one theory may do better on some counts, another on others. But it is worth listing the sorts of considerations that seem relevant to the matter.

If there were no theories that rivalled the intention-postulating theories, then that is all the justification the latter would need; for, generally speaking, better some explanation than no explanation. To illustrate this, consider the layman's explanations of the behaviour of his dog. If he can't say that the dog is barking up the wrong tree because it believes that the cat is up it, then he probably can't explain the dog's behaviour at all. This alone entitles him not to be crudely behaviouristic when handling his dog. Such an explanation, I suggest, is not necessarily an account that is 'true by correspondence to the facts' (there need be no identifiable thought in the dog's head), but that won't matter: the ascription makes the dog's behaviour intelligible, and is the only available explanation that does so. (We can, I suppose, say that this explanation is true in the sense that it coheres with all the behavioural evidence: the coherence theory of truth. But 'truth by coherence' is not enough to give us realism.) Indeed, it is probably even the case that a *false* theory is better than no theory at all. The phlogiston theory of heat would be one example. For, once you have a theory like the phlogiston theory, or Ptolemaic astronomy, then at least there is on the table something that can be tested; that allows, eventually, its deficiencies to show through, and hence may suggest how it might be amended or what should replace it. Our present problem, though, is not of this kind.

We want of our theories predictive and descriptive accuracy (within limits imposed by the subject-matter); internal logical coherence; external consistency — i.e. compatibility with theories in other domains; unifying power — consider the way Newtonian theory unified the explanation of the tides and the paths of projectiles; capacity for extension to new domains; clarity in the conceptual apparatus; and economy and simplicity. These values, particularly the last, 'simplicity', are very hard to assess. Nonetheless it is hard to avoid the conclusion that explanations lacking 'intentions', or 'goal representations' will, by and large, come out as superior to those that possess them.

Consider 'clarity' and 'economy'. It is unnecessary to argue that if we *can* eliminate the postulate of intentions without losing much in return, we'd be better off. For we have seen that 'intention' is a highly complex and confusing notion, and that the identity-conditions for intentions are most obscure. 'Intention' gets its misleading appearance of clarity from its home in anthropocentric common sense, from the fact that we sometimes express very specific intentions in language. But most purposive behaviour isn't preceded or accompanied by anything like this. As soon as we leave this very small range of examples, our decision what to call 'an intention', and our judgment about whether we've got one or not, becomes increasingly arbitrary; and hence the judgement between saying some action is guided by an intention to reach the goal, rather than that it merely results in a goal, will be correspondingly arbitrary. If the slogan 'no entity without identity' has any truth in it, then the problems with identification must gravitate back on to entification. To defend such woolly postulates as 'intentions' or 'representations' we'd need to establish that there were instances of behaviour which could not be explained without them; or which could only be explained in a highly unwieldy way without them. This is absolutely crucial, for, if this could be established, then other deficiencies of 'intentionalist' theorising can perhaps be overlooked; I have already argued that it's better to have some explanation than no explanation.

Given that this is in dispute, can we turn the original point on its head? That is, would the postulate of intentions or representations at least have the virtue that it allowed us to eliminate some strands elsewhere in the theoretical framework? Non-intentionalists argue that in terms of their framework, representations are unnecessary; could intentionalists reverse this argument and claim that some of the apparatus required in rival theories could be eliminated by this particular posit? I do not know the answer to this — I am not sufficiently familiar with the theories concerned, and 'intentionalist' theories are, to put it mildly, not exactly well-developed. However, it seems implausible. If we think just of the rival theory mentioned by McFarland in this volume, I cannot see how any elements of his theoretical apparatus would be rendered *redundant* by the postulate of 'representations of goals to be achieved'. But to defend this conjecture would take me away into a field where I am far from home.

Consider next the value of 'unifying power'. Here again the intentionalist seems to do badly. He will surely admit that there are numerous examples of behaviour that get the organism to some goal *without* that organism being guided by anything like a representation of the goal, or an intention. If that is so, then an intention-postulating theory will have less range and scope, less unifying power, than theories which treat all purposive behaviour alike, or at least as sitting on a continuous spectrum of sophistication and complexity. (However, this point will be qualified in the next section.)

Third, the non-intentionalist must do better in terms of the consistency of his theory with theories in other domains. Non-intentionalist theories (with the exception of crude behaviourism) have historically relied on, and often in part derived from, evolutionary theory, ethology, anthropology, and biology. They tend to be fully consistent with these, with physiology, and with newer ventures such as sociobiology. Intentionalist theorising, though — by and large — restricts its debts, and its analogies, to computer science: a dubious advantage, to my mind, given the colossal dissimilarity between brains and any existing computers. We have briefly discussed some of the problems that are bound to arise when we hunt for the neuroscientific basis of intentions or representations. I do not suggest that such theorising must or will prove to be strongly inconsistent with any of the other regions of brain and behavioural sciences. I suggest only that the links are at present a very great deal looser than are those enjoyed by non-intentionalist theories.

Insofar as theories can be evaluated in terms such as these, intention-postulating theories come off rather poorly by comparison with their more economical rivals. Note, though, that saying this in no way returns us to anything like the oversimplifications of early behaviourism. After all, what we are doing here is only suggesting that *one* — just one — of the psychological terms in everyday language may not be appropriate for use in science. Consider what proportion of the *OED* consists of 'psychological' terms! There are thousand upon thousand of them. Yet we don't expect the behavioural sciences to adopt and adapt more than a handful, any more than physics adopts more than a handful of everyday physical terms. Extreme (Watsonian) behaviourism failed because there is so much that it just cannot explain. This is scarcely surprising; it always was a priori implausible that so simple-minded a theory could serve to account for the most complex system we know. But it rejected *all* 'mental' terms; here I am only examining the possibility that a scientific theory might do without one of them: intentions. 'Representations' *tout court* would survive my comments, since 'representations of goals' are only one sub-class of the jumble of things that get called 'representations'.

## Exception? Language and representation

The most striking difference between humans and other animals is the human capacity for language, and his use of tools. Of course other animals communicate in some ways — by warning cries, threat or courtship signals, etc. — and several birds and monkeys can use simple tools. But there is all the difference in the world between using sounds to warn a conspecific of the presence of a leopard, and to ask the price of a lemon; and just as much difference between shaping a stick to catch termites, and constructing a wheelbarrow. I mention tool-use simply because it is generally so neglected, and yet it seems to me quite as significant as language (and probably required development in the same region of the brain). However I have to admit that it is language that concerns me in this section.

There is a very strong thesis which I shall not here defend or dispute, but which I mention because it allows me to put my point in its strongest form. It is argued by Macphail (1982, 1986), and he calls it the 'null hypothesis'. This hypothesis proposes that there is no quantitative or qualitative difference in intelligence among the vertebrate species, excluding man. He claims that there is no solid evidence that any of the cognitive feats ascribed to allegedly more intelligent species, like chimpanzees, cannot be rivalled by any other vertebrate — once one has taken into account and allowed for differences in perceptual capacity, motivation, physical capacity, and other such contextual variables.

I repeat: I am not concerned, nor competent, to defend this highly radical claim; it must evidently be hard to assess, if only because of the dubious nature of any attempts to grade intelligence, whether inter- or intra-specific. Hard to assess as it may be, it is also an hypothesis that sits up and begs to be examined: a Popperian paradigm of an important, but also fully exposed-to-test, scientific conjecture. (Were it to be plausible, though, note that the non-intentionalist would benefit: *if* it were unnecessary to postulate representations of goals in, say, goldfish, or even simpler vertebrate systems, then — since chimpanzees are, according to the null hypothesis, no more intelligent — it should be just as unnecessary to postulate them in any other members of the non-human vertebrate kingdom.) The point is that Macphail allows that humans outstrip other vertebrates in intelligence, and 'humans possess a species-specific language-acquisition device, and that it is this qualitative difference alone that distinguishes their intelligence from that of non-human vertebrates' (1986, p. 49). Whereas humans can solve most of the problems that non-human vertebrates can solve (once one has allowed for the contextual variables; e.g. humans can't fly, and so pigeons can do many things we can't), there's a vast range of problems which they, but no other vertebrate, can solve. This is 'so clear that no evidence in support of the assertion need be provided' (1982, p. 290).

If we accept the null hypothesis, then we accept a neat and simple dichotomy between humans on the one hand, and the rest of the vertebrate kingdom *en bloc* on the other; and the human possession of language is the most plausible explanation for the difference. Even if we reject the null hypothesis, we can still say that the difference between the intelligence of human and non-human animals is 'so clear that no evidence in support of the assertion' is needed; and again, language seems the most obvious explanation. The difference, like any differences in the natural order, should probably be regarded as one 'of degree' rather than 'of kind'; that seems to me to be one implication of taking evolution seriously. But that doesn't matter. Differences of degree can be colossal; I have never understood the insertion of the weasel-word 'only' into statements about differences 'only' of degree. The difference between the bumps in my lawn, and the Himalayas, seems to me significantly greater than that 'of kind' between wolf *canis* and the Tasmanian wolf, or the American and the European robin. Here we have a colossal difference of degree, and one which might make a difference — even at the expense of complicating theories in the behavioural sciences. If the capacity for developed language is an evolutionarily 'new' capacity, then it would not a priori be strange if 'new' explanatory structures were required to fit it. (As all will know, there is a long-running and often highly acrimonious debate about the capacity for language in apes. I don't need to take sides here; *if* language is, as I believe, crucial for consideration of the need to postulate intentions, and *if* chimpanzees have some capacity for linguistic communication, then maybe some chimpanzee behaviour might require us to talk in terms of goal-representations. If not, not.)

The fact that humans use language is independently a complicating factor in scientific explanation; so it would not be strange if it affected our puzzle as well. Cross-species comparisons in all kinds of problem-solving tasks are vexed by the ubiquity of language in humans. Even when these problems are not presented verbally, and do not call for a verbal answer, we simply do not know at the moment what role language might or might not be playing; the mode of solution might depend upon previous experiences that did exploit linguistic processing, and hence would implicate language indirectly. Other kinds of tasks are explicitly posed, considered, and answered, via language directly — i.e. very evidently by strategies not available to non-humans.

Returning, however, to our problem: the strongest argument in favour of positing representations is not unquestionable, but should nonetheless be acknowledged: namely, that we seem to have clear knowledge that our behaviour is, precisely, often governed and dominated by a conception of the goal we want to achieve. It is probably unhelpful to call this a deliverance of introspection; it is not that we examine our deliberations and discover that we have represented to ourselves some goal we want to achieve. 'Introspection' has been somewhat discredited of late, and rightly so; and we should accept that it carries little of the 'incorrigibility', 'immediacy', and 'directness' ascribed to it by post-Cartesian psychologists and philosophers. But we need not think of an 'internal inspection'; just the expression of what we think has guided our means–ends reasoning and activity.

I am not thinking of anything *outré*, or technical. I have in mind such everyday phenomena as claiming that we suddenly remembered a decision to buy foreign currency from our own bank today rather than from the airport bank tomorrow; or the relieved recognition that if it hadn't been for the note in the diary, we might have completely forgotten today's meeting. In the first example, suppose that you have a busy traveller who has really very little time to go to the bank, but who equally hopes to arrive at Heathrow at the last possible moment. Suppose further that he knows that his bank certainly has Yugoslav dinars, but that other banks often do not, and that this is the currency he needs. Given all that, he decides to get to his bank the next day. Then he puts the matter out of his mind, *until* the next day, when he remembers his decision — and therefore goes to the bank. He has, as it were, put a note on a 'scratch pad' mental diary; and the review of either his earlier decision, or the physical diary (which has a 'representation' in very literal form) explains why he goes to his bank, or his meeting.

These representations help guide our behaviour. They seem, too, to be phenomena that we want to construe realistically: phenomena needing to be individuated, and which 'really exist'. But the behaviour of other animals is also guided — by the cries of conspecifics, by the marking-out of terrain by excrement, and so forth. What is special about the 'guiding' of diary entries, or sudden recollections of an earlier decision? Simply that they cannot guide us unless their semantic content is understood. The marks in a diary must have meaning for the user; if someone translated every entry in my diary into Hebrew it would be meaningless to me. Put another way, it's no use tying a knot in a handkerchief if one cannot remember the content of the reminder of which it was intended as a shorthand.

Now: such phenomena as these are not the sorts of thing that science takes as *explananda*. But as familiar phenomena from commonsense explanation ('I went to the bank because I suddenly remembered my earlier decision ...'; 'I had completely forgotten the meeting, but fortunately glanced at my diary just in time ...') they illustrate how pervasive are instances of deliberation, previewing, casting intentions in words (and often writing them down) — thinking about the future, in short, and framing 'goal representations'. The earlier deliberation, resulting in some intention or other, seems required by any adequate explanation of the behaviours in question, as one of the factors — sometimes the most significant factor, sometimes holding less importance — that should be cited. Presumably nobody would want to deny that in a readily-intelligible sense of the term, a diary entry is a legitimate 'representation' of a decision. It can often be clear that a glance at a diary alters, modifies, or explains our behaviour. Some people do not need diaries, and keep their decisions 'recorded' in short-term memory — but the difference between written and remembered intentions seems insignificant. So I find it implausible to suppose that behaviours such as these can be handled without some postulate of 'intention' or 'goal representation'. Thus, even though I have provided no instance of purposive behaviour that is both appropriate for scientific (systematic) investigation, and requires the postulate of representations, we must and should expect that there will be such.

This is a very modest conclusion, though. It restricts 'goal representations' to language-using creatures, and even there argues for their utility only in cases where the deliberation, and framing of intentions, is explicit, prior to the action taken, and linguistic. Vast amounts of human purposive behaviour isn't like this at all. It is as yet an open question whether any behaviour of non-linguistic creatures requires the postulate of goal representations, and conversely whether human purposive behaviour that lacks such prior and explicit intention-formation requires it. It puts great weight on the fact of language: *because* this is such a consequential capacity, *therefore* it has made possible dramatically new behavioural chains, a novelty that requires corresponding innovations in the *explanantia*.

The issue remains open.

**Suggestions for further reading.** Any reader who wants a short and clear description of what 'intensionality' is should consult chapter 11 of: R.M. Chisholm, *Perceiving: a Philosophical Study* (Ithaca and London: Cornell University Press, 1957). On the question of theory-assessment in terms of 'values of scientific theories': many philosophers of science have considered this. It is discussed at some length in: T.S. Kuhn, *The Structure of Scientific Revolutions* (2nd. edn, Chicago: University of Chicago Press, 1970). Realism in science is extensively examined, although rarely in connection with the brain and behavioural sciences. A very full recent treatment is: M. Devitt, *Realism and Truth* (Oxford: Blackwell, 1984). A briefer but much-discussed view can be found in: W.H. Newton-Smith, *The Rationality of Science* (London: Routledge and Kegan Paul, 1981).

Causality is another topic on which much philosophical ink has been spilled. Van Fraassen's own bibliography (in the work cited) should be consulted; and for a full and detailed treatment see: T.L. Beauchamp and A. Rosenberg, *Hume and the Problem of Causation* (Oxford: Oxford University Press, 1981); and J.L. Mackie, *The Cement of the Universe* (Oxford: Clarendon Press, 1974).

Few have considered the difference, such as it is, between scientific psychology and commonsense psychology. The best source is still the classic work: L. Mandler, and W. Kessen, *The Language of Psychology* (New York: Wiley and Sons, 1959). I have recently tried to pursue the distinction and its implications in: K.V. Wilkes, 'Describing the child's mind', in J. Russell (ed.), *Philosophical Perspectives on Developmental Psychology* (Oxford: Blackwell, 1987). For further support of the view that the *explananda* of science and common sense may diverge where natural kinds are concerned, see: J. Dupré, 'Natural kinds and biological taxa', *Philosophical Review*, 90, 1981.

# PART III
# THE POSITIONS DEBATED

CHAPTER 10

# NARROW INTENTIONS

*Shawn Lockery*

It was the burden of my first contribution to show how beliefs and desires can be given neurophysiological interpretation, and to suggest that from what we know so far about the nervous systems of a few simple creatures, there is no reason to suppose that there is a fundamental incompatibility between explanations of behaviour at the neurophysiological and intentional levels. Throughout my first contribution I concerned myself solely with explanations that are intentional in the broad sense which includes explanations that make frequent use of all classes of mental states (including intentions *per se*) as well as those that confine themselves to beliefs and desires, or more generally, information-bearing and need-based states. That is to say, I thoroughly and quite conveniently ignored the role in explanation and physiological prognosis of intentions in the narrow sense of internal state attributions of the form 'x intends to $\phi$'. In the present chapter, I hope to redress the balance.

Intention, like belief and desire, can profitably be thought of as a theoretical term in folk- or commonsense psychological theories of behaviour. As such, it gets its meaning from the way it is used in explanations of behaviour, that is, from the causal role it takes in commonsense explanations of behaviour. Not surprisingly, commonsense is less than clear about the causal role of intentions, and to meet this problem, a field of philosophy — action theory — has arisen which specialises in this issue. The approach of the action theorists has been termed 'the method of assent': the idea is to probe our intuitions about the correct application of the term (and its cousins such as 'intentional' and 'intend') thereby deriving an analysis of the concept. Much blood has been shed over the issue but, within the camp of the causal theorists at least, there appears to be a consensus. An intention to $\phi$ is a state produced by beliefs and desires (or their functional equivalents) via the formulae of practical reasoning: Because John wanted it to rain and believed that every time he washes his car it rains, he formed the intention to wash his car. To $\phi$ intentionally is to be caused to $\phi$ by a particular kind of antecedent event: the intention to $\phi$ which, as we shall see, is itself a complex event comprising cognitive or informational as well as motivational aspects.

It is a philosophical commonplace that a very wide range of behavioural explanations are intentional in the broad sense of attributing information bearing and need-based states. These include, in addition to folkpsychology: decision theory, animal learning theory, economics and, of particular interest here, the Trade-Off Principle (TOP) which McFarland offers as the theory to eliminate goal representations. In defining the issue at hand, it is worth noting that these explanations, although intentional, do just fine without once positing as a causal state the intention to act. We see a hungry rat at a choice point in a maze. He goes to the right, we say, because he wants the pellet in the goal box and, having run the maze before, remembers that this is an appropriate turn. No mention of intention seems called for, indeed, it would seem out of place, yet the explanation seems perfectly adequate post hoc, and also useful should we in the future want to predict this turn.

What is going on here? If intentions to act are as central to explanation of human behaviour as they seem to be, how can information and motivation in the absence of intention succeed in explaining anything? Notice that many perfectly successful explanations of human behaviour do not mention intentions either. The suggestion is that an intention functions like a trigger: it has more to do with why the action came out of the barrel, so to speak, than why the target was the one it happened to be. Much about the content or aim of the action is already determined in advance of the intention by the information and needs or interests of the agent. Intention seems to add little to this story. Its principal role (in addition to attributing praise and blame) seems to be in explaining why certain behaviours did not occur despite the subject having had all the appropriate beliefs and desires. If so, then this helps to explain why we do not bother with attributing intentions to animals which nevertheless are subjects of belief-desire ascription: their complement of informational states and needs is (to us anyway) sufficiently simple that we do not observe a disconnection between the having of the information and need and the appropriate act.

Thus it would appear that we are dealing with a very special kind of mental state. One that seems to be reserved for intentional explanations when these are applied to very sophisticated believers and desirers. But this is not to belittle the intention to act. As many hold, including Montefiore in this volume, should scientists succeed in sinking the concept of intention, more than just the baggage will follow it to the bottom. Let us now assess the damage incurred during the first round.

This was McFarland's argument against the commonsense concept of intentional behaviour:

1. An intentional behaviour is an action the selection* of which is determined (or can be predicted or explained) by an internal representation of the goal of the behaviour.
2. But explanation according to the TOP can predict (and thereby explain) intentional behaviour without adverting to goal representations.
3. Therefore goal representations are otiose and may in actuality be causally irrelevant.

The argument as it stands has a couple of potentially serious defects. Although the conclusion follows from premises (1) and (2) — with the additional assumption that the TOP is more parsimonious — premises (1) and (2) are open to some serious objections.

Premise (1) appears to endorse a rather idiosyncratic view of the commonsense concept of intentional behaviour. I doubt that philosophers specializing in action theory would admit (1) as a statement of the necessary and sufficient conditions for intentional action. According to the action theorist, there is much more to the commonsense concept of intentional behaviour than the selection of (and commitment to) a course of action. This means that an action whose only relation to its goal is the goal's influence on the

---

*David McFarland uses the term 'guidance' but I think his usage of this term bears more of the sense of 'selection'.

outcome of the selection process is not an intentional action. Thus the behaviour that the TOP succeeds in explaining is not intentional behaviour and the argument fails to show that intentions are otiose.

Action theorists (e.g. Brand, 1984) have identified three necessary aspects of behaviours which are intentional actions. The first is that the action must fall within the pattern of a plan. Consider the following example (adapted from Chisholm, 1966):

Carl wanted to kill his rich uncle because he wanted to inherit the family fortune. He grabs his pistol and, believing his uncle to be at home, drives toward his house. Carl's desire to kill his uncle agitates him and he drives recklessly. On the way he hits and kills a pedestrian, who, as luck would have it, is his uncle.

Our intuitions here are clear. Although Carl intended to kill his uncle, his hitting him with the car was not intentional. The reason is that Carl intended to kill his uncle at his home with a pistol, not on the road with the car. That is to say, the incident with the car, though it achieved the end Carl had in mind, was not part of the plan.

However, no matter how important plans might be, merely acting in accordance with a plan is not sufficient for the action to be an intentional one. Stephan decides to make a pot of tea. He has just moved house and conditions are rather spartan. The room is bare, he crouches at a single low table, drinks the tea black for want of milk, and generally deviates from his usual routine. So doing, he inadvertently performs a Japanese tea ceremony (after Brand, 1984).

Stephan of course had no idea his actions fit the plan for the tea ceremony. One might say that he acted in accordance with the rules of the ritual, but clearly he did not follow it. Thus we cannot say that he performed the tea ceremony intentionally. This example suggests a further requirement for an intentional action: that the subject knows or at least believes that he is following the plan.

The requirements that an action fits into the pattern of a plan, and that the subject knows this, can be subsumed under what we might call the cognitive aspect of intentional action. The final essential aspect is the motivation to undertake the plan. Notice that no amount of planning issues in action without the concurrent motivation to act. In a similar vein, one can even knowingly act according to a plan and yet act unintentionally. This happens in cases of extreme coercion, for example.

As McFarland presents it (see also McFarland and Houston, 1981) the TOP amounts to a calculus of behavioural choice. Given an animal's repertoire of (mutually exclusive) actions, and its current needs, environmental inputs, and behavioural state, the theory predicts which actions will be expressed. This point seems to place the premise (2) in jeopardy. The TOP washes its hands of prediction (and explanation) once an activity is begun. In one of his examples, it predicts the circumstances under which the robot will undertake to wipe up the ink spilled on the carpet, but it does not tell us how the task is accomplished, that is, how the many actions within the cleaning activity are organised (the plan), nor how progress is monitored along the path to completion. In terms of the present examples, the TOP informs us under what conditions Carl will try to kill his uncle, but it says nothing about how the job will be attempted. Someone who is convinced that the within-task aspects of purposive behaviour are very much controlled by internal representations would not grant McFarland the second premise, and if the above analysis of the commensense concept of intentions is correct, this would include most people. This is because to follow a plan is to match one's unitary acts to an internally represented 'script' or action plan. Now it is perfectly conceivable that the TOP can account for the organisation of behaviour within an activity, and do so without mention of internal representations of goals or even plans. If so, McFarland's argument would be vindicated. But so far we have not been shown how the TOP can account for within-task behaviours.

In order to get his argument back into the air, McFarland has got to repair both the first and second premises. Regarding premise (1), he might simply reject the analysis offered by action theorists by claiming that his concept of intention does indeed capture the commonplace sense of the term. But this approach seems to be an unlikely one. For if an intentional action is any action whose initiation is governed by a goal-representation, then Carl's killing his uncle is an intentional action, and this really does seem to be strongly counterintuitive.

A second approach would be to grant that premise (1) does not capture what commonsense has to say about intention, and then argue that the TOP theory is not bound by the *explananda* chosen by the commonsense theory. I am here referring to Wilkes's remarks on the possibility that the categories of commonsense psychology may not be the most profitable ones to adopt in explaining behaviour. Ultimately the issue is not whether the TOP explains the behaviours as described by intention-laden accounts. Rather, the issue is whether the TOP can get the job done: can it explain the complete repertoire of bodily movements of the organism at issue — however it happens to group them — and not advert to goal representations? While this approach may have some promise, it must be remembered that the TOP (together with its close cousins in economics and decision theory) has by and large taken on board the very action types picked out by commonsense psychology. The latter has, of course, found it necessary to posit intentions to account for the vicissitudes of human action: why someone with all the appropriate beliefs and desires still refuses to act ('because the intention wasn't there'), why Carl evinced shock and consternation on killing his uncle ('things had not gone according to plan, and now he won't be able to dispense with the corpse discreetly, the police will arrive, questions will be asked, etc.'), why Stephan said 'What Japanese tea ceremony?' ('because he had no intention of performing one'). It seems to be very much an open question whether the TOP can achieve the same ends operating with basically the same unitary actions, meanwhile disavowing the use of the cognitive aspects of intending.

The best approach, the one that would make the strongest case possible against the intentional account would be to show that the TOP theory can play by the rules of the commonsense intentional theory and still win, that is, to show that the TOP theory can take any instance of what appears to be correctly motivated, plan-following action *as picked out by the commonsense intentional theory* and show that goal-representations play an indispensable role neither in the initiation of the action nor in its control once initiated. This amounts to correcting (1) to bring it more in line with the dictates of common sense and the action theorists, and then going to work on (2) which is badly in need of further argument.

The critical question here is whether a theory that trades solely in the choice between ready-made behavioural options can explain/predict the control of within-task behaviour. One solution would be to propose that within-task behaviour is governed by a behavioural program, where the initiation of the program is governed by the TOP. This would certainly do the job of accounting for the control of purposive behaviour within tasks. However, such a move would drop the TOP theorist right into the intentionalist camp: to follow a program is simply to follow a plan.

A safer tactic would be to elaborate the TOP slightly so as to allow for regulation of behaviour within tasks. One might imagine this could be accomplished through the concept of 'nested' optimisations, that is to say, trade-offs within trade-offs. Consider the case of the robot and the ink-spill. The initial decision to tackle the ink problem was a trade-off between this and the various other tasks in the system's behavioural repertoire. Why not suppose that once 'inside' the ink-wiping task a second-order trade-off principle applies: one that governs the choice between the various possible sub-task behaviours? Such a move would require the addition of some extra theoretical concepts, such as a within-task analogy of fitness (or efficiency) and means of producing local behavioural loops (e.g. wipe-recoil-wipe for the task of ink-cleaning), which could be achieved by implicitly represented motor programs that are common in neurobiology. None of these seem to violate the spirit of the theory and, more important, none are equivalent to goal-representations, or even the representations of plans, at least insofar as these would be explicit. (I take it that McFarland's argument is only aimed at explicit representations.)

Let us assume that McFarland *can* reshape the TOP to ward off the foregoing challenges. What about the lengthy objections of Montefiore? I admit to some difficulty in sorting out the various levels of his complicated disagreements with McFarland, but at one level the argument seems to be a *reductio* of the following kind:

1. Assume no action is intentional (the conclusion of McFarland's argument).
2. An utterance is meaningful only if the utterer conforms to the appropriate linguistic norms.
3. An utterer conforms to linguistic norms only if he/she does so intentionally.
4. But by assumption, this is impossible.
5. Therefore, no utterance is meaningful.

The crux of the argument is premise (3), since only if our account of meaning requires intentions does the argument bear on the conclusion McFarland hopes to establish. Above I drew attention to the distinction between following a plan and merely acting according to a plan. The similarity between plans and rules suggests that the same distinction can be drawn in the present case. Thus we can distinguish in principle between following a norm or (henceforth) a rule and merely acting in accordance with one. Only the former would be an intentional conformance with a rule, according to the action theory consensus, and this is what Montefiore seems to have in mind in premise (3). The question then becomes what conformance with a rule means in the context of linguistic norms, and if following a rule, but never merely acting in accordance with one, is sufficient to preserve coherence. If the latter, then the present argument does not go through.

There is a very plausible sense in which simply acting in accordance with a rule would seem inadequate to endow an utterance with meaning. Suppose Stephan's tea cup had burned his lips causing him to sputter 'cha', the Japanese word for tea. Even a native speaker would have doubted whether Stephan meant 'tea'. But this is an unfair example. Even in the most propitious cases, where there are no external circumstances suggesting as here that something besides naming was going on, a single instance cannot serve to fix the meaning of an utterance. The appropriate test of course is to ask whether the usage will generalize. If Stephan, now in Japan, were to encounter numerous instances of tea (none of them before seen by him), and correctly applied 'cha' to them, and never misapplied 'cha', then, and only then, would we be justified in attributing the concept to him and meaning to his utterance.

Thus we are led to conclude that if utterances in general were produced in such a way that could not plausibly be fitted to the model of commonsense intentional action, this would not prevent us from determining their meaning, or what amounts to the same, considering them to be meaningful. The point is that we can just as easily apply the generalization test to a machine as to a person: meaning is neutral with regard to the mechanism by which its tokens are produced. This is a good thing: although I generally do not like arguments from introspection, it does seem to me that the commonsense intentional model is at odds with how we speak. I would align the production of a sentence more with a skilled movement than, say, Carl's plan to do his uncle in. The whole process seems to occur at a level far below one at which one regularly and necessarily matches one's occurrent behaviour (mid-sentence, say) with a template. Nor can it be a case of the intentional becoming habitual (such as driving a car, athletics, typing, etc.), as the production of novel sentences demonstrates. At this point it is worth noting that model neural networks exist which are capable of passing generalisation tests in tasks such as pattern recognition and word pronunciation (Rumelhart and McClelland, 1986; Sejnowski, and Rosenberg, 1987). What is significant to the present discussion is that these models are designed without 'templates', algorithms, or rules. There is no way to fit their inner workings to the intentional model.

CHAPTER 11

# EXPLANATION — HOW NOT TO MISS THE POINT

*Kathy Wilkes*

What are the issues at issue? I agree with Noble's comment in his second-round chapter (pp. 262-3) that controversy is still alive; but it is getting surprisingly difficult to say just where, and why. Let me try to list some of the themes that *seem* to be in contention.

First, and most clearly: whether 'the traditional goal concept, which involves internal representation of a desired or required state of affairs' (McFarland, chapter 4, p. 41) is necessary — as McFarland of course thinks it is not — in accounting for animal behaviour. This 'accounting' is taken in quite a strong sense: it requires realism (of some kind) about 'intentions', or 'explicit representations', so that they are the sorts of things that can 'control', 'cause', or 'guide' behaviour. Much of the disagreement here, although not all, rests in the obscurity of the term 'representation'. (See for instance the multiplicity of adjectives used in this volume to qualify the term: 'explicit', 'implicit', 'tacit', 'degenerate and non-degenerate', 'declarative', 'procedural', 'figurative'; and more besides.) Montefiore in his chapter 14 rightly draws attention to the unenviable facts (a) that we seem not to be able to do without (something like) the notion of a representation, and (b), that there is yet a major and unsolved problem of clarifying it. Possibly someone should indeed 're-write virtually the whole of these debates in terms of a deeper, more extended and more carefully detailed discussion of the varied actual and possible uses of this ubiquitous term' (chapter 14, p. 260). My present inclination is to bet that parallel distributed processing (PDP) research just might give us a basis from which to start. In any event, the obscurity of that notion is something that certainly needs highlighting, so perhaps our occasional muddle here is no bad thing.

Second, slightly less clearly: what sort of 'accounting for' we want 'the traditional goal concept' to provide (or what we want to deny that it provides). In this book we find free use of 'causes', 'is responsible for', 'explains', '(continually) guides' and more besides. This leads into the rather more specific question of whether explanation *via* intentions, or goal representations, is a species of causal explanation. And that forces one to ask just what is needed if $A$ is to be 'the cause' of $B$: 'being a cause', 'serving to explain', and 'being responsible for' are not synonymous expressions.

Third, less clearly still: whether non-intentional explanations (physiological; or mechanical-causal) could ever replace or substitute for explanations in intentional terms. But here 'intentional' is taken in the broad logical sense, often spelled 'intensional'; this includes a very wide range of psychological phenomena (thinking, wanting, deliberating, looking for, expecting, evaluating, attending, information-retrieval, motivation, etc.), of which 'forming or having intentions', or 'representing a goal to be achieved' is only one species. Montefiore and McFarland seem, at least occasionally, to be taking on board the bigger issue: of the alleged chasm between 'a causally determinate and/or statistically regular order' on the one hand and 'the order of teleology — of goals, intentions and norms' on the other (Montefiore, chapter 14, p. 238). But this question is clouded by the two other issues listed above: first the related but more limited problem of the dispensability or not of one kind of intensional phenomenon, 'intentions', or 'representations of goals to be achieved', construed realistically. We might, or might not, manage without *these*, even though we might not manage without 'desires', 'plans', 'purposes', 'beliefs', 'expectations', 'attentiveness', 'information', and dozens more. The second cloud is the relationship between explanation and causality, not to mention that between physical causality and some rival kind. Just how does the explanatory role of intensional ascriptions come about? Lockery hopes to 'identify a representational state with a physical state' (chapter 8, p. 157). This would get us representational states which explained actions by being (physical) causes of them. Noble thinks that this is probably mistaken; such states explain behaviour, sure, but we should not 'conceive of intentions as being like physical causes of our movements'. My own view is messier: in everyday (commonsense) explanation we explain actions by ascribing intensional states, but these are usually not causal claims (since I am generally anti-realist about these ascriptions); in scientific explanations we shall want to be realist, and some intensionally-characterised *explanantia* will undoubtedly be required. My argument here is rendered the stronger by the fact that such ascriptions are not only required, but are routinely *found*, even in hard-nosed neuroscience: as for instance when we discuss the 'expectancy generator' function when explaining habituation in the rat.

To structure these 'second-round' comments, I shall first pick up two points of my chapter 9 with which Dennett (correspondence; and his chapter 13) seemed least happy: the discussion of explanation, and of natural kinds. He found my earlier comments on these subjects either blandly vague, or wrong-headed. But brooding on — and saying more about — these two issues will allow me to weave in further comments on some of the other chapters in this volume.

## Explanation again

The reason for gesturing, in chapter 9, towards the diversity of things that count as 'explanations' was this: it allows us to see more clearly why it is that the contributors to this volume at times appear to be talking past each other, and why it is so difficult to focus 'the' issues at issue. There was no attempt, of course, to botanise the diversity of explanation-types; if so, then (as Dennett rightly suggested in correspondence) it would have been more to the point to distinguish 'why' questions from others, or to borrow Haugeland's taxonomy (Haugeland, 1978) of (a) *derivational-nomological* (b) *morphological*, and (c) *systematic* explanations. But citing Haugeland's trio, and distinguishing 'why' questions, would have served only a very small part of my concern. The object was rather to exploit van Fraassen's comments on the context-, purpose-, and audience-relativity of questions and answers to suggest a more extreme position than Haugeland's: that explanations can take practically any form, depending both on how the *explanandum* is formulated, and on the audience, and on the context. Thus we'd get Haugeland's trio; plus unspecificably-numerous further 'types'. Removing puzzlement is the name of the explanation-game; puzzlement can be expressed as who? why? what? which? when? where? with what? how? by what means? (and doubtless more besides). Puzzlement can be removed, depending on the context, by anything at all from (at one extreme, perhaps) a strict and formal deductive-nomological schema, to (at the other) a remark like 'because it's a bank holiday'. Thus, although taxonomizing will be useful no doubt in carefully-structured contexts, it is at least not obvious that attempts to botanize patterns of explanation in unrestricted contexts would be any more than hand-waving. Moreover, all talk about *the* 'explanatory power' of physiology, intentionality, or whatever, must be subject to this context- and purpose-relativity.

This allows us to ask whether we do indeed typically have 'rival explanations': whether in any interesting cases we have to decide between explanations couched in intensional or teleological terms (leaving aside for the moment whether or not intensionally-described phenomena can be said to be *causes* of actions) and those that resile from intensional terms. That is, I wonder whether it might not after all be 'seriously disputable that in many ... cases other types of explanation can be provided showing those which may have been given in terms of goals pursued and of means chosen in furtherance of that pursuit to be at best irrelevant and at worst positively misleading' (Montefiore, p. 58). There are indeed some such: for instance, Lockery shows that if we explain the behaviour of a bi-metallic strip in terms of 'information content', this would be an explanation much inferior to one that went via the correlations between temperature change and curvature adjustment. Or, a different example: once, the weather seemed explicable only by postulating anthropomorphized gods and forces; now we can and should do better. But in the domain of action that can be described as purposive ... what is the 'it' for which we are seeking an explanation? Signalling just is, in some contexts, extending an arm. But when described as a 'signalling', it is already conceptualised as an action done for a purpose, and no explanation which ignores that aspect is going to remove the puzzlement of anyone who wants to know about *his signalling*. If described merely as an extension of the arm, then — if the inquirer is a physiologist — purposes, intentions, beliefs and so forth might be well-nigh irrelevant. But so far forth these are not rival explanations for the same *explanandum*. So they are, simply, not rivals at all.

Thus, although endorsing Noble's claim (p. 87) that 'within an intentional context a "machine" description of what happens fails to make reference to the most significant facts' I would want to explain why this must be so by linking 'significance' to the precise characterisation of the *explanandum* — to the puzzlement of the inquirer. I find it increasingly difficult to find any real-life cases where there is genuine, honest-to-goodness, 'rivalry' at all between intensional and non-intensional explanations of what is indeed one and the same *explanandum*. There are of course real-life cases where there might be rivalry between two different intensional, or two different non-intensional, explanations: in particular, between one which postulated goal-representations (intentions as controllers of behaviour) and one that did not. We shall need to say more about this shortly, because it will link up with my attempt to underline the differences between common sense, and scientific, explanation. But a brief and parenthetical comment that attempts to debunk the apparent chasm here: I repeat that neuroscience repeatedly, consistently, and without apparent embarrassment, describes events in its domain in terms that are 'functional', 'teleological', and 'intensional': see absolutely any neurophysiological textbook. Although countless examples *could* be given, the following will by themselves prove the point: 'receptor cells'; 'information'; 'expectancy generators'; 'texture gradient detectors'; 'reward neurons'. The behavioural sciences tend to be *more* 'intensional', the physiological sciences to be *more* 'extensional' — but that's about all we can say about this alleged gulf.

There is yet another reason why asking for explanations of purposive behaviour in (neuro)physiological terms, and why expecting explanations of screen displays in machine terms, is wrongheaded. Explanation isn't transitive. This is a point I emphasised in chapter 9, but here I want to underline it; because, *given* the brute fact of the context- and purpose-relativity of explanations, I think its significance has been overlooked by most of the chapters in this volume. We now explain purposive behaviour by (in common sense) appeal to desires, intentions, plans, perceptions, beliefs and the like; in the sciences by (perhaps) goal representations, perhaps by goal and cost functions and trade-off principles, by talk of information, information processing, motivation, expectancy, attentiveness, etc. Computers have several levels of description, from (say) ADA at the top to the assembly language and then the machine code at the bottom. PDP systems need a somewhat different explanatory framework citing different sorts of 'levels'. The brain will need yet another — consider as an example of a 'middle level' the discussion of the 'comparator function' which is performed, according to Sokolov's explanation of habituation, by the rat's amygdala. At any level the *explanantia* that suffice for the level above can in turn no doubt (one day) be explained themselves by the next level down; and so on. But 'jumping' levels almost invariably fails to remove puzzlement — fails, that is, to explain.

This, to my mind, is one of the more encouraging features of Lockery's programme. By starting off with systems that are neurophysiologically simple relative to humans, there are fewer 'levels' of organisation that interpose themselves between something like 'attentiveness' on the one hand, and a description of (say) a pattern of connectivity among neurons on the other. I doubt that this is contentious (except in so far as the 'levels' required in a hierarchy of neuroscientific taxonomy are at present largely uncharted); but my point is that purposive behaviour is in no way peculiar in this respect. I won't 'explain' — to take Putnam's familiar example — why square pegs can't fit through round holes by describing their atomic lattices: even though the lattice description is *in some sense* responsible for the brute fact that things with angles won't go through gaps without angles. So Noble's denial that intentions should be conceived as being like physical causes, and his general disdain for mixing the level which talks of programs or intentions with that which talks of electronic events or neurons, is true but is not quite an objection to Lockery, because unlike Lockery Noble is supposing a somersault over several levels, from macro to micro. For, in between intentions and any 'purely' physical level will come several layers of subordinate, functionally (and often intensionally) characterised subroutines. Lockery hasn't so many hurdle-levels to leapfrog over. I see no reason whatsoever to suppose that causal-explanatory relations may not be findable between *adjacent* levels of a system — and Lockery's physiologically-accessible invertebrates are, precisely, examples where the physiology is getting a lot closer to the psychology than we find in human behaviour.

## Natural kinds again

'Natural kinds' is an expression renowned for its vagueness. That should perhaps be a reason for avoiding it, and Dennett is sure that 'the invocation of natural kinds' is 'obscure and of dubious value to *anyone*, not just scientists' (chapter 13, p. 237). I doubt we can avoid it, though; doubt that we would not lose more than we gained. For, to cite someone who (for different reasons than

Dennett's) thinks that science has very few natural kinds at all, Paul Churchland:

> The problem of natural kinds form the busy crossroads where a number of larger crossroads meet: the problem of universals, the problem of induction and projectibility, the problem of natural laws and *de re* modalities, the problem of meaning and reference, the problem of intertheoretic reduction, the question of the aims of science, and the problem of scientific realism in general (1985, p. 1).

At the moment I am not concerned with universals, meaning, reference, *de re* modalities. All the other items on Churchland's list, though, concern us directly. It does not matter much to me, unlike Dennett, that we can't *define* a natural kind. I can think of few if any interesting terms, outside of developed science, that have tidy definitions. (Only boring ones, like 'bachelor', or 'square', have definitions. The biggest misconstrual of analytical philosophy is that it should start with the injunction 'Define your terms!') Of course there will be borderline cases of natural kinds; there will be kinds nested within kinds, and so forth. But it is a phrase with a useful core of intelligibility, and it will not be difficult to explain why I need to introduce it. We could harmlessly substitute for 'natural kinds' something like: 'scientifically profitable *explananda* and *explanantia*'. Cf., Fodor (1981, p. 8): '... if we want a science of mental phenomena at all, we are required to so identify mental properties that the kinds they subsume are natural from the point of view of psychological theory construction'. 'Naturalness' here he glosses in terms of the likelihood that the chosen kinds can generate laws or generalizations; e.g.:

> there is a level of abstraction at which the generalizations of psychology are most naturally pitched ... It would be hard to overemphasise this point, but ... theories about the nature of mental properties carry empirical commitments about the appropriate domains for psychological generalisations. It is therefore an argument against such a theory if it carves things up in ways that prohibit stating such psychological generalisations as there are to state (*ibid.*, p. 8-9).

This shows one way in which kinds, and laws, connect. It is wholly compatible with what one might call a 'futuristic scepticism' about whether natural kinds are in any sense 'basic' to the furniture of the world. Quine, whose article of 1968 is one of those from which discussion took off, suggests that natural kinds are crutches for scientific advance, to be thrown away once we have gone beyond, not only intuitive similarity, but even have no further need for theoretical similarity. For instance, 'once we can legitimize a disposition term by defining the relevant similarity standard, we are apt to know the mechanism of the disposition and so by-pass the similarity' (p. 136). So one might agree with both Quine, and (for different reasons) with Churchland, that natural kinds are not permanent features of the scientific landscape; while insisting (with Quine at least) that we need them, and are stuck with them — and all their risks and imperfections — for the foreseeable future. And the less developed the science, the greater the crutch-style assistance they bring.

Of course Dennett is right to say that '[s]cience does honest work about lots of types that are not obviously or intuitively natural kinds' (chapter 13, p. 237). But I think he is right for the wrong reasons. (1) Science aims to *discover* those kinds that are genuinely natural (subject to the Quinean qualification that this may be an intermediate goal; that we need the natural kinds in order to *get at* the more fundamental mechanisms which will allow us eventually to by-pass them). Of course scientists may initially bunch together and examine things that are *not* natural kinds. Our intuitive similarity-standards may prove illusory or over-crude on examination. (Cf., the marsupial mouse — not a mouse; wolf *canis* and the Tasmanian wolf look similar but are of different species, as do and are European and American robins.) Nonetheless, I would still claim that it is precisely because the behavioural sciences have not, in general, much consensus about natural kinds (not much consensus about their central *explananda*) that they are 'underdeveloped'. (2) Science can treat of much more than natural kinds, but will do so by applying what it has discovered from the study of natural kinds. This is a further illustration of what I discussed in the first round. When theories 'intersect', to use Cartwright's happy phrase, there just won't be handy laws to apply to the phenomena in any straightforward sense. Several laws — each of which treats of kinds that are natural to their own domain — will compete; moreover, the initial conditions may be special and even unique to that *explanandum*. I do not argue that science cannot handle events that are not, as described, members of natural kinds; my point is rather that in order to handle them, the sciences must apply a complex set of laws which have themselves been developed and tested on their home terrain: with natural kinds.

Natural kinds are what scientific laws, symmetry principles, whatever, are about. They are thus the key intermediate *explananda* for a science (any science) that has not reached the ultimate goal of being able to by-pass them. They are the nodes around which scientific explanation centres. If that is so, then — to turn back to our present concerns — few would wish to deny that psychology at least is at present theoretically chaotic. There is, to put it mildly, no consensus whatever on how to characterize the central *explananda*, let alone *explanantia*, of the discipline. (See here the comments of Montefiore and me about the term 'representation'.) Since Charles Taylor's work is what originally provoked the discussion of most of the participants in this volume, it will be appropriate to quote him in this connection (Taylor, 1970, p. 54):

> The search for a conceptual framework, for a concept of the 'normal' course, is no less vital in the sciences of behaviour than it is in the physical sciences. Only in the former field it seems to have met with success. One can describe the state of disarray and contention in which we find the sciences of man as arising from deep disagreements over the conceptual frameworks which are appropriate.

Clearly it would be helpful to find psychologists saying much the same thing, so that this comment is not (erroneously) seen as the sneer of a philosopher — Taylor or myself — about one of the special sciences. But that is all too easy to provide; *vide* Eysenck:

> Many of [his 200 Ph.D. students] know more statistics than I do and many of them are very good at manipulating apparatus and writing programs for the computer. The thing they fall down on is looking for the right questions to ask. They go for the things that are popular and are considered interesting but that are really of no importance at all. (Cohen 1977, p. 115)

Or Hudson:

No, you barely wouldn't [believe that assorted psychologists were involved in the same discipline]. In fact, candidly, they often aren't. The latent metaphorical systems are different, the language is different, all the assumptions are different, and what counts as a decent piece of research is different. ... And, certainly, they don't have the same conceptual apparatus — they don't use the same system of ideas. (*ibid.*, p. 168.)

The same point can be made by taking any *explanandum* term that is used as, say, a chapter-heading for an introductory textbook. 'Memory' is a familiar example. There is virtually no agreement about how best to subdivide types of memory; candidates are short-, medium-, long-term, and 'working' or 'scratch-pad' memory; procedural versus declarative, semantic versus episodic, iconic, non-cognitive, somatic etc. Twenty two different kinds of memory storage system have been postulated; but I expect you could find psychologists prepared to defend every figure between 3 and 22. The astonishing varieties of the several amnesias, to take the other side of the coin, show equally clearly that 'memory' cannot be thought of as unitary. For instance: amnesia can be anterograde, retrograde, or both; some amnesiacs can remember skills (like the Tower of Hanoi puzzle) while being unable to remember any *facts* — such as the fact that they have seen the puzzle often before; some memory failures seem due to an inability to store information, others to a failure to retrieve it; some diseases (e.g. the Korsakoff syndrome) might spare some remote memories, whereas others (Huntington's, Alzheimer's) do not; the list could continue long (and see Butters and Miliotis, 1985). And memory, of course, is but one of the psychological key terms about which dispute rages. Other examples might be 'recognition'; 'intelligence'; or 'consciousness' — contrast Freud (1964, p. 70), 'What is meant by consciousness we need not discuss; it is beyond all doubt', with Joynt (1981, p. 108), 'Consciousness is like the Trinity; if it is explained so that you understand it, it hasn't been explained correctly.' But such a list could continue long.

The lack of an acceptable and shared taxonomy of *explananda* and *explanantia* explains why psychology not only has no 'theory' worth the name (but rather hosts of competing mini-theories); but does not even have a 'paradigm'. It did once have both theories and paradigms: witness Wundt's, or Titchener's, structuralism; or early Gestalt theory. To put the point very bluntly, the science of psychology yet needs to work out which of its *explananda* and *explanantia* are more like force, mass, energy, gold, donkeys, and molecules; and which are more like carpets, ashtrays, fences, editions of *Hamlet*, and ornaments.

This evidently complicates our present discussions. The scientific interest lies in discovering how to characterise behaviour and the mind-brain so that it is maximally amenable to systematic study. What is dispensable or not for *this* enterprise may prove to be a somewhat different question from what is or is not dispensable to the explanation of behaviour that is not so characterised.

## Explananda in science and common sense

Without attention to such concerns, no systematic psychology of behaviour will emerge. By contrast, commonsense psychology neither wants nor needs explicit taxonomizing — just as our talk in common sense about carpets, fences, ashtrays etc. cannot be indicted for 'failing' to pick on natural kinds, so in our 'Clapham omnibus' remarks about the behaviour of others, we have no special interest in deploying *scientifically* fruitful terminology. Common sense isn't after systematicity, economy, sharply-defined terms; it revels in the rich, nuance-ridden, overlapping chaos illustrated by Roget's *Thesaurus*. Laws and generalisations are rarely sought or cited; the 'generality' of our commonsense descriptions and explanations is a function of our mastery of the language. That is, we can use a term like 'generous' consistently — but this is a far cry from saying we have laws or generalisations about what generous people typically do. This distinction between common sense and science (which, as I said in chapter 9, is one 'of degree'; but degree-differences can be colossal) is one which is taken for granted by McFarland (this volume), when for instance (p. 43) he comments 'In order to move from a common-sense view to a scientific view of apparent intentional behaviour ...' I am less clear that Noble and Montefiore give the difference the importance I ascribe to it. Lockery accepts it, with reasonable qualifications; Dennett thinks I overstate it. *That* the explanation of much behaviour can only be given in teleological, intensional idioms, and even idioms that cite 'intentions', I accept. That behaviour *as classified in ways appropriate to a science of behaviour* can only be handled by reference to 'the traditional goal concept which involves internal representation of a desired or required state of affairs' (McFarland, this volume, p. 41 — who of course argues against this) I doubt (with a few qualifications).

What I take it this means is that *of course* scientific (systematic) explanations in terms either of goal-representations, *or* of goal-directedness and cost- or goal-functions, *or* via neurophysiological ('hardware') nitty-gritty, will never replace our commonsense and unsystematic everyday explanations of the behaviour of another. But equally, and for exactly the same reasons: no more can everyday statements of common sense about fences be replaced by statements in the terminology of the physical sciences. Crudely: there are no fences in physics. And now we can return to one of the topics listed at the beginning: whether intensional phenomena are 'causes' or not. Well, they might be. 'Cause' is a pragmatic notion; *sometimes* the presence of oxygen can be cited as 'the cause' of a flame (particularly, perhaps, when oxygen was not expected). We describe things as causes when they interest us, when they seem important to us, when we can juggle and manipulate them. Maybe all true singular causal statements instantiate *some* general law (this is Davidson's [1970] thesis of the Nomologicality of Causality). But statements of commonsense causality — supposing of course that psychological phenomena can be said to be causes of behaviour — may be as far removed from any known law as is a statement like 'the event described on page 1 of today's *Guardian* caused the event described on page 4 of the *Morning Star*'. The two events concerned might have descriptions under which some true law or generalisation covering these events could be sought (suppose the first was the 1976 earthquake, the second the destruction of Tangshan). But the common sense statement picks things out under descriptions under which they are not 'natural kinds', under which they are not amenable to law-citation, under which they are not appropriate for science. So one moral to draw is that *even if* intensional phenomena 'cause' behaviour, a 'translation' into *law-governed* causal terms may be one that leaves the original *explanandum* far behind. (Incidentally: by and large I accept Davidson's argument for the anomalous nature of psycho-physical relations — IF he is talking about psychological and behavioural phenomena as described in common sense. Once we shift towards the scientific-psychological *explananda*, then we'll want to work to eliminate anomalies.)

This brings me to two problems which (to my mind) are central to the main debate with which this volume is concerned. One of these is — I think — a pseudo-problem: whether or not goal-representations, or intentions, are essentially cited in the explanation of purposive behaviour. I think it is obvious that they are.

Common sense psychology cites them; commonsense psychology cites them even when the behaviour of non-human animals is in question. This may perhaps be the 'anthropomorphism' of which McFarland complains in his own 'second-round' comments: we work from the inside, and use the explanatory apparatus (on the Clapham omnibus) which we know and love from our own case, and which — above all — works rather well *for the explananda which we are considering*. But the failure with which McFarland should be concerned is not the anthropomorphisation; it's the adoption, as and when we are thinking of systematic scientific explanation, of the wrong *explanantia*-terms — those of commonsense psychology.

Common sense, as I noted earlier, still routinely comments that 'the sun is rising', or that someone is 'possessed'. Everyday discourse is slow to adapt to scientific discovery but rather, in jackdaw fashion, holds on to anything that allows it to express what it wants to say economically, amusingly, trendily — with no particular concern with 'truth by correspondence with the facts'. In other words, common sense is usually not bothered about the *literal* truth of its ascriptions. (I think I am here for once departing from Lockery's view of everyday psychological statements.) Literal truth matters: if we are (*inter alia*) concerned with whether 'explicit representations' are required as elements of a causal and scientific explanation of purposive behaviour, then those representations must, in some sense — which the chapters in this volume obscure rather than clarify, but at least they display the difficulty of clarifying the notion — exist. If $A$ causes $B$, then we'd better 'have' an $A$. In general, though, I strongly suspect that common sense isn't much interested in literal truth-by-correspondence. It isn't much interested in causal explanations. It's trying to make behaviour intelligible, to give it an acceptable explanation (and here see the remarks earlier about the radical relativity of what counts as an explanation); and that might — *or might not* — require an explanation in causal terms.

Second: since the difference between common sense, and scientific, psychology is one 'of degree', then *of course* there will be hosts of puzzling borderline cases. So also in physics. (Physics has served as psychology's superego; superegos, however, get distorted and idealised — and that has certainly happened with physics *vis-à-vis* the behavioural sciences.) Nancy Cartwright (1983) has recently, and most valuably, emphasised the way in which exciting current physics is a seat-of-the-pants, guess-and-by-golly, enterprise; an enterprise in which many of the fundamental 'laws' concerned are true only of highly artificial experimental products, and which may fail to hold of many real events in the real world. The hard, explanatory, work may be done by lower-level laws (which she calls 'phenomenological'); by models, by approximations, by fudge and mudge. But what this means is, first, that we must spell out precisely what the *explanandum* is to be; second, to cast around for whatever laws or generalisations look to be helpful (this is where I believe that natural kinds crop up); and third, to examine and specify the contextually-relevant features of the event in question.

Perhaps this point needs elaboration. Some *explananda* are so couched that they fall neatly and simply under the explanatory scope of a specific science. For instance: 'why was a total eclipse of the sun visible at place p, but only a partial one at place p*?' Some *explananda* cross scientific domains, and then, when 'theories intersect', matters are more complicated; for example, '[al]though both quantum theory and relativity are highly developed, detailed, and sophisticated, there is no satisfactory theory of relativistic quantum mechanics' (Cartwright, p. 51). Finally, most *explananda* not only cross scientific domains and require reference to laws and natural kinds in different spheres; they also require reference to specific and perhaps idiosyncratic initial conditions. To adapt one of Cartwright's examples: the plants failed to flower partly because I planted them too deep, partly because the compost was too warm at the time of planting, and partly because of the severe frosts in May. In these latter cases most of the explanatory burden may be sustained by citing these particular facts, which will sometimes (but not always) be 'causal'. The more that theories intersect, and the more that specific or unique factors are relevant, the closer we come to *explananda* typical of common sense.

Insofar as the authors in this volume are discussing all forms of purposive behaviour without restriction, then — to support a claim made earlier, but this time providing slightly different reasons — it will be *trivially* true that 'a purely physiological theory is deficient' (Noble, p. 81). For the same reason purely machine events will be 'deficient' with respect to explaining appearances on a screen display. But, again, this would not be a feature special to the brain and behavioural sciences; it will apply to any phenomenon at all which intersecting theories are needed to explain, and where initial conditions may have to assume most of the explanatory, puzzlement-removing, burden (after, of course, the *explanandum* has been specified and the puzzlement of the audience known). Equally it will be no particular limitation on physiological theory. Meteorology alone can't explain why leaves fall off trees, although meteorological considerations need to be adduced; so in this sense meteorology is 'deficient'. Sciences avoid 'deficiency' only in those rare cases where the *explanandum* is as described amenable to explanation via the laws of that discipline; put loosely, where the *explanandum* is a 'natural kind' phenomenon in the conceptual apparatus of that science, such as an eclipse — so that the laws of that science *unproblematically* cover it.

## Language and intentions

Montefiore and McFarland seem to be approaching agreement on at least one point: that intentions are needed for any adequate account of linguistic behaviour. In my first chapter I was saying something compatible with this when discussing diary-entries, or 'thoughts in words that run through the head', which are often cited in order to make some feature of the behaviour of language-users intelligible. (I can, incidentally, accept McFarland's 'second-round' comments about the sort of 'control' that these linguistic representations exercise. Since I am tolerant about what can be called 'a cause', I can agree that a diary-entry may be no more than 'a stimulus to be weighted among all the other stimuli that will be taken into account when deciding what to do', rather than something that 'continually guides' behaviour. After all, a match may 'cause' a forest fire, but doesn't 'continually guide' it. But if we are realistic about intentions, and also need to cite them, then there is at least one kind of behaviour whose explanation is likely to be incomplete without reference to them; hence *some* 'representations of goals to be achieved' is indispensable.)

What of non-human animals, though? Here McFarland's chapter 12 confuses me. At times it looks as though he is claiming that inten*s*ionality isn't needed to explain their behaviour. For example, he says 'If I accept Montefiore's argument ... then I cannot deny that I use intentional processes ... However this does not mean that my ordinary, non-linguistic behaviour is intentional' (p. 215). But 'using' intentional (intensional?) processes isn't necessarily a matter of being guided and controlled by goal-representations! This would be a far stronger claim than that 'representations of goals', which 'instigate and continually guide' behaviour — a tiny sub-class of intensional phenomena — aren't needed. I would reject the former claim; but so I think must McFarland, when he says (e.g.) that 'rats are capable of some cognitive evaluation' (p. 223). 'Cognitive evaluation' is *highly* intensional. I believe that McFarland thinks I have misunderstood him here, but if so I am not clear what has gone wrong.

I conclude myself that I want to be a realist about 'representations of goals to be achieved' at least in the explanation of some of the behaviours of language-using animals. I want to admit them as elements that often need to be cited — but *not* necessarily as 'continually controlling' elements — in the explanation of such behaviours. I assume that if I knew much more about creativity and deliberation in music or painting I might want to take a similarly realist attitude about non-verbal 'representations of goals to be achieved' in musicians and artists. I am left agnostic about 'representations of goals' in non-human animals, or human behaviours that do not obviously require linguistic talents. If we look at representations more generally, and not only at goal-representations, I assume that animals can be ascribed non-linguistic (or protolinguistic) representations, in the following sense: *if* we gloss 'the dog thinks the cat is up the tree' as 'the dog has a cat-up-tree representation' then non-human animals have representations. But the gloss is almost wholly uninformative, since 'representation' is here as much a dummy-term, and no more helpful, than were the Cartesian and Empiricist 'ideas'; we would still need to know whether to be realistic about them (and what that would *mean*), whether they are 'explicit' or 'tacit' (whatever those adjectives mean). Commonsense explanations I believe — for the reasons given above — to be redolent red herrings if what concern us are the demands of science and scientific explanation. In common sense we can *usefully* (and untendentiously) ascribe representations to other animals — but we needn't take ourselves to be saying anything that is literally true. As for scientific explanations: empirically we are some way away yet from pinning down the neuroscientific functions and patterns that might allow us to support the postulate that representations exist; my guess is that support is more likely to come from Lockery-style investigation of simpler systems, or PDP modelling. But at present we are driven back to the remaining alternative, which both McFarland and I defended in different ways and for different reasons: that what is needed is some principled way, independent (as yet) of neuroscience, for preferring theories which cite (explicit; 'solid') representations from those that do not. There my strategy was to look at 'values of scientific theories', and suggest that we might find reasons for preferring one theory over a rival from this source.

Our discussions of these issues over several years have left me more confused at the end than I was at the beginning. But that's to some small extent an advantage in itself (the removal of complacency). In this second-round chapter I have suggested that many of the problems *might* be pseudo-problems — to be dissolved rather than solved; certainly I align myself with the 'theft over honest toil' school of philosophers who prefer problem-dissolution to problem-solution. However that might be, one question has emerged as indissoluble, crucial, and critical: what counts as 'realism' in psychology. This needs serious thought, which would and should enrich and deepen the ongoing examination of realism in the physical sciences.

CHAPTER 12

# THE TELEOLOGICAL IMPERATIVE

*David McFarland*

After writing chapter 4, I discovered a considerable parallelism with Dennett's *Evolution, error and intentionality*, which he kindly sent me in preprint. Much of the time, Dennett is preaching to the converted, as far as I am concerned. Under the heading 'Is function in the eye of the beholder?' is the following passage:

> 'Pending the completion of our mechanical knowledge, we need the intentional characterisations of biology to keep track of what we are trying to explain, and even after we have all our mechanical explanations in place, we will continue to need the intentional level against which to measure the bargains Mother Nature has struck' (Dennett, 1987, p. 315).

This is the well-worn biologist's justification for evolutionary studies, except that a biologist would have used the word 'functional' instead of the word 'intentional'. It is, however, an argument about the utility, rather than the veracity, of the functional viewpoint. I am not suggesting, here, that there is anything wrong with the adaptationist approach, rather that Dennett does not go quite far enough. Dennett comes close to my position when he says: 'We cannot begin to make sense of functional attributions unless we abandon the idea that there has to be one, determinate, right answer to the question: What is it for?' (p. 319). Any product of evolution by natural selection has no single function, nor is it a compromise between a few competing functional requirements. It is the result of trade-off among a myriad of conflicting pressures; the phylogenetic, ontogenetic, energetic and utilitarian costs and benefits. This is where Gould (1980) misses the point with the panda's thumb. Natural selection is a designing process which starts with a particular state of affairs. In the panda's case the starting point for the evolution of a 'thumb' is a wrist bone, the normal starting point not being so readily available. That is to say, in the ontogenetic process the wrist bone precursor was more evolutionarily accessible than the normal thumb precursor. Gould takes the view that the thumb is not perfectly adapted to its role, because it started out as a wrist bone. Unlike Gould, Dennett sees no problem here. 'Mother Nature doesn't commit herself explicitly and objectively to any functional attributions; all such attributions depend on the mind-set of the intentional stance, in which we assume optimality in order to interpret what we find. The panda's thumb was no more really a wrist bone than it is a thumb' (p. 320).

On the subject of human intentionality Dennett reaches the following conclusion:

> 'The design process itself is the source of our own intentionality. We, the reason-representers, the self-representers, are a late and specialised product. What this representation of our reasons gives us is foresight: the real-time anticipatory power that Mother Nature wholly lacks. As a late and specialised product, a triumph of Mother Nature's high tech, our intentionality is highly derived, and in just the same way that the intentionality of our robots (and even our books and maps) is derived. A shopping list in the head has no more intrinsic intentionality than a shopping list on a piece of paper. What the items on the list mean (if anything) is fixed by the role they play in the larger scheme of purposes. We may call our own intentionality real, but we must recognise that it is derived from the intentionality of natural selection' (Dennett, 1987, pp. 317–8).

Some of the wording, here, I find unfortunate, and liable to lead to confusion. I take it that the sense of the last sentence would be unchanged if it read 'We may call our own intentionality real, but we must recognise that it is derived from the process of natural selection.' Whether or not the process of natural selection is an intentional process is a matter of the way intentionality is defined. I would prefer to call it a goal-achieving process, agreeing with Dennett (1987) that there is no (explicit) representation at all in the process of natural selection, and concluding that natural selection is therefore not a goal-directed process. If it is not goal-directed it cannot be intentional, because I see intentions as goals-to-be-achieved (McFarland, 1983), and argue (this volume) that the to-be-achieved goal must be explicitly represented if it is to direct behaviour.

Turning now to Dennett's evolutionary stance (above), it seems to me that Dennett, like Noble (this volume p. 90) is pointing to the (to me) obvious fact that the precursors of our intentional behaviour must have been acted on by natural selection. To paraphrase Noble, there must be 'stored information that is used in forming the antecedent conditions of a particular intentional action'. That this information is organised in a particular way today suggests that it once conferred, and probably still does confer, an evolutionary advantage. This is not to say that a biological evolutionary analysis must shed much light on particular intentional behaviour, although it may be the case that particular intentions have survival and reproductive advantages (chapter 6). My problem with the observations on evolution by both Dennett (1987) and Noble (chapter 6) is that what they say is true, not only about intentional behaviour, but about the evolution of very many aspects of behaviour. They do not tell us what special significance evolutionary theory has for the analysis of intentional behaviour. I say this because I do think that evolutionary theory does have a special role in the analysis of intentional behaviour. It accounts for the fact that we naturally talk and think in teleological terms. It accounts for the fact that we find it very hard to divorce ourselves from the purposive anthropomorphic view, which I propose to call the teleological imperative. It accounts for the fact that Dennett finds it necessary to write *Evolution, error and intentionality*, in an attempt to dispel this view.

Dennett (above passage) seems to suggest that humans have an evolutionary advantage (over other species) in being able to represent goals, but he does not say what type of influence these representations have on behaviour. If Dennett is suggesting that these representations directly control our behaviour, then I would disagree, because I do not think that such a scenario is workable, for reasons that I have outlined (chapter 4). Moreover, even if this scenario were workable, it would not give us an advantage over other species, since if it were workable for us it would be workable for them. There is no obvious ostensible difference between the goal-seeking behaviour of humans and that of other species. It may be, on the other hand, that they influence our linguistic abilities, our thinking and language-using processes. Is this the kind of advantage to which Dennet is alluding? I agree that such a state-of-affairs would give us humans an evolutionary advantage, in being able to represent our goals to ourselves and to each other. Whether such representations are likely to be accurate I will discuss later. It is here that I see the relevance of much of Montefiore's contribution.

Montefiore (chapter 5) argues that the concept of intentionality is indissociable from any adequate analysis of meaning or linguistic behaviour. It is indispensible for our understanding of our various thought processes, including references to the future; reflexivity and self-consciousness; commitment and responsibility. Without wishing to contradict these arguments, I would like to offer two caveats: The first is that these arguments say nothing about non-linguistic behaviour, either that of ourselves or of other species. It remains a possibility that intention is confined to linguistic behaviour (with its concomitant thought processes), and plays no role in the type of goal-seeking behaviour that we have in common with other species. The second caveat is that we cannot assume that our linguistic behaviour has evolved because of its survival value. It seems to me that the selective forces that have shaped our linguistic abilities have more to do with the reproductive potential than with the survival of the individual. Linguistic abilities are closely connected with communication, social behaviour, and politics, the evolutionary advantages of which are primarily reproductive. If anyone doubts that such selective forces are important in primates, they should read de Waal (1982). The implication of this view is that our linguistic abilities equip us to divine the truths of the political world, rather than the physical world: a point I will return to later.

I suggest that our evolutionary inheritance predisposes us to interpret the world in terms of meanings and purposes, as if the rivalries of our political life were relevant to the inanimate world. This is the teleological imperative. The result is that we attribute purpose where there is no purpose, and seek for meaning where there is no meaning. To insist that there must be a meaning to life, a purpose behind our suffering, an intent behind every action, is to take up a political stance. It is saying, in effect, that a satisfactory explanation must be made palatable to me, as a linguistic, purpose-assuming, teleological-thinking human being. Examples of this stance occur in this volume: 'It is strictly inconceivable that anyone should ever be able to provide a proof of the total dispensability of concepts of effective intentionality. This is not because human beings have somehow been so programmed by the processes of evolutionary selection as to be unable to do otherwise than make use of these concepts... It is, rather, that a concept of intentionality must be embodied, or be at work, in the explication of the meaningfulness of any piece of discourse whatever — including, most notably, any claim to offer a proof of the dispensability of all such concepts' (Montefiore, p. 59). That this is a political stance can be seen from a later passage. 'The conceptually graspable meaningfulness of one's own argument is a surely necessary predisposition of its presentability as argument, whether to oneself or to others. But then, it must surely equally follow that, if one could show a reference to intentionality to be necessarily implicit in the very concept of (discursive or conceptual) meaningfulness, then to present one's own argument as being in principle wholly intelligible in exclusively non-intentional terms must be as self-defeating as to present it as being itself devoid of conceptual meaning. (But notice the importance of the word 'wholly' in the preceding sentence. As will become clear later on, I do not, indeed cannot, deny that there must always be perspectives of non-intentional explicability from which any observable sequence of behaviour may be seen as explicable — fully explicable, indeed, so long as one remains within the limits of that perspective, even though the perspective itself may have to be seen as only a partial one)' (p. 61).

Obviously, self-defeating propositions are possible. If I maintained, verbally, that 'I am incapable of using language', I would, presumably be deluding myself. If I accept Montefiore's argument that intentionality is a necessary part of language, then I cannot deny that I use intentional processes, because to deny something I would have to use language. Presumably, I could not even think (without deluding myself) that I have no intentionality, if my thoughts are of the linguistic type. However this does not mean that my ordinary, non-linguistic, behaviour is intentional. As Montefiore acknowledges, a non-linguistic, non-intentional perspective on behaviour is possible, even though the perspective may have to be seen as a partial one. A crucial question here is whether our intentions ever control our (non-linguistic) behaviour.

In maintaining that our intentions do not control our behaviour, I am not contradicting Montefiore, nor is this a self-defeating view. There are a number of points to be made here. The first is that it is part of my thesis that our linguistic behaviour and thinking is not designed to be wholly intelligible, it is designed to be politically effective. So, to say that my argument is not wholly intelligible does not worry me much. Secondly, if our language is constrained by being organised on an intentional basis, then there may be some aspects of reality which may be difficult, or impossible, to express. My language is a crutch, which I am forced to use because of my disability. I would like to throw it away and be able to express myself freely, but I cannot. My disability arises from the fact that I am designed (by natural selection) to be self-deceiving. I do not have access to my true thoughts and motives, and when I try to express myself it always comes out in intentional terms. If it does not come out this way, it is not perceived as having meaning by other people. Some may try to express themselves in non-linguistic art, music, or mathematics, but I am not sufficiently talented in these directions. The third point is that my main claim is that our (non-linguistic) behaviour is not controlled by intentions. There is nothing incoherent in asserting this, but it may be argued that I am being incoherent in thinking it. If all our thought processes were organised on a linguistic basis, then it might be possible to argue that it would be incoherent of me to think that my behaviour was non-intentional. I have already suggested (p. 57) that we are designed to assume that our own, and other people's behaviour is purposive, so how can I now say that my own behaviour is not purposive? It may be, however, that not all our thought processes are organised on an intentional basis. Indeed, since part of my argument is that behaviour control (in the strict sense of the word control) by intentions is incompatible with the necessity for trade-offs in decision-making, I more or less have to assume that such trade-offs are achieved by some non-intentional, non-linguistic type of thought process. Before turning to this possibility, I will mention some implications of my position for Dennett's application of his intentional stance to vervet monkey behaviour.

Dennett (p. 111) notes that shortly before a monkey in a bush moves into the open, it often gives a MIO (moving into the open) grunt. Other monkeys in the bush may repeat it, but if there is no such echo the original grunter will often stay in the bush for about ten minutes before repeating the MIO grunt. When the grunt is repeated by one or more other monkeys, the originator moves cautiously into the open. Dennett asks what the MIO grunt means. I take it that he is asking about the proximal function of the behaviour, rather than meaning in the linguistic sense, but I am forced to conclude that he is not after either of these types of explanation. To illustrate my point, I have chosen an example from a less complex animal.

Before a pigeon flies away from a feeding flock, it usually gives a flight 'intention-movement' consisting of incipient take-off behaviour. The other birds usually continue feeding, but if a pigeon flies off without giving the intention-movement, the other birds take off in alarm (Davis, 1975). The intention-movement can be interpreted as meaning 'I am making a routine departure', by which I am suggesting that the intention-movement has a communicative function. I am not suggesting that the individual pigeon means (in the sense of intends) to communicate anything to the other pigeons. Indeed, it could be that when a pigeon takes off in a hurry it fails to give the intention movement simply because it takes off quickly. I suggest that a pigeon departing in a leisurely manner performs the incipient take-off behaviour purely as part of the dithering that animals often show when slowly changing from one activity to another. Human observers, and other pigeons, learn to interpret this as flight-preparation behaviour. Pigeons are programmed to take alarm when one of their number departs without any flight-preparation behaviour.

It may be that the functional significance of the MIO grunt lies in the number of monkeys that do not answer. I do not know, but I would not want to presuppose that the grunt has a meaning in any intentional sense. Even though Dennett may recognise that the individual monkey may not mean (in the sense of intend) to communicate to the others, his approach is still essentially anthropomorphic. In adopting the intentional stance, he is saying 'let's pretend that the monkey does mean to communicate to the others, and see where this line of inquiry gets us'. This approach is appealing to us precisely because it is framed in teleological terms, and involves a way of thinking with which we are familiar. But does it really ask the right questions?

It seems to me that the right question, from a functional viewpoint, is to ask what would happen if these signals were not given. In the case of the pigeons it is not difficult to see what would probably happen. If no pigeons produced flight intention-movements, then leisurely take-off would be indistinguishable from hurried take-off, and the warning function of the hurried take-off would be lost. The birds would then remain without a warning system, or the individual that spotted a predator would have to give a specialised alarm call, as do many passerine birds. The problem here is that the pigeon giving the alarm endangers itself by pausing to give the alarm and by attracting the predator's attention. As the members of a feeding flock are unlikely to be kin, alarm calling would be a form of altruism that would be inherently deleterious unless supported by some sophisticated reciprocal arrangements. As things stand, all that is necessary is that pigeons find hurried take-off alarming. In the case of vervet monkeys, I do not know what would be likely to happen if no MIO grunts were given. All that I am saying is that this is the question to ask if one is enquiring about biological function.

If Dennett is not enquiring about biological function, and is not asking about the meaning of the MIO grunt in the linguistic sense, then perhaps he is using the intentional stance to enquire about the design of the individual. This approach may be fruitful when applied to behaviour that is the result of cognition, but it is not clear to me that MIO grunts are the result of cognition. In the case of the pigeons (assuming my sketch of the situation is roughly correct), there is little to be said about the design of the individual. All that is involved is that each pigeon is alarmed at the sight of another pigeon taking off without any flight-intention-movements. The rest is simply due to the circumstances in which the communication takes place. Without knowing more about the circumstances, and the biological function, of the vervet MIO grunt, it is difficult to say much about the design of individual monkeys. It seems to me that the intentional stance is likely to be fruitful only where there is reason to believe that cognition is involved. If this is so, then there is a problem about anthropomorphism. The intentional stance is based upon a human perspective. It is based upon an essentially teleological framework, which accords with our normal linguistic way of thinking. However, it may be that some other species have a completely different form of cognition, which is not linguistically based. (Indeed, I have argued above that we also have such a form of cognition in addition to our linguistic cognition.) If this is so, then the intentional stance is not likely to be an appropriate tool with which to analyse animal cognition.

Dennett concludes that, because the vervets live in a world in which secrets are virtually impossible, there is little news that the individual can impart to others. The vervet lifestyle is too simple for them to be able to make use of most of the features of a human language. He concludes that the MIO grunt is not properly translated by any familiar human interchange, and that the intentional stance can tell us little about vervet beliefs, because the monkeys do not really mean anything by their vocalisations — they do not really believe anything.

It seems that I have come to the same conclusion as Dennett by a different route, but have I? Dennett's vervets that have no secrets are similar to my honest robots. They can hide nothing, so they have nothing to lie about. I find it hard to believe that a primate, good at little except politics, can find itself in such a position. However open their society, the individuals must be in competition for mates, leadership, and power. It may be that their debate is not a vocal one, but I suspect that somewhere amongst the grunts and pheromones war is being waged by devious means. I suspect this because an open primate society, like an open robot society, is not an evolutionarily stable situation.

## The role of representations

The main issue, as I see it, is the role of representations in the control of behaviour. I have argued (chapter 4) that there is no hard evidence for explicit representations that control behaviour in the manner of a 'set-point', or 'sollwert'. It may be that hard evidence has been too difficult to obtain, and I have to admit that such evidence may be obtained one day. However, this possibility does not justify the high profile that these concepts have in much of the psychological literature.

There is, however, some good behavioural evidence for the existence of 'declarative' representation with a role in animal learning. The evidence is not conclusive, but it is persuasive. The best that I can do here is summarise the situation briefly.

In addressing the question of how animals organise their knowledge of the consequences of behaviour, Dickinson (1980) considers the nature of the internal representation that encodes the learning experience. He distinguishes between procedural representations and declarative representations of knowledge. A procedural representation directly reflects the use to which the knowledge will be put in controlling the animal's behaviour, whereas a declarative representation corresponds to a statement describing relationships among events in the animal's world which does not commit the animal to any particular course of action. The distinction corresponds to that of 'knowing how' and 'knowing that'. These concepts originated with Ryle (1949) and have been taken into human cognitive psychology (Anderson, 1976), but I think it is easier to explore them in the animal context, free from the complications of language.

In a declarative system, knowledge is represented in a form that corresponds to a statement or proposition describing a relationship among events in the animal's world. This form of representation does not commit the animal to use the information in any particular way. In a procedural system, however, the form of representation directly reflects the use to which the knowledge will be put. For example, Holland (1977) exposed rats to a tone–food relationship by occasionally presenting an 8-second tone and then delivering food pellets into a receptacle. Holland noticed that the rats developed a tendency to approach the food receptacle during the tone. This observation might suggest that during learning, the procedure of approaching the food receptacle is established, so that the learned information is stored in a form that is related closely to its use. The alternative possibility is that the rat learns that the tone causes the food, and thus establishes a declarative representation. The observation that the rat tends to approach the food receptacle during the tone then would have to be accounted for in some other way, because a declarative representation is passive in the sense that it does not control the animal's behaviour. The procedural representation thus provides a more parsimonious explanation of the rat's behaviour.

Suppose, however, that after the tone–food association is established, the rats are exposed to a food–illness relationship (i.e. they associate a distinctively flavoured food with sickness) to the point where they refuse to eat the food when it is presented. The rats now will have formed two separate associations, tone–food and food–illness. The question is whether they are capable of integrating the two. On the one hand, a procedural account of learning would imply that the rats should not be able to integrate the two procedures, which have no factors in common. A declarative system, on the other hand, provides a basis for integration because both representations have the food term in common. Holland and Straub (1979) showed that rats can integrate information from such associations learned at different times. Rats exposed to a food–illness following tone–food showed a disinclination to approach the food receptacle when the tone was presented again.

There is now little doubt that animals can integrate separately formed associations, and this is explained most easily in terms of a declarative system. However, under certain circumstances there are failures of integration, and these failures point to the possibility of an underlying procedural representation (Dickinson, 1980).

In a declarative system, there must be some way of translating the stored representation into overt behaviour. Various mechanisms have been suggested (Dickinson, 1980), but these need not concern us here. The important point is that, although a procedural theory offers a more parsimonious explanation of simple learning situations, a more complex theory may be necessary to account for the observed phenomena, and this may require some form of declarative representation. Once we accept that declarative representation is a necessary ingredient of our explanation of behaviour, then we have to admit to some form of animal thinking, which involves explicit representations. However, we have to be careful to distinguish between evidence for declarative representation and the facility that this concept affords scientists attempting to explain behaviour. It may be that the notion of declarative representation is merely a convenient crutch upon which to support current learning theory. Let us accept, for the present, that declarative representations do play a role in animal thinking. Does this imply that some aspects of animal behaviour are goal-directed, intentional and purposive? In other words, can the declarative representation act like a goal-representation that controls behaviour? Dickinson claims that it can.

Dickinson (1985) highlights the two dominant opinions: (1) The mechanistic stimulus–response view, according to which a particular behaviour is either an innate or an acquired habit which is simply triggered by the appropriate stimulus. (2) The 'teleological' view, which maintains that some activities are purposive actions controlled through the current values of their goals through knowledge about the instrumental relations between the actions and their consequences.

In my view, a number of problems are raised by the fact that Dickinson (1985) portrays rather extreme versions of these two different views. He contrasts 'responses' and 'actions'. The former is elicited by stimuli, and (by implication) the animal gains no feedback about the consequences of the response. The latter is 'controlled at the time of performance by the animal's knowledge about the consequences of this activity. In other words, the teleological model claims that, at least, some behaviour is 'truly purposeful and goal-directed' (p. 67). One issue here is whether behaviour, as 'controlled at the time of performance', is goal-directed or not. As we saw in chapter 4, I have argued that it is not.

Another issue concerns 'goal revaluation'. Dickinson (1985) maintains that the type of control (stimulus–response or goal-directed) over any particular activity can be determined by a goal revaluation procedure. Specifically, if an animal's behaviour changes appropriately following an 'alteration of the value of the goal or reward' without further experience of the instrumental relationship, the behaviour should be regarded as a purposive action. I do not dispute, in the face of Dickinson's persuasive evidence, that some form of revaluation occurs. The question is whether 'goals' are revalued or whether some other entities are revalued.

These issues are best illustrated by discussion of one of Dickinson's own experiments. A crucial experiment was carried out by Adams and Dickinson (1981a), who trained hungry rats to lever press for one of two types of food (sugar or chow) while they received the other on a schedule designed to ensure that lever pressing and food presentations were uncorrelated. Thus for sugar the rewards were contingent on lever pressing, while for chow they were non-contingent. In another group of rats the roles of sugar and chow were reversed. They then devalued the contingent foods (counterbalanced design) for one group of rats (A), while maintaining the value of the non-contingent foods. For another group (B), the non-contingent foods were devalued and the value of the contingent foods was maintained. Food was devalued by allowing the rats to have access to the food in the absence of the lever, and injecting them with lithium chloride soon after they ate the food. The lithium chloride makes the rats mildly ill and induces an aversion to the food with which it is associated.

Both (A and B) groups were then given an extinction test in the lever-pressing situation. The result was that the contingent (A) group pressed at a lower rate in the extinction test than the non-contingent (B) group. To check whether the aversion procedure had been differentially successful, reacquisition tests were then given. These showed that both the contingent foods in group A and the non-contingent foods in group B had lost their capacity to act as rewards.

Dickinson's (1985) interpretation of these results is that the animals for which the contingent food is devalued (group A) perform less vigorously in the extinction test because the goal (obtaining this food) had been devalued. The animals for which the non-contingent food is devalued (group B) perform more vigorously because their goal (the contingent food) had not been devalued. The reacquisition tests show that the food itself is devalued in both groups. His conclusion is that 'performance of this particular instrumental behaviour really does seem to be controlled by the knowledge about the relation between the action and the goal' (p. 72). 'From my point of view ... the main implication of our results concerns the nature of the cognitive processes controlling instrumental behaviour. My colleagues and I (Adams and Dickinson, 1981b; Dickinson, 1980; Mackintosh and Dickinson, 1979) have argued that teleological control of instrumental behaviour cannot be explained, at least at the psychological level, in terms of internal associations which have just excitatory or inhibitory properties. Rather, we argue that the knowledge about the goal-action relation must be encoded in a propositional-like form so that it can be operated on by a practical inference process to generate the instrumental performance' (p. 78).

While accepting that the results of these, and other, studies suggest that rats are capable of some cognitive evaluation of the consequences of their behaviour, I do not agree that any teleological element is required by these results. The problem, it seems to me, is that Dickinson anthropomorphically interprets the instrumental paradigm as a goal-directed paradigm. He assumes that the animal has a goal (to obtain food) and learns what behaviour to perform to obtain the goal. An alternative interpretation is that the animal simply learns what behaviour to do to improve its situation, where improvement is measured in terms of the overall, in-built goal function (as outlined in chapter 4). It may be that obtaining food will improve the animal's situation (i.e. move its state to a less costly condition), but escaping from the apparatus may seem to the rat to improve its situation even more. The animal is continually evaluating its perceived situation and deciding what to do on the basis of the evaluation. It may well be, as the revaluation experiments suggest, that knowledge about the behaviour–consequence relation is encoded in a proposition-like form and is operated on by a practical inference process to generate the instrumental performance. This is simply another way of saying that the animal makes use of declarative representations in evaluating the likely consequences of its behaviour. As I have argued in more detail elsewhere (McFarland, 1989) the goal-directed paradigm is not a necessary ingredient of this scenario.

At this point it may be useful to ask how our robot (introduced in chapter 4) would proceed in an instrumental learning task. My claim (in chapter 4) is that the behaviour of individual animals (and people) is guided, not by any goal-representation, but by myopic hill-climbing behaviour. Hill-climbing by gradient-maximising is a means of achieving goals that does not involve any goal-representation. The animal, or robot, surveys the options available at each point in time. These change according to the external circumstances and the internal state. The options present themselves already evaluated in various ways. So far, in the case of our robot, the evaluation process has been entirely preprogrammed. In adapting to the new environmental circumstances, however, the robot could learn to alter the constraints on its behaviour, so as to perform better in terms of its own goal function. It could not learn to alter its own goal function to make it more like the cost function of its new environment. Although an animal which could do this would greatly increase its overall fitness, we have to remember that all learning must be based on feedback from the consequences of behaviour that can be evaluated in terms of a set of criteria. These criteria are provided by the goal function. Learned modification of the goal function could not, remember, be based on information about the cost function, unless we are prepared to allow that the animal understands the evolutionary function of its own behaviour. In other words, the goal function is a fixed property of the robot which cannot be modified by learning, except where the learning is entirely preprogrammed (McFarland and Houston, 1981). Preprogrammed learning, of the kind discussed above, could involve a contingent change in the goal function. Thus a very sophisticated robot could embody a rule such that when in a French kitchen it automatically switched to a preordained goal function (see p. 51).

In considering the robot (or animal) in an instrumental learning situation, we are concerned with the means by which the robot assesses the consequences of its own behaviour. In the final analysis, and by means of some (unknown) intervening mechanism, the robot must assign more or less weight to the behaviour that produced the consequences that improve the state (remember that the state includes the perceived — and calibrated — external environment). Thus if using a new mop produces results that are better than usual, more value will be assigned to that activity. This means that the behaviour will be more likely to occur in the future. Similarly, if washing the dishes more quickly produces more breakages, less value will be assigned to that aspect of behaviour. This is merely Thorndike's (1913) Law of Effect, which is useful as an empirical summary, but says nothing about the mechanisms involved in learning.

In the case of instrumental learning (the kind of learning we want our robot to achieve), Dickinson (1980) notes that 'instrumental responses appear to be purposeful being directed at the goal of achieving the environmental change ... The obvious way to find out whether information about the goal of action is represented in the underlying associative structure is to look at an animal's integrative capacity' (p. 103). He notes that a large number of experiments have attempted to do just this, and discusses the example of an experiment by Adams (then unpublished). Dickinson concludes (p. 109) that 'Adams' experiment on the devaluation of rewards leaves us with little doubt that integration can occur and that some form of declarative representation is also required'. I have no quarrel with this conclusion, but I do disagree with the way Dickinson initially sets up the problem. He notes (above) that instrumental responses 'appear' to be purposeful, and then claims that the way to find out whether information about the goal is represented in the underlying structure is to look at the animal's integrative capacity. The problem here is that it is the goal as identified by the human observer that is being investigated. He assumes that the animal's goal is to obtain food, demonstrates that the animal makes use of declarative knowledge, and concludes that it is knowledge about the goal that is the subject of the declarative representation. I do not find this line of argument very convincing, because it could be knowledge about the consequences of behaviour that is stored in a declarative manner.

Dickinson (p. 105) notes that 'extended practice of an instrumental act seems to produce a transition of control from the declarative to the procedural form, thereby setting up a habit. A habit can be viewed as an action we perform automatically in a given situation without direct reference to the goal of that action.' However, a habit could also be viewed as an activity performed automatically in a given situation without direct reference to the consequences of that activity. It is not necessary to invoke the concepts of goal-direction, purposiveness, or intention, to account for those experiments that point to the use of declarative representations by animals. The question of the exact role of declarative representations remains an open one for me, because I do not see any compelling reason to link declarative representations and intentionality.

Returning to our robot, we can envisage a situation in which the consequences of a particular activity are better (or worse) than usual in the sense that they improve (or worsen) the robot's state. To learn from this novel situation, the robot would have to remember the consequences of the behaviour and the situation in which it occurred. For example, it might store the information 'activity A in situation E produced consequences C, when I was in state X'. In other words the state changed from X to Y as a consequence of activity A in situation E. The learning process might result in a procedural change, such as do activity A when in situation E and state X. On the other hand, the robot might simply store the information for future (unspecified) use. To store the information in this way, it would have to be represented in a declarative form. In other words, the robot would know that certain relations existed between X, E, A and C, without tying the knowledge to any particular set of circumstances.

On some future occasion, the robot could make use of its various declarative representations of the consequences of behaviour in trading-off alternative possible courses of action. In my view, such a robot will be better designed than one which operates on the teleological principle of selecting a goal and then pursuing it. Let us take window cleaning as an example. Suppose that clean windows is a desirable state of affairs. The robot has an explicit declarative representation of clean windows. That is, it knows what clean windows look like. The question is how to attain this state of affairs. On the teleological model, the robot learns that polishing produces clean windows, it wants clean windows, so it polishes in order to attain clean windows. In other words, its behaviour is directed by the clean-window representation. This means that the robot will perform the behaviour (polishing) necessary to clean the window, so long as the behaviour continues to produce the desired results. If the polishing cloth became contaminated with oil so that polishing no longer made the window cleaner, then the robot would presumably stop polishing and take some corrective action. This is fine so long as the robot is merely a window-cleaning machine, but problems arise (as discussed in chapter 4) if it also has other activities in its repertoire.

The alternative design is that the robot reviews its behavioural options and sees which is most likely to maximise utility. To do this the robot would have to be able to evaluate each potential activity in relation to its probable consequences. We can see this if we arrange matters so that the robot has only one feasible activity relevant to two different tasks. For example, the activity of polishing is necessary to attain clean windows, and it is also necessary to attain clean brassware. In the teleological view the robot integrates knowledge of the goal with knowledge on the consequences of polishing. 'My goal is clean brassware... polishing cleans brassware... so I will polish the brass until it is clean.' The fact that polishing cleans windows is not seen as relevant. However, the optimal solution, and therefore the behaviour that the well-designed robot should follow, takes account of other considerations, thus: 'It cost some time and labour to obtain the materials for polishing the brassware, so while I am polishing the brassware should I not also polish the windows?' Let us assume that the motivation to polish the windows is somewhat less than that to polish the brassware. The robot will start by polishing the brassware, but after a while a new consideration arises. 'The brassware is nearly clean, so should I not now switch to the windows, because (1) my total costs (of having dirty brassware and windows) will be less if both brassware and windows are nearly clean than if the brassware is completely clean and the windows still dirty (assuming quadratic goal functions, see McFarland and Houston, 1981). Thus if I am interrupted (and lose the momentum gained by having the cleaning materials in my possession) it is better to have two jobs half done than to have one completed and the other not started.' The point here is that the behaviour is controlled, not by the goal-representation, but by trade-off considerations. This conclusion need not imply that explicit (declarative) representations do not exist, but rather that they do not control behaviour, and therefore the behaviour is not goal-directed. It may well be that animals (and robots) make use of declarative representations in integrating knowledge about activities and their consequences. In fact, I see no reason why there should not be quite complicated cognitive processes involved in both associative learning and in the control of behaviour. Indeed, this is not a new idea; 'act-outcome' representation has often been cited as the key to intentional behaviour (e.g. Irwin, 1971; Gallistel, 1985). While I do not go along with this view of intention, I am happy to agree that behaviour–outcome representations would provide a vehicle for behavioural flexibility and the incorporation of novelty into the behavioural repertoire. My point, however, is that these cognitive states have a role in the control of behaviour that is no different from that of other (non-cognitive) motivational states. They simply provide new stimuli for the trade-off process. This brings me to a point made by Wilkes.

Wilkes (chapter 9, p. 181) finds it implausible to suppose that diary entries, and other ostensible representations of goals, can be handled without some postulate or intention or goal representation. As I understand them, her points are that the evidence of explicit representation of the goal is readily apparent, and there is no doubt that such representations control behaviour. However, they do not control behaviour (in my view) in the proper sense of the word control. Behaviour that is controlled is instigated, and continually guided by reference to the goal representation. Moreover, it is guided in such a way as to resist disturbances from outside influences including the influences of other behavioural control systems. This principle is the very opposite of the trade-off principle, which requires continual compromise among behavioural systems. In my view, the person seeing a diary entry 'telephone mother' takes this, not as a representation of a goal-to-be-achieved, but as a stimulus to be weighted among all the other stimuli that will be taken into account in deciding what to do. The outcome may depend upon the availability of a telephone, whether the route to the telephone is compatible with some other task, etc.

The entry in the diary is indeed a declarative representation which does not commit the person to any particular course of action. It is not a written-down intention in the sense that it represents the goal of goal-directed behaviour. Indeed, such a representation would have to be a procedural representation, directly reflecting the use to which the knowledge is to be put, since it is the essence of goal-directed behaviour that the behaviour is directed (the procedure) by an explicit representation of the goal.

In conclusion, there is some confusion in my mind as to what people mean by intentional behaviour. I hope I have dispelled the notion that intention is some kind of goal-directed behaviour. I am happy to entertain the notion that declarative representations provide food for thought, and that these may be representations of act-outcomes, goals, etc. We can talk about them to each other, indeed I claim that nature intends us to do so (the teleological imperative), but we should not claim that they are responsible for our behaviour.

CHAPTER 13

# COMMENTS

*Daniel C. Dennett*

Given the limited space provided for each of us to reply to the others, I have chosen to concentrate on just three, chosen not because I agreed with everything in the others, or found the points I concentrate on to be the most important sources of disagreement, but just because I found that I knew what I wanted to say about these, and could manage it in relatively short compass.

## Comments on McFarland

I agree wholeheartedly with McFarland that the explicit representation of goals is less important, less prevalent, less a necessity for goal-seeking behaviour, than the prevailing opinion supposes. That is why I have insisted over the years that the theoretically perspicuous classification of intentional systems should sidestep the question of internal representation, by including all entities that are predictable from the intentional stance, whatever their innards. In my terms, then, McFarland asks the question whether there is a theoretically important subset of intentional systems that are in fact what common sense proclaims them all to be: systems guided by explicit internal representations of the goals their behaviour tends to achieve. His answer is that so far as he can see, the only role for explicit goal representations is in those agents that have the special behavioural option of communicating (and, on occasion, miscommunicating) information about their internal goal-states. The only behaviour *directed* by represented goals is the behaviour of reporting those goals to others.

Certainly the subclass of intentional systems capable of linguistic communication is a theoretically interesting subclass in many ways, and while I am in sympathy with this boldly minimalist account of the role of representations of goals, and particularly applaud McFarland's analysis of the truthfulness conditions on robot communication, I have doubts about some of the background assumptions. I am inclined to think that the lines that can be drawn within the class of intentional systems are less crisp, and less objective, than his admirably clear and systematic account suggests. Most fundamentally, I think McFarland understates the extent to which his formulations depend on interpretation schemes which derive their warrant from tacit optimality assumptions. This leads him to suppose the distinction between explicit representations and other internal mechanisms is crisper than in fact it is.

McFarland is well aware of the pitfalls inherent in his use of the assumption of perfection, but I think he ignores the extent to which the assumption gets carried along in spite of his acknowledgments. We start with the myth of the 'perfectly adapted animal', which maximises its inclusive Darwinian fitness. No such creature exists, as he notes, because of such sources of noise as evolutionary lag. So we move in the direction of realism by advancing from the hypothesised cost function (which describes the perfectly adapted animal) to the goal function (which is supposed to describe the *optimal* performance of the *actual* design in the individual phenotype). This is still an idealisation, but, shall we say, a more proximal, less distal, prescription of competence. We need the hypothesised cost function so that we can make sense of the goal function as an approximation of it, tracking it along a deflected course. McFarland shows clearly that an individual's goal function is itself an optimisation relative to assumptions about what a computer scientist might call the default values of features of both the animal and its environment. If the animal loses a leg, or if the environment shifts suddenly to present problems or opportunities beyond the scope of the plasticity of the animal's design, the goal function will prescribe behaviour that is no longer optimal relative to the animal's *real* needs, powers and opportunities. But that goal function can still be used to predict and explain the sub-optimal behaviour, he notes.

So far so good, but what of the determination of the goal function itself? We can specify any number of subtly different notional environment–body pairs relative to which we can derive a goal function, but which is the 'right' one? Every mismatch between hypothesised cost function and our candidate goal function can be allocated to evolutionary noise *or* treated as evidence that we should adjust either our cost function or our goal function to bring them into closer registration. Every mismatch between the actual world–body pair we are observing and the notional pair used as the basis for the candidate goal function can be allocated to insufficient plasticity/sensitivity in the 'actual' goal function *or* treated as evidence that we have posited the 'wrong' goal function. (See Dennett, 1983, on notional environments, and Dennett, 1987, on the grounds for attributing 'error' to a system.)

Presumably, McFarland is counting on Nature to give us a fairly obvious set of answers to our questions here, and this reliance is surely largely justified. Consider the set of explanations that begin with:

> organism $O$ is in a predicament where it *ought* to fly away, but it *won't* fly away because . . .

Here are some obvious completions:

> $O$ is a frog, and flight in frogs is vastly too distant in the adaptive landscape to be included as a live option in the cost function, let alone the goal function. (Or, as a philosopher would say, *ought* implies *can*, and frogs can't fly.)
> $O$ is a domesticated chicken, and although it will 'try' to fly away (it still lists flying away as the option of choice in its goal function), its wings no longer work well enough for this to be the optimal strategy in the real world.
> $O$ is a piping plover whose current goal function mistakenly favours the injury-feigning distraction display in this circumstance, since its discrimination system is too crude to 'recognize' this circumstance as one in which distraction-display is futile and dangerous — not cost-effective.

But what of the other cases that are judgement calls? Every time a bird that *can* fly (and typically does fly away in circumstances like these) fails to fly away when it seems to us that it should, we are left wondering whether the mistake is the bird's or ours. If we can find nothing to *settle* that wonder, our continued use of any particular goal function to characterise that bird (or its kin) depends on a sort of dramatic license. That is not at all to say that we shouldn't continue to exploit the methods McFarland espouses, but that we shouldn't fool ourselves about their having any sort of bedrock objectivity.

The same relativity to interpretation haunts McFarland's attempt to show that plasticity of behaviour is not in itself a conclusive sign of goal-representation, as some have argued. As he notes, in each animal or robot there must a goal function that is fixed innately or hard-wired, if only to be the standard relative to which alternative soft-wired goal functions can be evaluated, but this is a minimal limit, since by exploiting that fixed standard, an agent can in principle adopt any number of subsidiary goal functions, rather the way a fixed von Neumann machine can emulate any number of vastly different virtual machines. Any such plastic adaptation can be accomplished via what I have called *transient tacit representation* (1982-3), not explicit representation, so in principle there can be unlimited plasticity in the face of environmental novelties without explicit representation of the goals sought, and McFarland shows that there are certainly varieties of striking plasticity that are thus accomplished.

But there is plasticity and then there is plasticity. We can always account for $n$ different degrees of freedom or plasticity by postulating $n$ distinct partially redundant goal functions, each tacitly represented by a group of parameter settings, as McFarland says. But when $n$ gets large, the efficiency of this scheme is jeopardised. At some point the benefits of a more compact, systematic, partially generative system of grouping these parameter settings (a system with slots for variables, for instance) may outweigh the costs of designing and implementing it. Then we are *on the way to* undeniably explicit representation, with 'terms' and a 'syntax'. My point is that where along that path we decide that the systematicity and flexibility of the system earns it the accolade of explicit representation is probably a matter of arbitrary, theoretically idle, opinion.

McFarland concludes his argument about 'myopic hill-climbing' with a claim that was initially puzzling to me: 'Hill-climbing by gradient-maximising is a means of achieving goals that does not involve any goal-representation' (p. 54). How, I asked myself, can the continuous trade-off be 'calculated' or 'computed' (or if that begs the question, how can it be *implemented*) unless the outcome of each possible trade-off is somehow to turn on or favour or single out some sort of internal *representative* (not 'representation') of the 'chosen' option? The answer is, it can't be. Something must 'stand for' each contestant in the trade-off, but this thing is not, in McFarland's understanding, a *representation* of the goal, or of the action with the goal as its defining consummation. But what this means is that this representative is more like a proper name than a description; the alternative modes of action are just Tom, Dick, and Harry to the trade-off system that determines that for a little while the organism will Tom, and then, when the position on the hillside changes, it will begin to Harry for a bit, and once it has finished that, it will commence to Dick. That's only metaphorical, of course, and in any case the stand-ins or representatives or whatever are not real, explicit representations. But as the population grows, will these non-representations *turn into* representations? Or is there a sharp distinction still to be drawn?

Let us compare two apparently opposing design principles, and ask ourselves if there might be a watershed regarding their application by Mother Nature. The CIA has its notorious Need to Know Principle: tell each operative in a project as little as he needs to know in order to accomplish his role in the mission. This principle has its applications, and also its limitations. Some projects become stymied or grotesquely inefficient or blind because of overcompartmentalization of the relevant knowledge. The contrary principle, instantiated in fiction if not quite so obviously in fact in the organization of 'élite' commando teams, is Every Team Member Should Know Everything. The agents should be versatile, interchangeable, capable of taking over each other's roles, capable of appropriate improvisation and instant recognition of the import of novel and unanticipated shifts in the environment.

These principles have their analogues in the design of robots or organisms, and the watershed apparently is determined by the complexity and unpredictability of the environments in which the system must operate. If the system designers can count on a stereotypic American kitchen, the Need to Know principle works quite well, but even here, there are pitfalls. Suppose the lights go out in the kitchen. Will the robot be able to adjust its goal priorities appropriately, 'recognising' that without electricity, it cannot run the vacuum cleaner, but could get on with the washing up, counting on the power being restored in time to permit it to recharge its batteries?

The engineers wanting to add this capability have several design options to cost out ranging from the cheap 'kludge' (build in a rigid, relatively dumb but usually appropriate priority-shifter that is triggered by lights-out) to the deluxe 'expert system' (build in information about the environmental (power) requirements of the various tasks, the symptoms that are their harbingers, together with problem-solving methods for dealing with untoward, unexpected developments). Should the robot have the wits to check the fuse box, see if the fridge is still working, unscrew the light bulb and try replacing it? The more such versatility we build in, the more our system risks becoming an ungainly collection of mutually interfering modules, unless it is radically and elegantly redesigned (somehow — no one knows how, yet) with a central *lingua franca* of representations — of goals, of their enabling and disabling conditions, the symptoms of those conditions, etc.

McFarland is sanguine about the engineering opportunities of the 'dumb' approach, and he is certainly right that its prospects should not be underestimated. Rodney Brooks (1987) has begun to demonstrate the surprising power of stupid, insectlike robot systems designed by piling more and more modulating modules on top of a basic, and very simple, control system. But the question of whether there is something of a natural barrier (rather like the speed of sound for flight) standing in the way of the indefinite elaboration of systems without explicit representation is not settled by any of McFarland's observations. He has not yet addressed himself to the issue of whether the enlargement of $n$ becomes problematic at some value.

But he has concluded that once communication is added to an agent's repertoire, explicit representation of goals is worth the price. Perhaps there is an interaction between these costs and benefits. There are several possibilities to explore, ranged between two poles:

1. as $n$ becomes large for increasingly versatile, adaptive creatures, the watershed is passed, and they come to be designed as generative goal-representers; this new capacity is then a *necessary precondition* for the subsequent evolution of the novel behaviour of communication.
2. as the 'social' environment becomes more complex for some species, the benefits derivable from communication begin to create a sharp selection pressure in favour of systems with enough explicit representation to permit such communication. Once such representation systems begin to emerge, they bring along a happy side benefit: greatly increased versatility and sensitivity in goal-seeking, thanks to the efficient representation of those goals and their enabling conditions.

Robots that can communicate can also do many other things that their mute cousins cannot. Is it that they can communicate because they can do these other things, or that they can do these other things because they can communicate? This is the next question to which I would like to see McFarland's ingenious mind turned.

## Comments on Montefiore

With most of Montefiore's analysis I have no quarrel. He develops a substantial set of interlocking prerequisites for what I would call full personhood (not every intentional system is a person), and it is quite similar in spirit and content to my own list of requirements in 'Conditions of Personhood' (1976). The crucial step that divides us comes early in his analysis:

> So long as there are, or may be, or may have been human agents to whom responsibility may be attributed for the devising of such rule-following machines ... we can have no compelling reason to attribute any sense of normative expectation or commitment to the machines themselves (chapter 5, p. 63).

I don't see any argument for this claim, and don't myself believe it. Montefiore goes on to deny that he is attempting any sort of a priori argument against the possibility in principle of a conscious, intentional robot, but insists that in any such case 'there would have to be grounds for construing at least some of their behaviour as being, in part at least, autonomously intentional' (p. 64). I agree, but wonder if we would agree on what 'autonomously intentional' means. Autonomy, to me, is not a particularly vaunted property; the Viking spacecraft had a theoretically important sort of autonomy when its designer-controllers realised that it was moving too far away from them for their control signals to be effective; they turned control over to it; it ceased to be a sort of electronic marionette, and became a *self*-controlling robot (for a description, see my *Elbow Room*, 1984a). This, I suspect, is not enough autonomy for Montefiore, but I doubt that a debate over that point would be fruitful.

On another front, I was struck with the parallel between Montefiore's discussion of the requirements for rule-following and the ongoing puzzlement among some biologists about the requirements for something being an adaptation. The wings of insects, we are now told, developed from scales whose prior function was thermoregulation. What about the very first mutant insect whose slightly protruding scales had non-zero thermoregulatory capacity? Were *those* scales an adaptation for thermoregulation? Why do some biologists — e.g. Stephen Jay Gould — think it is important for there to be a history of successful thermoregulating ancestry before we can interpret a structure as an adaptation *for* thermoregulation? For the same reason, I gather, that Montefiore thinks that there is a conceptual requirement that a single instance of rule-following should occur in a historical (biographical) context. My prior acts of rule-following are the ancestors of my act today; without them, my lone act has no pedigree; it lies on no trajectory that can be extrapolated into the future. This is all very well, so long as it isn't inflated into a principle that would permit us to infer that there could be no first instance of rule-following, no first adaptation, no first mammal. All these very real categories must have evolved gradually from predecessors that were not 'full participants', 'genuine adaptations', 'true mammals'. The lines *must* be fuzzy.

## Comments on Wilkes

When it comes to explanations of the behaviour of animals (including human beings), is there really all that much difference between the layman's preoccupations and those of the scientist? Of the various disagreements I have with Wilkes, this strikes me as the most fundamental, so I will concentrate on it.

Wilkes contrasts the biologist's (generalised, projectable, systematic) interest in the concept of fitness with the layman's interest in idiosyncratic, ungeneralisable particularities, such as 'what George will do when he discovers that his youngest son has become a skinhead'. I am not convinced. When the biologist gets interested in any particular case of fitness, he must indeed determine some approximation of it via a consideration of many complicated, local factors of the particular case (e.g. in a particular case of snake mimicry, the local frequency of poisonous snakes with a red and black band around their necks, the visual acuity of the resident predators, etc., etc.). If on the other hand he is interested just in fitness as an abstraction (the way mathematical population geneticists typically are), he can ignore such specifics and just pick numbers out of a hat until he gets the sort of case he wants to study. Similarly, the chemist can ignore such complexities as levels of concentration, variation in kinetic energy, etc., if he is interested in the abstract concept of valence, but if he actually wants to make fine-grained particular explanations and predictions of reactions, he will have to gather data on the complexities. And if the layman is interested in just what George will do, he had better gather lots of complex and idiosyncratic facts, while if he is just curious about the phenomenon of paternal love in the abstract, or loyalty or anticipation or fear, then there is an undetailed bird's-eye view he may adopt.

Even less convincing, in my opinion, is Wilkes' claim that '*Explananda* that are not natural kinds — which are not, in other words, amenable to *systematic* explanation — are subjects for commonsense rather than for science'. Perhaps there is a large and important difference between 'common sense' explanation and 'scientific' explanation (though I doubt it), but I am sure that the invocation of 'natural kinds' will not mark it. For, contrary to received philosophical opinion these days, I find the doctrine of natural kinds obscure and of dubious value to *anyone*, not just scientists. So far as I can tell, no philosopher has succeeded in giving a halfway decent *definition* of natural kinds, though it is easy enough to point to paradigm cases: supernova, gold, carbohydrate, plant, animal. But science treats of much more than these. Are earthquakes and avalanches natural kinds? Are lakes? (If lakes are, then why not puddles?) Are prisoner's dilemmas a natural kind? Boom-and-bust cycles? Are evolutionarily stable strategies a natural kind? Are genes, for that matter? Science does honest work about lots of types that are not obviously or intuitively natural kinds. Indeed, the biologist Michael Ghiselin and several philosophers of biology have recently argued that species are *not* best considered to be natural kinds, but individuals — just like George.

I certainly agree that explanations are not all of the same type. I distinguish physical stance explanations, design stance explanations and intentional stance explanations. There are finer distinctions that also seem well-motivated to me, but I don't yet see why we can't use them all in science — and in everyday 'commonsense' explanations.

# CHAPTER 14

# ROUND TWO

*Alan Montefiore*

In chapter 5 I tried to sketch out a linked set of arguments in support of the thesis that we — self-aware, language-using creatures that we are — find ourselves committed in and through our own awareness of ourselves as 'embodied reasoners' to two radically different ways of describing and accounting for ourselves and our world. The one account is that of a causally determinate and/or statistically regular order; the other is of the order of teleology — of goals, intentions and norms. We cannot, according to this thesis, conceive of either order without finding ourselves having, at some point or another, to make reference to the other; but neither can we effect a remainderless reconciliation between them. The reason for this is that they involve fundamentally different presuppositions as to the structure of time and of our own temporality.

One of the most effective ways of getting at the sense of an argument is by way of a characterisation of the opposition against which it is or seems to see itself as being directed. For my part, I found my initial challenge in trying to show why what I took to be David McFarland's initial standpoint — whether put forward in all 'scientific' seriousness or, in part at least, with the intent of fruitful provocation — was one that rested on a radical incoherence. (This is not, of course, to deny that it might for certain purposes prove to be a simplifying device with powerful heuristic advantages.) As I understand McFarland's own second round contribution (chapter 12), he has now to some extent shifted his position — but not as yet, or so it seems to me, as far as, in some sense or another, he must.

First let me try to set aside what seems to be a fairly substantial misunderstanding. McFarland says (on p. 214): 'I suggest that our evolutionary heritage predisposes us to interpret the world in terms of meanings and purposes... The result is that we attribute purpose where there is no purpose, and seek for meaning where there is no meaning. To insist that there must be a meaning to life, a purpose behind our suffering, an intent behind every action, is to take up a political stance ... Examples of this stance occur in this volume.' He then quotes by way of such an example a passage from my chapter 5: 'It is strictly inconceivable that anyone should ever be able to provide a proof of the total dispensability of concepts of effective intentionality. This is not because human beings have somehow been so programmed by the processes of evolutionary selection as to be unable to do otherwise than make use of these concepts ... It is rather that a concept of intentionality must be embodied, or be at work, in the explication to be given of the meaningfulness of any piece of discourse whatever — including, most notably, any which may claim to offer proof of the dispensability of all such concepts.' This last remark has, of course, a specifically polemical function, and was indeed made with specific polemical intent; and if polemical, then in one sense of the word, certainly, political. But — it must surely go without saying — there is no suggestion whatsoever in this argument, either explicit or implicit, of any view at all with respect either to the meaning of life or as to a purpose behind our suffering.

McFarland then goes on: 'That this is a political stance can be seen from a later passage.' And he quotes me once more: 'Inasmuch, then, as the meaningfulness of one's own argument is a surely necessary presupposition of its presentability as argument, whether to oneself or to others, it must equally surely follow that if one could show a reference to intentionality to be necessarily implicit in the very concept of meaningfulness, then to present one's own argument as being in principle wholly intelligible in exclusively non-intentional terms must be as self-defeating as to present it as being itself devoid of meaning ...' Again, this is, of course, an argument designed to secure a certain kind of hold on one's opponent, and I have no particular objection to characterising such a design as political. Indeed, it seems as if it was *qua* political move at least in part an effective one. For McFarland now continues in two (to my mind) significant, even remarkable, paragraphs that are too long to reproduce here, but to which the reader may well find it worthwhile to return (pp. 215-6). These contain, first, an admission: 'If I accept Montefiore's argument that intentionality is a necessary part of language, then I cannot deny that I use intentional processes, because to deny something I would have to use language ... However,' he continues, 'this does not mean that my ordinary, non-linguistic, behaviour is intentional ...' But here, surely, we run into certain very real difficulties. True — the argument to which McFarland is referring is directed to linguistic, i.e. symbolic meaning-bearing behaviour as such and, as such, can carry no strictly necessary implication for any form of behaviour that is strictly non-linguistic. But — and this is very far from being any mere debating point — any precise line between linguistic and non-linguistic behaviour turns out to be peculiarly hard to find.

What, for example, of the movements of my own arm, hand and fingers, co-ordinated, of course, with those of my eyes, as I guide my pen across the paper in the act of writing the first version of this present sentence? These movements are integral to this act as it actually takes place. This is not, evidently, to say that they might not have had their behaviourally quite different functional equivalents if I had performed the same act in terms of sentence production through use of a typewriter, dictaphone or word-processor (not to mention the fact that I might, in writing larger or smaller, have moved my hand across the page in a multitude of interchangeable if different ways). However, I take it to be beyond need of further argument here that *some* physical changes in my bodily disposition are strictly necessary to the performance of any of these functionally equivalent acts of sentence production. Furthermore, what of all those innumerable other acts which, while involving no obviously linguistic behaviour in themselves, are yet indisputably part of the overall performance? The movement towards my desk, the opening of my note-book, the switching on of the electricity, and so on and so on? The fact is that there are not one but at least two different types of problem involved in any attempt to draw (what I should take to be an in principle impossible) a determinate line between linguistic and non-linguistic behaviour. The first lies in the artificiality of any attempt to draw a sharp line between what one might seek to identify as actual linguistic production as such and all the various forms of surrounding 'non-linguistic' enabling and stage-setting activity; the second lies in the fact that the multifarious physical activity involved in whatever forms of bodily behaviour serve as the vehicle of my linguistic behaviour are manifestly part of and continuous with my bodily activity overall. Moreover, for the most part not only am I not in conscious control of most aspects of this activity, but I am very largely not even consciously aware of it as going on at all.

In other words, it seems that McFarland is bound to find it in principle impossible to cordon off such damage as may be done to his position by any (politically?) forced admission of intentional concepts to the area of (his account of) linguistic behaviour by drawing a sharply definitive or definitional line around it; once admitted to this central area they start seeping out.

Thus, it is hard to know what exactly to make of his claim that 'In maintaining that our intentions do not control our behaviour, I am not contradicting Montefiore, nor is this a self-defeating view ... it is part of my thesis that our linguistic behaviour and thinking is not designed to be wholly intelligible, it is designed to be politically effective. So to say that my argument is not wholly intelligible does not worry me too much.' Setting aside for one moment questions of evolutionary design, there need surely be no argument — nor could such argument be very fruitful — over whether or not any given pronouncement or thesis was or could be 'wholly intelligible'; for 'total intelligibility' has surely to be understood as one of those 'ideas of pure reason' whose function is essentially heuristic, but which could not in actual fact ever be encountered by finite human intelligence or exhibited in any given context of human discourse. Nor, certainly, is it any part of my thesis that our linguistic behaviour and thinking is or is designed to be wholly intelligible to ourselves or to anybody else. There is at no point any theoretically determinate end to further possibilities of understanding or misunderstanding. But what, surely, *must* worry McFarland would be any suggestion that his argument was wholly *un*intelligible. (I do not, of course, make any such suggestion. I believe his argument to be mistaken, but I take myself to have at any rate some understanding of it; I could not otherwise, of course, believe it to be mistaken or set out to show it to be so.)

It is on this, surely unremarkable, claim that my thesis in fact turns, namely that our linguistic behaviour and thinking cannot paradigmatically be represented — still less represent itself — as wholly *un*intelligible; and on the, it still seems to me not very much more remarkable, claim that such intelligibility as it may have or must claim for itself is bound up with the presupposition of its own intentionality. It would — no doubt whatsoever — be absurd to suppose that our conscious intentions exerted anything like a 100% degree of control over our behaviour, linguistic behaviour and thinking included. But it would surely — and by now it would seem on McFarland's own however sideways admission — be equally absurd, self-defeating indeed, to suggest that none of our linguistic behaviour or thought was governed in any way by any of our intentions at all. To make the point in a perhaps unduly *ad hominem* way, when McFarland moves backwards and forwards between considerations of total intelligibility and/or control and considerations of total *un*intelligibility and/or lack of control, I can readily take the effective force of his argument as having a political design; but I am still bound to suppose that in his production of the words that he uses — 'political', 'control', 'behaviour' and so on — he is intending them to carry meaning broadly common to his and my and our readers' understanding, and, consequently, that the gestures by which he produces them were, broadly speaking, produced in response to his own meaningful intentions.

McFarland then goes on to argue: 'if our language is constrained by being organised on an intentional basis, then there may be some aspects of reality which may be difficult, or impossible, to express.' Well ... yes and no. What must here — presumably — be at stake is the expression of non-intentional aspects of reality. Nobody, I take it, would seek to deny that reality, as we conceive it within the terms of 'our own' predominantly scientific and secular culture, contains many non-intentional aspects. Of course, elements of intentionality and normativity will enter, in inextricably constitutive ways, into the formation of that culture and, more specifically, into the characterisation of whatever particular aspects of reality in non-intentional terms; concepts of non-intentional characterisation are, *qua* concepts, as intentional and as subject to constraints of normative reiterability as any other. But what McFarland may still have in mind is the genuinely impossible-fully-to-express possibility that the 'truth' about reality would, if it could be given, *have* to be expressed in wholly non-intentional terms.

According to the broadly Kantian type view of which I tried to give some sort of sketch in chapter 5, this possibility may indeed seem to impose itself upon us, not merely as one possibility among others but as one from which we cannot escape. That is to say, (i) that from the standpoint of an observational and experimental science — two terms which, incidentally, we can now see to be much more closely interconnected than they once appeared to be — we have no choice but to look for a way of structuring (at any rate macroscopic) events and their temporality such that we may always conceive of what is the case at any given moment of time as the (causally or statistically 'determined') outcome of what has gone before; (ii) that this standpoint, or a standpoint of this general sort, is indispensable to us in our conceptualisation of our experience as that of an objective and common world; and (iii) that no conceptualisation of experience that is not that of such a world is open to us as the kind of beings that we find ourselves to be. Up to a point at the very least, one might see a view of this sort as presenting notable advantages to anyone seeking to pursue the sort of research programme in which McFarland is interested. For it not only endorses, it actually insists on the necessity of a perspective within which *all* physically identifiable phenomena — the production of sounds, marks, movements, etc. — must be characterisable and in principle explicable within the same fundamental set of non-intentional terms. Within this perspective there are no impossible lines of conceptual discontinuity to be drawn between what is to count as linguistic behaviour and what is not; there are no 'no-go' areas for the McFarlands of the laboratory world. The whole of the non-intentional universe, and in one sense that means everything that there is to be observed, is open to their investigation.

On the other hand, of course, an intentional perspective is according to this view as fundamentally indispensable to our own understanding of ourselves as is that of non-intentionality. If it is the ambition of a McFarland-type scientist to be able in principle to provide one complete and exhaustive account of the human subject and human reflexivity, then — on this sort of view — it is an ambition that, though entirely proper, is nevertheless in principle doomed to irresolvable frustration. Moreover, no ground can in principle be provided for declaring either perspective to be truer of reality than the other; or rather, no determinate sense can be made of any reference to a reality of which the truth might be reflected through one perspective rather than the other, since neither perspective can in fact be articulated in terms which do not in the last resort involve reference to the other. 'Reality' is, on this view, of irreducibly dual aspect (at least). Or, if references to dualisms have become altogether too loaded to be any longer acceptable, 'reality' we might say, in perhaps more acceptable terms, is marked by irreducible complementarities.

If McFarland's and my views seem here to stand in starkest opposition to each other, this is in part, no doubt, because we are at the same time in effective agreement as to the existence of some sort of basic incompatibility between the commitments of intentional and causal-cum-statistical concepts. Here it would seem that we should both, from our otherwise different standpoints, disagree with someone such as Dennett, who, while agreeing very firmly with me on the indispensability of what he calls the intentional stance, has in his various writings provided as full and as ingenious (and as readable) a set of arguments as virtually anyone else designed to show that the impression of any such basic incompatibility rests in the end on nothing but illusion. These arguments would treat intentions and rational calculation as causal factors among others, as fully determined in their occurrence as any other causal features of the world — but also, and by the same token, factors that contribute in their turn to the control of the onward production of behavioural events. It is on this point, of course, that McFarland takes issue with Dennett as well as with myself.

At the heart of Dennett's disagreement with me, as I understand it at least, lies a difference of understanding of the nature of rational thought. Before taking up this quite fundamental issue, however, it may be as well to try and deal with a number of lesser possible misunderstandings. In view of the great clarity, ingenuity and, indeed, general importance of Dennett's writings on these matters, it is worth doing so in some little detail.

First, then. In an earlier set of comments on my chapter 5 which Dennett sent to me, he gave expression to a certain (indeed quite understandable) disquiet at my apparently strategic use of the expression 'and "full" participant in discourse' (see p. 65). 'What,' he asked me, 'would a world be like in which the "communicators", the "scientists", etc. were all of them only 99 percenters? (Would it be, say, a world inhabited by robot "scientists" who only *seemed* to have genuine intentionality? This is the absolutism I suspect.)'

I readily acknowledge that my use here of the word 'full' could have been misleading — even though I did take the rather easy-going precaution of enclosing it in inverted commas, and of glossing the expression 'full participant' as meaning 'nothing more mysterious — nor rigorously precise — than paradigmatically acceptable as a standard member of the relevant speech community'. The fact of the matter is, of course, that there is and strictly speaking could be no such thing as a definitively 'full' participant in discourse. My thought — my intention — in introducing the expression was rather the following. I took it as a central feature of my argument that 'to have the capacity for language is to have at least the potential for reflection on that capacity; the user of language is at least potentially capable of a self-aware self-recognition as such.' But I wanted precisely to avoid any suggestion, (i) of either an empirical claim or a definitional insistence that every user of language to however limited a degree must himself or herself (or perhaps even itself) possess the capacity for further and more sophisticated progress; and, (ii) of any clearly determinable cut-off point on some empirically given scale of potential capacities. My point was rather that the potential for reflexivity is a property of language itself. It is a property not so much of the individual, quasi-Cartesian consciousness as of the conceptually determined need for each participant in discourse, as participant in an essentially inter-personal or social enterprise of reciprocal checks and counterchecks, to have available in principle the resources to signal to himself and to others his recognition of the position in discourse which he or they may occupy at any given point in the open system of exchange. That is to say that the enterprise of language in which he is engaged must contain within its possibilities the means necessary for all of its participants so to identify themselves to themselves and to others, and to recognise and acknowledge each other's self-identifications.

Of course, very young beginners, mental defectives, some mentally afflicted and, for all that I am prepared *here* to argue one way or the other, some animals at least may be said to participate to some extent, and indeed be practically accepted as to some extent participating, in discourse without them being supposed to have gained (or retained) any insight into or mastery of reflexive modes of speech or thought; and many of them may in fact lack the empirical potential for acquiring it. I am *not* arguing either that such cases may not be very common, let alone that they do not exist. Nor am I trying to argue that we may not often have good, even compelling, reason to regard as 'fully' intentional behaviour that we may find it natural to characterise as only 'semi-' or 'quasi-' linguistic or, indeed, as not linguistic at all. I am arguing simply that it is in the context of our own paradigmatically linguistic behaviour — the relatively sophisticated behaviour of, for example, those who indulge in argument or reflection about the appropriate characterisation and analysis of their own linguistic and reflective capacities — that we find ourselves willy nilly committed to the use of intentional concepts. It is here that we find ourselves committed to an intentional stance that we cannot coherently renounce; and that being so, on looking back from this standpoint, as it were, we may find it most plausible to treat as similarly intentional forms of behaviour which, from our 'fully' conceptualising vantage point, we can see as standing in one form or another of continuity with our own.

*What* forms of continuity, the question may be pushed at this point, should we count as being continuous enough for these purposes? This is in effect one of the two main questions which a reader of our first round contributions thought it appropriate to put to me. It still seems to me that to try and answer this (clearly important) question in any detail would be to go well beyond my present brief. However, my general feeling would be that if we try to go on thinking the situation along the lines suggested by (some version of) the 'Kantian dualism' model, we shall be led to hypothesise in something like the following way: (i) That all events of which we may acquire observational or experimental knowledge must in principle be susceptible of a causal-cum-statistical characterisation, ordering and explanation of some sort: (ii) That whenever we may find it indispensable, or at least of an overwhelmingly plausible aid to understanding, to characterise what we, or other people or animals or whatever, do in goal-directive or intentional terms, we still know that there must exist as always this other causal-cum-statistical perspective within the terms and limits of which everything which occurs may also be observed, characterised and explained. Whether criteria of identity might in principle be available by reference to which one might be able to give clearly meaningful content to any assertion that 'exactly the same' events might be characterised in one way (from one perspective) or the other depending simply on the context of interest or concern is, in my view, more than doubtful. (Indeed, this point, though made in very different ways by different philosophers, is basically a familiar one.) However, (iii) it *would* be very plausible to hypothesise that for beings situated, as it were, at the point of intersection of two such perspectives — for embodied rational beings, as first and most compelling example, but perhaps for other less rational, less reflexive beings as well — the occurrence of certain characteristic, even characteristically detailed, patterns of causally-cum-statistically characterised states and events should present itself as a *de facto* necessary and sufficient condition for the occurrence of similarly characteristic patterns of goal-directive states, activity or reflection and vice versa. In which case, (iv), and on the assumption that such a supposition had received 'sufficient' confirmation in a 'sufficiently' broad range of cases, it may not be unreasonable to suppose further that, whenever observation discloses the existence of causal-cum-statistical states and patterns of events closely analogous to those already known to occur within symbolically communicating systems in established connection with their states or activity of expressed intention or reflection occurring also within systems that are as such incapable (or apparently incapable) of symbolic communication, the behaviour and 'outlook' of such systems may plausibly be presumed to have an at least rudimentary intentional or, at any rate, goal-directive aspect as well.

However, for present purposes, as I said, all this must be regarded as no more than bare indications of lines of possible further speculation.

I am also considerably intrigued by Dennett's remark to me that, while he is 'in great sympathy with the line of argument about (what I would call) the inescapability of the intentional stance in our own cases ... I think that even as you express it, it leaves a loophole of sorts. The Churchlands, for instance, could grant that *some* norm-presupposing mutually adopted stance ... is a necessary condition for pursuing science ... but hold out for the possibility that it could be radically (and unimaginably ...) different from the folk psychology of to-day. When the schmientists of the future gather, they will not sit around trying to *persuade* each other of the *truth* of their beliefs, but will in some other way compare rival ways of situating themselves in the world, appealing (somehow) to some mutually honoured norms.'

What exactly is the point that Dennett feels should be conceded here — even though he regards it as 'so lacking in detail as to be negligible'? In terms of contemporary resonance, however indeterminate in detail that resonance may be, the stakes would in fact seem to be anything but trivial. One may think of Thomas Kuhn, of Richard Rorty, of Foucault, of Feyerabend, of Jean-Francois Lyotard among many others who, in one way or another, either have or have been taken as having argued that the assumption of some ultimately common framework of universal reason or 'objective' truth of the world is but an enlightenment myth to be discarded, by those who have seen through it, in favour of an in principle endless and undecidable plurality of incommensurably different 'grand stories'. No doubt, there *can* be no sense to any supposition that there might be just one and one only correct and determinate way of describing the world. But that does not mean that one can attribute any better sense to the supposition of a plurality of conceptual schemes so radically different from each other as to rule out all possibility of constructing communicative passages between them; or that one can meaningfully give up the assumption of an ability common to all participants in discourse to distinguish between the broadly correct and the broadly incorrect (in basic situational terms, the broadly true and the broadly false) usages of whatever the terms of their own local and no doubt always imperfect mastery of language.

In fact, the point at issue here is of such fundamental importance that it seems worth trying to set it out once again. To be engaged in discourse (of whatever sort) is to be engaged in essentially normative activity. To engage in normative activity is only possible to those who can in principle recognise (though not necessarily infallibly, of course) others as likewise participant in that activity, and who can furthermore recognise elements of the behaviour of others as normative and as constituting prima facie evidence of their having 'got it right or wrong' in terms of their own attempted following of the common norm. This is the argument to the necessary possibility in principle of a public or interpersonal check. But it is at the very heart of this ability to recognise a check for what it is that one should have a firm grip on the distinction between making something to be the case on the basis of one's own unilateral decisions or preferences and acknowledging it to be the case *whether one likes it or not*. It is this latter acknowledgement which constitutes that minimal recognition of and respect for truth without which there is no capacity for meaning — because without it there is no capacity for distinguishing between the successful and unsuccessful, the correct and incorrect attempts at following a rule or norm and hence in effect no ground for genuinely normative behaviour at all.

So while we may, perhaps, conjure up some picture of 'the schmientists of the future' sitting around comparing their rival(?) 'ways of situating themselves in the world' without any of them being necessarily committed to claiming the provable invalidity of the others' yet somehow rival accounts, we cannot, as indeed Dennett allows, suppose them not to acknowledge respect for certain 'mutually honoured norms'; but this means, by the same token, that we cannot suppose them not to acknowledge certain common criteria of truth and falsity. That is to say that the very meaningfulness and reciprocal intelligibility of their apparently merely different ways of situating themselves in the world is bound to their ability in principle to acknowledge the truth — a truth that may be characterised as 'objective' in contradistinction to their own purely 'subjective' feelings and preferences — of the checks that each others' linguistic and associated intentional behaviour provides on each others' linguistically normative performances.

Moreover, over and above that respect for the 'objectivity' of checks that is called for by the norms of meaningfulness itself, a way of situating oneself in the world can only function as such in so far as it is, within its own terms of reference, responsive to the world's actual configurations. Granted (the obvious point) that there is no way of articulating these configurations other than via one conceptualisation or another, it remains the case that no way of situating oneself can be entirely free-wheeling. If a way of situating oneself is to function as such, there must inevitably take place some sort of process of mutual accommodation between it and the 'actual facts' of one's situation. So while it does, certainly, remain theoretically possible for an indefinite number of different accounts all to accommodate equally well the underdetermining facts of a nevertheless common world, they must still be commensurable in terms of those associated and interlinking descriptions by virtue of which alone they are intelligible as being indeed different accounts of one and the same world. They must, furthermore, be comparable in terms of their ongoing success or failure in accommodating that world as it continues to develop — unless, of course, it turns out that the logic of their mutual relationships renders them extensionally equivalent, in which case there would be no factual content to their alleged 'rivalry' after all. (This is not, it hardly needs saying, by any means an impossible nor even a disreputable scenario. Different religious accounts of the world, for example, may certainly be said to function as ways in which men situate themselves within it, and may differ widely in religious and prescriptive content while yet being equally adaptable to whatever facts of whatever situation. It remains the case, however, that they will only be intelligible to and discussable by those who share at least to some degree a common respect for common conceptual norms and who have in common an ability to recognise such facts as may constitute the ever indispensable checks on how the performances of the different participants in discourse stand in relation to these norms.)

The stakes in all this debate are in general, then, anything but trivial. For immediate purposes, however, it is perhaps even more important to insist once more on the point that the ability to follow norms, including the ability to assess the normative performances of others, is inextricably bound up with the ability to integrate over time. And it is here that I should try too to respond to the other main query very fairly addressed to me by the first press reader: ' ... it is unclear how he [Montefiore] wishes to link the fact that intentions point to the future with the idea that rule-following behaviour is necessarily not "one-off". The latter idea may require that the agent be able to conceive of other similar cases, but this won't explain his ability to represent a future state of affairs, which may never have been actualised before.'

In fact, it is no part of my 'intention' to seek to *explain* anyone's ability to envisage or to 'represent' a future state of affairs which may never have been actualised before. Moreover, this reference to the possibility of the future state of affairs never having been actualised before introduces a certain number of interesting but complicated red herrings. For one thing, whether any given state of affairs is to be seen as occurring for the first time or not must depend *inter alia* but always crucially on the level of generality of the description through which reference to it is made. For another, any properly general discussion of these matters must presumably cover equally the ability to envisage or 'represent' past states of affairs which were never in fact actualised, or of which one is ignorant whether they were actualised or not, as well as possible temporally present but spatially remote states of affairs of which, again, one may be uncertain whether or not they actually obtain. Indeed, from this overall angle, the most relevant issue would seem to turn on the sense or senses that we may or must here attach to the notion of 'representation', a notion that I found myself being led to treat with some wariness in my first contribution. The *present* point, however, if one may put it that way, surely concerns the future as future and the connection between intentional reference to the future and the fact that normative or 'rule-following' behaviour is necessarily not 'one-off'. My argument, if it is successful, is still only designed to show something of what we have to presuppose of ourselves — of what, indeed, we find ourselves 'always already' presupposing of ourselves by virtue of our own undeniable engagement in conceptual or discursive activity, an engagement that is undeniable, to repeat the by now familiar point, in as much as any denial must itself perforce recognise itself as itself discursive.

The way in which I see the connection is — overbriefly — as follows. We may start once again from the position that to think, to speak, to engage in meaningful discourse is to participate in an essentially normative activity. To engage in normative activity is not merely to behave or to perform in a certain way. It is to behave in a certain way with a view to meeting certain demands, to satisfying certain criteria, *to achieving certain ends*; it is to hold oneself open or ready to respond by way of appropriate adjustments to the checks that one must in principle recognise that one may always encounter. It hardly needs repeating, perhaps, that it is no part of my thesis that anyone thus engaged in normative activity must at all times carry within his or her consciousness determinate representations of these ends, criteria or possible checks and possible responses to them as part of its explicit content. One might say rather that to engage in normative activity is to be adjusted in a certain way to time and to one's own temporality. Crucially this involves the reflexive capacity to presuppose one's own self-identity over a period of time; for in as much as normative or 'rule-following' behaviour is necessarily not 'one-off', to engage in it carries with it the necessary assumption that this the present occasion is not the only one on which one might find oneself engaged in activity governed by the same norm. Moreover, though one can, certainly, envisage occasions which might present themselves as the last on which an agent might conceive himself as following a particular norm or even, in a case of ritual suicide, for example, following any norm at all, such occasions cannot in principle be typical; not all or even most occasions can be last ones. Typically, then, to engage in normative activity is to be adjusted in a certain way towards the future; and to engage in the normative activity of participation, in one way or another, in meaningful discourse is, typically, to stand in relation to oneself in a position of potential self-awareness of one's own openness to one's own future, as well, of course, as of one's own continuity with one's own past, and of the bearing of one's meaningful intentions upon it.

None of this need or should be taken to imply that all intentional activity is normative — nor even, perhaps, that all normative activity is intentional, or at any rate consciously so. One might, for example, best understand as normative a great deal of behaviour that is not only best classified as habitual, but whose habitual disposition has never been consciously acquired and whose social significance may not easily be made explicitly recognisable to those most closely concerned (c.f. Pierre Bourdieu's concept of 'habitus'). But I am not here seeking to map the whole general territories of the normative or the intentional. The thesis for which I here argue is — to return to my initial formulations — that there is at least one central area in which the concepts of an effective intentionality are strictly indispensable, that this is the area of participation in meaningful discourse, that in this area the intentions in question are paradigmatically to be understood as those involved in the rule-governed production of appropriate sounds, marks or gestures in such a way that they be intelligible as bearers of symbolic meaning, and that any agent or subject presumed by itself or others to be engaged in such activity must *ipso facto* be presumed to be not only identical with itself throughout the relevant periods of time but, moreover, capable in its normative stance of taking appropriate account both of its past and of its future. Whatever may or may not be the case in other areas of intentionality or normativity, in this central paradigmatic area we are committed to the recognition of our own intentionality by virture of the very same sets of considerations that commit us to the acknowledgement of the normativity of our own discursive activity. These same considerations likewise commit us to this vision of our own temporality, the temporality of subjects whose own self-identities over time are as much tied to their capacity for directing themselves in terms of their conceptions of a possible future as it is to their capacity for a remembering re-presentation of the past.

Dennett, if I understand him aright, would once again find himself in deep selective disagreement with what I am here trying to argue. In his very interesting paper on *Evolution, Error and Intentionality* (Dennett, 1987) he argues powerfully for his view that even our own human intentionality and capacity for normative behaviour (for the failure of error as well as for the success of 'getting it right') is at bottom to be understood as in principle nothing more than vastly more sophisticated versions of the capacities possessed by what he calls a 'two-bitser', that is to say a machine capable of distinguishing between coins for whose acceptance it has been designed and all those other coins or similar shaped and weighted objects which it has been designed — hopefully — to reject. I cannot, of course, attempt to engage with all the detail of his argument here, but I must at least try to clarify what I take to be the points of main disagreement.

First, however, a point of no little importance on which we do *not* disagree. Dennett believes that however subtly we may seek to refine the meanings of the terms through which we may characterise our own beliefs and intentions, there must always remain within them some itself indeterminate element of indeterminacy.

So do I. That is, I agree with him not only in the view that there is in general principle no privileged access to the facts of our own fully determinate beliefs and intentions; I agree with him also in the view that there are no such facts.

Why does this matter so much? Dennett seems to believe that what he calls 'the doctrine of original intentionality' is tightly bound to a belief in real, determinate meanings and intentions; and certainly he sees himself as opposed to the doctrine of original intentionality. Do I see myself as committed to maintaining this doctrine? That must depend, of course, on what exactly I am to take it to mean. At any rate, it is here that I suspect some of the sources both of misunderstanding and of disagreement to lie.

Artefacts, in my view anyhow, two-bitsers, for example, or robots of very much more complex purpose and ingenuity of design, typically have only a 'derived intentionality', that is an intentionality derived from that of their designers and makers. This we may take to be true even of robots which are so designed as to have monitorial access to their own internal states and the capacity to build on to and extend their own operations in such a way as to take their performance far beyond what their designers may themselves have foreseen or what they are now capable of predicting in advance of their occurrence. Dennett argues that we too may be regarded as artefacts, designed in our case by 'Mother Nature' acting through the devices of evolutionary selection, the major difference being that 'Mother Nature' is not to be thought of as having been working to any conscious design — is not, indeed, to be credited with any intentionality of her own at all. Unless, of course, we are with Dennett to call the '*blind* and *unrepresenting* source of our own sightful and insightful powers of representation' 'the intentionality of natural selection'.

It will be evident, no doubt, that my own inclination must be to treat this so-called 'intentionality of natural selection' as no genuine sort of intentionality at all. It would be altogether foolish, however, to relapse back into reliance on some stipulative use of or equally stipulative refusal to use any given word. So what really is at stake here? Dennett says: 'Certainly we can describe all processes of natural selection without appeal to such intentional language, but at enormous cost of cumbersomeness, lack of generality and unwanted detail. We would miss the pattern that was there, the pattern that permits prediction and supports counter-factuals.' As must be tediously clear by now, I belive not only that we can so describe all processes of natural selection, but likewise all processes of human (let alone other forms of organic) behaviour without appeal to intentional language, and yet in a sense leave nothing out — nothing, that is to say, concerning the occurrence or non-occurrence of what may be ascertained to take place or obtain in observable space-time. There would, no doubt, be comparable cost in terms of cumbersomeness, etc., though at certain levels of enquiry there might also be compensating gains in terms of detailed understanding and effective power. However, and this belongs to the very core of my thesis, while we may be pushed by the demands of convenience into appealing to intentional language in our descriptive engagements with the processes of natural selection, there is no insuperable problem in principle in seeing how we could dispense with it altogether; in the case of our own active and reflective/reflexive engagements in meaningful discourse, on the other hand, we can see why in principle we could never dispense with the 'intentional stance'.

The dispensability in principle of the intentional stance is what seems to me, then, most sharply to distinguish the normative-intentional characterisation of artefacts, be they two-bitsers or the most sophisticated of Dennett's hypothetical robots, from the normative-intentional characterisations that we find ourselves having *in*dispensably to apply to ourselves as we find ourselves participants in meaningful discourse.

I fully agree with, indeed I argue for, the view that there is every reason to suppose that normative-intentional characteristics only occur when certain non-normative-intentional conditions also obtain; and I have also argued for the view that it may indeed be reasonable to attribute 'genuine' intentionality to those animals and perhaps other organisms or entities in which we may discover or even build in non-normative-intentional conditions of sufficiently analogous similarity. But I see no prospective sense in the ascription of such conditions or characteristics to 'Mother Nature' or to the processes of evolutionary selection as such.

If I am to adopt Dennett's title of 'the doctrine of original intentionality' as appropriate to what I should myself have been more inclined to dignify as 'the doctrine of indispensable intentionality', the originality should in no way be taken to lie in some peculiar determinacy of original intentions, let alone in any guaranteed privileged access to them. Nor should it be taken to lie in the absence of any plausible evolutionary explanation of why intention and meaning-forming creatures should have appeared and survived in the way that they have. Indeed, I should be more inclined to suppose that our own temporal nature as beings fundamentally turned towards both past and future is largely independent of any capacity we may have to give determinate content whether to our memories, our expectations or our intentions, and in the last resort, therefore, independent of our capacity for self-awareness or any sense of our own self-identity (which are dependent on these things). People suffering from severe disturbance to their memory or ability to plan for the future even to the smallest degree do not in general seem to lose their sense of having had a past or of being turned towards a future; on the contrary, it is in many cases precisely their awareness of having forgotten their past and of not knowing or being able to decide where they are going that they find so upsetting. Conversely, as I understand the matter, there are some mental conditions in which the sufferers appear to retain full intellectual grasp of the past and of the likely course of the future while having lost all sense of its 'reality'; this too has its own very different but also very frightening aspect.

All the same, the expression 'original intentionality' may capture something of true importance. This lies in part in the sense in which the intentionally acting agent finds himself acting under the necessary supposition that his own intentions make — under normal conditions at any rate — a genuinely 'originating' or initiating contribution to the ongoing course of events as one of their effectively necessary conditions. This effectiveness, of course, is not something that Dennett would dispute. On the contrary, it is, as we have already seen, a point on which he and I are agreed against McFarland. However, for Dennett the agent's own intentions may or, indeed, must be seen as themselves belonging on an equal footing to the same onward-going complex of causally linked events and states of affairs. The one peculiarity of the position is that the agent himself or herself cannot possibly know the full details of that linkage and must accordingly make the best estimates of the situation of which he or she is capable. His estimates, on the Dennett view, are genuine estimates, as genuine as are the decisions that flow from them. They have their full share of causal efficacy and so the agent has in principle his or her own full share of freedom of choice and responsibility. The fact that his estimates and his decisions were themselves causally fully determined in no way means that they were somehow inevitable. But it is here, it seems to me, that Dennett loses the other and equally important part of the sense of 'original intentionality'; and it is here, no doubt, that we do find ourselves in some sort of fundamental if not entirely straightforward disagreement.

Let me return to my view that artefacts typically have only a 'derived intentionality', unless, of course, there are quite special 'grounds for construing at least some of their behaviour as, in part at least, autonomously intentional' (see chapter 5, p. 64). Dennett quite explicitly disagrees with this view: 'I don't see any argument for this claim and don't myself believe it' (p. 235). He goes on (fairly enough) to express some suspicion about my use of the expression 'autonomously intentional' — but also his doubt as to whether 'a debate over that point would be fruitful.' Certainly, I should be prepared to say with him that the kind of autonomy that the Viking spacecraft acquired when its designer-controllers turned control over to it 'is not a particularly vaunted property'. But what I understand by 'autonomous intentionality' in this context is that intentionality from whose perspective present and future states and events are not merely not fully ascertainable on the basis of knowledge of the past, but remain in part not fully determined by it; and, from this perspective, that absence of full causal determination must be presumed to apply to the formation of intentions and decisions themselves. This is that other sense of 'original intentionality', in terms of which an intention must see itself as not only originating but as in some degree also properly original.

I am not here suggesting, of course, that the formation or carrying out of intentions are to be thought of as events like any others that may occur in the ordinary temporal sequence and pattern of events except only that they have no causally determining antecedents — that they are, as it were, genuinely random events. Like Dennett, I should take this to be a senseless suggestion. My thesis is rather that thoroughgoing causal-cum-statistical discourse, on the one hand, and the discourse of normative intentionality, on the other hand, present us with two different ways of structuring time and hence with two different ways of characterising such events: that these two different ways of structuring time, though each irreducibly parasitic on the other, are nevertheless incompatible in that the governing principle of the one is that all that is of the past or present may be fully described or characterised without any implied reference to what may occur in the future (except in so far as that future has likewise to be thought of as determined or shown to be statistically probable by those very descriptions or characterisations), while within the terms of the other no complete characterisation of the past and present is possible without reference to a future within which what is going or not going actually to occur remains in part open and characteristically *un*determined by the characterisation of its past: that both these different ways of structuring time figure among the indispensably necessary presuppositions of our discourse taken as a whole: and that there is at least as strong reason for according ontological primacy to the intentional mode of discourse as to that of the causal-statistical. To this thesis I added in my first round contribution one or two excessively sketchy speculations as to how we may look to cope with this situation of apparently partially incongruent temporality. I shall not attempt to pursue them further here — though it seems to me virtually certain that they will continue to be pursued by others far better qualified to do so than myself.

Here we may return rather to what, a then unexpected number of pages ago, I took to lie at the heart of my disagreement with Dennett, namely a difference of understanding of the presuppositions of rational thought. As I struggle to work out the direction that my argument is to take, to decide what I am to say and in what order, what marks or noises I am to produce as the vehicle of my thought or attempted communication, I have to suppose the order of my production to be determined by my own attempt to follow the guidance of certain norms in their complex relations with each other, norms that are internal to the activity that I am engaged in, rather than by the relations in which the behavioural movements through which my reasoning activity is in fact carried on stand to all those innumerable preceding movements, states and changes to which they undoubtedly are related and from which *as* behavioural movements they can no doubt be shown to follow; for these lie well beyond the bounds of any argument constructing activity whatsoever. In this sense I have to suppose the order of my reasoned argumentation to be, as it were, self-determined, that is, determined by the principles that are at once constitutive of its own structure as rational argument and of my own activity as that of a reasoning agent. Of course, as embodied reasoning agent I can only develop the thinking of my argument in, through and as a given temporal sequence. But I have to suppose the 'origin' of this temporal embodiment of rational order to lie not in what temporally preceded its appearances in the overall order of the world, but in the principles of rationality and meaning from which it proceeds. And if anyone tries to mount an argument to show that this supposition may nevertheless be nothing but an illusion, he will find his own very argument to be rooted in precisely the presupposition whose illusoriness he is trying to prove.

And if indeed this is what I have to suppose, or something very much along these lines, then I cannot suppose in the same movement of thought that the order of my thinking and of my argument, far from having its own constitutive principles, was in fact already determined by factors not only temporally prior to my first engagement in the argument, but presenting in themselves no rational or meaning-bearing characteristics at all. I have thus to suppose that the order of my thought, to the degree that it is successful as thinking, is not a causal order and that the sequence of my argument is determined by other than purely causal factors.

None of this is to say that I do not also have to recognise that there must, as always, be other perspectives or stances from which the order of my performances may be observed and studied, not as embodying segments and structures of meaningful discourse but simply as behaviour, or as sub-behavioural physical sequence; and from such perspectives all that is observed may *ipso facto* be presumed to be subject to causal-cum-statistical explanation. Nor is it to say that I have to (or should dare to) presume the order or content of any given argument or thought sequence that I may actually produce to be determined by purely rational considerations. On the contrary, I am not and, indeed, could not consistently account myself to be a purely rational being; ironically enough, the very possibility of such knowledge as I may hope to acquire of myself depends on my knowing myself as embodied being and, as such, a member of the causally structured temporal order. I must, therefore, know that the actual order and content of all my thoughts and arguments must be to some extent, or from one perspective, open to explanation as causally determined by all sorts of factors external to their own inner rationale — though, my empirical self-knowledge being, as all empirical knowledge, necessarily mediate and imperfect, I must know too that it can never be complete.

My thesis in no way seeks to deny any of this. It maintains only that in the order and in the act of my would-be rational endeavours I cannot suppose myself to be entirely causally determined. I can suppose such a thing of myself neither as producer of my own reasoning thought nor as I seek to follow, to understand and to assess what I take to be the meaningful discourse of others. Nor can I suppose it of those others whose apparently meaningful discourse I seek to understand in the act of my seeking to understand it. Nor can they — or you, my listener or my reader — suppose it of me, as they — or you — seek to understand and to assess my argument. (Though what they or you can or must suppose of me *qua* pure observers of my not discursively interpreted behaviour is, of course, very much another story.)

Kant, so it seems to me, put the gist of this very well, and with unaccustomed brevity and clarity, near the beginning of the third and last chapter of his *Groundwork of the Metaphysic of Morals*: 'but we cannot possibly conceive of a reason as being consciously directed from outside in regard to its judgements; for in that case the subject would attribute the determination of his power of judgement not to his reason, but to an impulsion. Reason must look upon itself as the author of its own principles independently of alien influences.'

This, my contribution to round two of our debates, has by now become already much too long, and I have as yet said nothing by way of direct reaction or response to the first round contributions of my three other fellow-contributors. In fact, much of what I have here tried to say, or to a large extent to re-say in hopefully less obscure or condensed ways, has very considerable bearing on what I should likewise need to say by way of situating myself in response to Denis Noble, Kathy Wilkes and Shawn Lockery as well. If I have thus focussed on the positions and arguments presented by McFarland and Dennett, it is no doubt that I perceived them as posing the most immediate and direct challenges to my own; but this is by no means to say that the other three contributions do not present me with challenges of equal interest and importance. Indeed, once embarked on a difficult and fascinating argument it is always tempting to go on ... and on! However, there comes also always a time when enough has to be enough. So let me come to a present halt with just two further remarks.

First, a remark which is in effect little more than a reiteration of a point made in chapter 5. On reading and re-reading the texts of my fellow-contributors, I am again struck by the very great use there made of the concept of a 'representation'. Already in chapter 5 I tried to express a certain sense of uncertainty, if not indeed of distrust, that I have come to feel for this concept. The problem, no doubt, is not that no proper use can be given to the term 'representation' nor, indeed, that there is not an indispensable need for it or some closely allied term or set of terms. It is rather that it comes all too naturally to gather a number of different if interconnected uses, and that it is often far from easy to see how it is shifting between them. In particular, it sometimes seems as if the term is in effect functioning as a would-be, albeit impossible, bridging concept between the two incommensurable forms of discourse — the causal-cum-statistical and the normative-intentional. Perhaps we do in fact need two not wholly assimilable but nevertheless not totally unconnected versions of the concept of a representation — versions whose difference as well as whose point of connection would lie in the different forces at work in the concept's contained reference to the present, depending on the temporal structuring of the form of discourse in which it was being used.

At any rate, one may feel reasonably confident in saying that the sense or senses of the term 'representation' can in no way be taken for granted. Indeed, it might almost be possible to re-write virtually the whole of these debates in terms of a deeper, more extended and more carefully detailed discussion of the varied actual and possible uses of this ubiquitous term. For the moment, however, we may simply note once again that it will in any case be a mistake to suppose that one might be able to define intentionality in terms of representations. It is, rather, by reference to the subject's way of relating to its own temporality, and in particular to its own future that one may hope to distinguish between the two versions of the concept of a representation rather than vice versa.

Finally, another tentatively speculative suggestion. Throughout this whole discussion it has been almost irresistibly apparent that time, as one might say, is of the essence of the matter — time and the way in which the subject relates to or incorporates the time of its meaningful, intentional activity and the time of its own embodiment. If we are indeed confronted with a (transcendentally) inescapable need to postulate and to make use of two never wholly commensurable ways of structuring time, two never wholly commensurable forms of discourse, this amounts to a confrontation with a somehow inextricable duality of our own being. In the spatio-temporality of our embodiment we normally take it to go unproblematically without saying that we occupy a certain extended portion of space within which it is possible to define all sorts of other sub-spaces, without our feeling constrained to look for the 'reality' of our spatial identity in the determination of any very rigorously precise boundaries to our selves. My — no doubt rather simple-minded — suggestion would be that we might, for the purposes of our spatio-temporal embodiment, take it to be equally unproblematic that we occupy a certain extended portion of time, within which it will always be possible to define all sorts of other sub-portions of time, without our feeling constrained to look for the 'reality' of our 'present' existence in the determination of any very rigorously precise boundaries to our selves. How far such a suggestion might help lead to a softening of any apparent strains in the relations between causal-cum-statistical and normative-intentional ways of structuring our differently experienciable world is a question that I am not in a position to embark on here and now. But it might well bear further consideration in some possible future round of these debates.

CHAPTER 15

# WHAT DO INTENTIONS DO?

*Denis Noble*

It is intriguing to see how the debate in this volume differs from the university seminars that originally formed its foundation. The live seminars were full of controversy, some of which has been eliminated from the written chapters. This arises partly because issues on which disagreement was not as profound as first appeared have been worked through to the point at which no-one any longer wishes to formulate them in print. For example, we once thought it important to classify the types of behaviour that could be said to be goal-directed and to see whether a line could be drawn at some point to demarcate intentional from non-intentional behaviour. The basis of this classification was the idea that the types of behaviour could be arranged on an organisational basis into a spectrum starting from simple direct causation, which was then elaborated by adding feedback regulation, representation of goals, and so on, with the hope that intentionality might either lie in a sufficiently complex goal-directed type of behaviour or be shown by this process to be unnecessary as an explanatory concept. That attempt slowly disappeared, in part I suspect because we reached agreement on the view that some of the features of nearly all the types that might be distinguished could also appear in what we normally call intentional behaviour. Intentionality does not lie in particular feedback loops or sets of equations.

But it also seems to me that some of the controversy has disappeared from the surface of the discussion almost inexplicably. In this chapter I shall argue that much of it is really still there, indeed that it has re-emerged in a deeper form, but that in the process of debating with each other over such a long period of time we have become adept at phrasing the arguments in a way that anticipates the counterarguments. Like seasoned chess players, we are no longer arguing with each other's immediate or even medium-term moves, we are extensively covering ourselves for possible long-term moves. If this analogy is to be helpful, the way to unearth the real argument is therefore to move straight to the end game.

## Are intentions responsible for behaviour?

Fortunately, McFarland has done this, at least for one of the main issues at stake, at the conclusion of his second piece when he writes (p. 228) that 'we can talk about them (declarative representations) to each other, indeed I claim that nature intends us to do so, but we should not claim that they are responsible for our behaviour'. The question of what is responsible for our behaviour is one of the central issues, for it is via the notion of responsibility that the particular scientific and philosophical arguments about intentional behaviour achieve relevance to many other issues in philosophy, jurisprudence and politics, and, via the influence of this general cultural environment, the way in which we pursue the activity that we call science. I want therefore to look more carefully at the question of what can be said to be responsible for behaviour.

Before I discuss McFarland's conclusion, it is important to clarify the notion of responsibility involved here. The simplest sense of 'responsible' is that involved in immediate physical causation. We can in this sense say that the Mexico earthquake was responsible for the deaths of a large number of people. This sense clearly involves no element of intentionality, other than in some religious contexts. It is because we do not usually mean responsible in this weak sense that we would not attribute intentional responsibility to, say, an epileptic fit or a heart attack. From this one might conclude that the relevant sense of responsibility has nothing to do with ordinary physical causation. While it *is* true to say that it cannot be simply in virtue of physical cause that intentions might be responsible for actions (that is one reason why I insisted in my first chapter that intentions should not be regarded as causes in this sense) it would be wrong to conclude that the relevant notion of responsibility has nothing at all to do with physical causation. To hold that view one would have to think that rational cause has nothing to do with physical cause. As will be evident later in this chapter, I do not think that things are so simple. To say that there was a reason for a particular act does not lead to a notion of responsibility if there really is no sense in which the rationality enters into producing the act. For an agent to be responsible (rationally speaking — though that does not mean that his behaviour must be entirely or even largely rational) there must be some sense in which the agent is causally responsible. I will indicate later how I think that rationality enters into physical causation via the operation of selection.

To return to McFarland's conclusion, he refers deliberately to 'declarative representations' rather than to intentions for, as he writes earlier (p. 225), he does 'not see any compelling reason to link declarative representations and intentionality'. The reason for this is that declarative representations could have an important biological role in themselves — as signals to others that manipulate their behaviour in any way that may be advantageous to the signaller. And, clearly, that advantage need not depend on the signals being either true, or linked to an intentional state. For this to be so, of course, must mean that the sense in which they can be said to be declarative is merely that in which they are revealed to any other organism capable of being influenced by the signal. Since they are not to be linked to an intentional state, they cannot be declarative in the usual sense of the word.

Indeed, the circumstances in which the independence that McFarland postulates would cease to hold will be precisely those in which the signals form part of what we call a language, i.e. in the circumstances where it is possible for the signaller to be interrogated on the significance, reasons and purposes of his signals. For, in that context, to say that 'my aim is $x$' (the way in which in our language we would 'signal' that we have a declared representation of a goal $x$) is to say that 'I intend to do $x$', except in those cases where we are deliberately lying. And, as I argued in my first chapter, we cannot do that all or even most of the time without undermining the basis on which the lying, on those occasions when it is used, can have the effect that it does. The compulsive liar is not simply as a matter of fact ineffective, he is necessarily so in a context of rational use of language.

But this means that, while McFarland's conclusion may be correct for non-language users, it can hardly be so for language users. I would say rather that if 'we can talk to each other about them' (declarative representations, but *ipso facto* in this case, our intentions) then it cannot be the case that they are not responsible for our behaviour.

Now, I may unwittingly be responsible in part for the plausibility of what I will call the 'no-responsibility' view. For I argued strongly in my first chapter (p. 81) for the view that intentions are not legitimate physical causes of particular neural events. It may seem a short move from here to the claim that intentions are not responsible for our behaviour. If they don't in some sense produce our acts then they can't indeed be held responsible.

It is therefore very important to clarify what I mean when I say that intentions are not causes of neural events, particularly in view of the fact that Lockery speaks (p. 118) of 'causal interactions characteristic of beliefs and desires' as something one may expect neural states to exhibit. I don't in fact disagree with Lockery on this (at least I don't think I do), but from the way he and I use the language of causation, it might well appear that we are on a headlong collision course.

First, it should be noted that I did not argue for the view that intentions are not responsible fc. our *actions*. I argued rather that they cannot be expected to be located as parts of the causal sequence of neural events without making reference to entities that can be understood only in talking about states like intentions, just as the machine events that occur when my Pascal program (p. 82) is run cannot be understood as representing the convergence properties of the function *fncon* without making reference to the program and its mathematical/logical properties. At some point the machine analyst has to see that a loop is involved — and this is to start shifting the explanatory power to a program level.

To put the point another way, Lockery's project of looking for intentions, desires, beliefs, etc. in studying the properties of the nervous system is inconceivable without prior assumptions about what kinds of things intentions, desires and beliefs are. Hence his need to find criteria for determining whether mentality occurs before sharpening the electrodes. Those criteria are not physiological. There would otherwise be nothing to distinguish the causal sequences of neural events that occur during intentional acts from other possible neural causal sequences. It will be the fact that the causal sequences can represent the logic of intentional acts (which is what I understand Lockery to mean when he talks of 'causal interactions characteristic of beliefs and desires' being exhibited by neural states), and have been selected precisely because they do so and that that confers biological advantages, that will give the physiologist a claim to have found intentions etc. in his study of the brain, not that he will find any peculiar properties of the synaptic events or action potentials. What will be peculiar will not be 'local' events at all.

The role of selection here is crucial. A physically sufficient causal sequence may or may not represent a rational sequence — most do not. Moreoever, when it does, it is not the rationality that directly 'forces' a particular physical sequence to occur (that kind of thinking leads readily to theories of the type favoured by Eccles and requiring entities like 'liaison brains' to mediate the force — see p. 82). It is rather that the biological advantages of some forms of rational behaviour have led to the physical sequences concerned being selected.

This paves the way for an important development. Once a rational sequence occurs, and if it is effective enough, it needn't relinquish control until the physical system representing it breaks down. A computer that has been successfully programmed to play chess at a master level will do just that for as long as its electronic components function as specified. The reason for that is not that the program 'forces' certain machine events to occur (much as we may be tempted to say so, just as we are tempted to say that intentions cause certain neural events). In fact the machine events occurring during a game of chess occur just as naturally, and by the same physical mechanisms as when the computer is doing anything else, including just idling or running a nonsense program. Yet it is clearly true to say that what is responsible for the game that the computer plays — right down to its quirks and characteristics — is the intentionality represented in the program, and its associated data bank. So having selected a particular series of machine states because it represents the logic of a particular kind of action, it is perfectly correct to say that the machine is obeying that logic. If you want to blame something for having lost the chess game, for example, you blame the cleverness of the program. It would be odd indeed to try to express this blame by referring to a particular set of machine events ('if only the machine had not gone to address XYZ, I would have won!' does not make sense).

The view therefore that intentions are not causes of neural events does not, in itself, lend weight to the 'no responsibility' thesis. On the contrary, my argument was intended, amongst other things, to clear the way for dissociating arguments about causation at a neural level from arguments about what is responsible for our actions. I will try here to outline the nature of that dissociation.

For as long as we conceive of intentions as being like physical causes of our movements, just as particular external stimuli, or internal ones like epileptic seizures may be, we open the way to the question what is it about intentions that makes them able to bear the notion of responsibility any more than epileptic seizures and external stimuli. And the answer, of course, is that if they are indeed of the same type then there would be nothing about intentions that would enable them to bear the required burden.

It is therefore essential for them to be of a significantly different type to enable the concept of responsibility to apply. The point of my Pascal program example was to show that it is easy, in the computer age, to see how things can be of such a different type. There we found that what I called a 'program state' (such as a convergence property) could be of crucial importance in understanding the behaviour of a machine, yet for it to be quite incorrect to say that it (the program state) was simply an identifiable set of machine states that could be a physical cause of subsequent such states.

Yet we should notice that far from weakening the relation between the program state and the machine behaviour, this fact strengthens it. For if the program state were merely a particular set of machine states then there would be nothing to identify those machine states as being of any more significance than billions of others, equally efficacious in producing subsequent machine states. But, of course, they *are* more significant by virtue of the fact that they have been selected (by the process of programming) precisely because they enable the machine to express certain logical relations.

Now logical relations are, in a very obvious sense, stronger than physical causation. There is a 'must' about them which does not apply to physical causation. That is why, when a fully debugged (and logically correct) program fails, we blame the physical causal sequence not the program. We say that the machine broke down or that a stray signal was picked up. We then repair or protect the machine and re-run the program.

By analogy, it is the *rationality* of intentional behaviour that is relevant to its ability to carry the burden of concepts like responsibility, not its ability to compete with the physical causes of our behaviour. A diary entry (to quote the example discussed by Wilkes (p. 180) and McFarland (p. 227)) is not, on this view, simply a stimulus to be weighed with all other stimuli; it has a significance that is only apparent in the context of a rational intentional scheme. That is not to say, of course, that trade-offs of the kind McFarland envisages do not occur. It is rather to say that the significance of the diary entry does not lie merely in its being an event. It cannot therefore be a mere stimulus, coming as it were out of the blue.

It is important to note that I am using the word rational here with a fairly wide meaning. Moreover, I am not implying that behaviour is or even can be totally rational, but rather that rationality enters in in ways I will illustrate later. The concept matters even when we refer to *ir*rational behaviour, for we would not be able to do that if it was not evident how it could have been rational.

Before I leave this part of the argument I must elaborate on what it means to say that logical relations are stronger than physical causation. For it will be clear to some readers that even in allowing the two to be compared I am edging close to what many would regard as the fundamental error of confusing the language of reasons and that of causes. Worse still, I may appear to be in conflict with my first chapter in which I argued (p. 82) for intentional and physical causation being very different. They are, but that does not mean that they are in no way related. On the contrary, part of my argument in this chapter is that via the process of selection acting on the features that express rationality precisely those physical sequences that mirror the rationality (i.e. allow it to be expressed) have emerged. One way of looking at this is to say that the physical sequences expressing rationality (and once again I must emphasise that this includes what we would call irrational action — it includes all acts to which the notion of rationality is relevant, not merely those we would say are actually rational) are an extremely small subset of the possible physical sequences. They are characterised by virtue of the fact that the information they contain and the way in which it is processed are causally efficacious in producing rational behaviour.

The sense therefore in which logical (or rational) causation may be said to be stronger is that over and above the fact that any physical sequences are causally efficacious, those that express rationality have been selected precisely because of that fact. Not only are the sequences causally efficacious in the ordinary way, they themselves have been caused to occur by virtue of selection for rationality.

I am well aware of the fact that this line of thought may (perhaps must) lead to at least a partial blurring of the distinction between empirical and conceptual matters. In this I follow much of what Quine (e.g. in *From a Logical Point of View* and *Two*

*Dogmas of Empiricism*) or Davidson have to say. Anyone familiar with the outcome of my discussion with Charles Taylor (see p. 93) will not find my position here at all surprising. This is not the place to justify the position. I wish merely to make it clear that I am aware of the fact that it raises some very deep and fundamental philosophical problems. Any comprehensive defence of a compatibilist position on intentionality and physical causation must, I think, raise these issues. They are also at the heart of the question of the nature of the complementarity involved (see p. 78) and they can be avoided only at the cost either of trying to deny intentionality (or at least denying that intentions are ever responsible for behaviour) or of admitting a fundamental conflict between intentional and physical causation.

## Lockery's programme of research

We are now in a position to assess more critically what is involved in the programme of research on intentionality in animals outlined by Lockery. In general, I accept most of his treatment of the problem of intentionality as it may influence the development of neurophysiology. But there are points in his treatment where he comes dangerously near to identifying as empirical issues matters that cannot really be so. And in some cases I suspect that the relationships could be construed the wrong way round.

The statements on which I want to comment are the following (the numbering is mine):

I  'whether a system actually has mental states is ultimately a question of physiology' (p. 118).
II  'the functional roles of representational states often include causal relations not just with environmental conditions and behaviour, but between the internal representations themselves' (p. 135).
III  'to find the neural correlate of a mental state analogue is to describe a physiological state with a particular functional role in the shifting pattern of physical states within the nervous system' (p. 144).
IV  'Because the language of thought is literally a physical code, different sentences have different physical properties ... These physical differences confer on each sentence unique causal

powers in the interplay between sentences: exactly those which mirror the logical relations between sentences' (p. 151).

V 'To identify a representational state with a physical state we must show complete causal role isomorphism' (p. 157).

It is instructive to transcribe some of these statements into their equivalents with regard to the relation between what I call program states (p. 85) and machine events. From I we then get:

I' 'Whether a system actually has program states is ultimately a question of machine engineering.'

It then becomes clear that something is wrong. It is indeed a matter of engineering whether the machine has the *potential* to have certain program states. But, if we know that it already exhibits the behaviour required to ascribe the relevant program states, no amount of investigation of the machine engineering can cast doubt on whether the program states exist. Thus if we have a computer that can play chess, it is no longer a relevant *empirical* question whether the machine architecture allows that. The question is not whether it allows it, but *how* it allows it. I would argue similarly that no amount of physiological investigation of our nervous system can possibly change the fact that we have mental states and intentions.

I suspect that what Lockery has in mind here is not that physiological investigation might upset our own mentality, but rather that we need to find criteria for ascribing mentality to other organisms and he is saying that *his* ultimate criterion is going to be physiological. I would argue that this can be misleading, for it cannot be a matter of physiology alone. That is why in his programme of research he needs to make reference to states that are not themselves purely, or even primarily, physiological. As he notes elsewhere (p. 154) 'local physiological facts are not by themselves sufficient to settle the question what function a segment of the nervous system is performing'. I am not sure how far Lockery's concept of local may extend, but this statement bears a close relation to my proposition (p. 87) that 'we may not even know where in the world to draw the boundary of the system we include in our explanation'.

I think therefore that we must reformulate I to read something like

I″ 'Whether a system, other than man, has mental states is a question that may become a question of physiology.'

Statements II, IV and V raise the question of the possible conflict between Lockery's frequent reference to the causal role of mental states and my, equally frequent, attempts to deny a physical causal role.

The conflict here is not all that deep. It depends on various uses of the word cause. What I mean when I say that intentional states do not *cause* neural events is that we must not look, *pace* Eccles (p. 82), for a peculiar mental force that, perhaps via some intermediate, 'makes' the nervous system do what it does. I do not mean to say that there cannot be causal efficacy of any kind, any more than I would wish to deny causal relations between program states.

But it is important here to note that the notion of cause involved changes as we move from machine to program states, and even more so as we move to mental states.

In the case of my Pascal program (p. 82), the convergence properties of my function *fncon* might indeed be said to be responsible for (is this a kind of cause?) the behaviour of the machine. But the relation here comes closer to that of a logical causation (see p. 84) than that of physical causation. Similarly I would argue that causal relations between internal representations, and *a fortiori* between mental states, will have more the characteristics of rational causal relations. Thus, if a sequence of behaviour is totally rational then the relations will be capable of being expressed logically (here I use logical in the sense that also includes 'rule-dependent'). These kinds of relations will be evident in the physiology *only* in so far as it makes reference to the information content of the states involved, and their logical relations to each other. Lockery recognises this when he writes 'What is involved is the effect of information stored at one place on information stored at another' (p. 157). Such 'effects' are not simply causal in the physical sense, for they must depend on the rules for the processing of the information, which at the physiological level will appear contingent (actually some of them will remain so even at the information level, just as some of the rules of any language are). What is not contingent, what is necessary, is that there *are* such rules and that they are not likely to be discernible from the physiology alone.

Statement III introduces the concept of functional role in identifying neural correlates of a mental state analogue. Here I will note simply that this need for reference to functional role is crucial. Suppose, in my Pascal program example, we burrow down from the program level. First we identify the crucial program statement (UNTIL...) that immediately determines the outcome. Then, via knowledge of the compiler, we work out the machine states that encode that statement. We then run the program and we detect pulses of information passing from the central processor to the addresses of the memory locations we have found (just as a lot of neurophysiology consists in measuring traffic along pathways). We know from this alone that these machine addresses are important because the processor keeps insistently coming back to them. But that is about all we would be able to work out from a machine analysis. Further progress would depend on seeing the functional role, which would immediately take us back to the program level. I want to note here that this argument does not depend on programs (as we understand them) actually existing as such in the brain.

## The temporal topology of intentional explanation

Moreover, the reference to functional role is not necessarily merely a device that, once identified, allows us to continue our analysis at a purely neural state level. To explain why this is so I must return to the question of time scale that was raised briefly at the end of my first chapter (p. 99). There I noted that it would be wrong to think of neural events and intentional states matching each other on a simple time scale. Shawn Lockery has pointed out to me that my argument there might be misconstrued as meaning simply that, whereas individual neural events occur on a time scale of milliseconds, it is more usual for intentional states and acts to occur over seconds, minutes or hours. And, if that were all there were to it, then we could switch from talking about individual neural discharges to talking about the variations in, for example, the levels of various hormones or transmitters so that our time scales would match more closely. There is something in this point, of course, and no doubt there are better matched events to refer to than individual neuronal discharges. It would nevertheless be a deep misunderstanding of my point to think that a mere change of time scale in the sense of changing the time unit would solve the problem. As I noted in my first chapter (p. 99) it is not merely a question of how fine-grained our measurements may be.

I am certainly not saying that we may miss the picture because the information may be too grainy.

Perhaps the use of the phrase 'time scale' is itself misleading. The phrase 'temporal matrix' or even 'temporal topology' might serve better. The reason for this is that the point I am making depends on two crucial features of program level and intentional explanations that do not apply to neural and machine event explanations:

*First*, neural and machine events can indeed be ordered on a 'straight line' time scale. This is because the ability of the identification of such events to explain lies in the requirement that they be events that can be idealised to have causal impact *at the time they occur*. In this idealisation they are, as it were, blind to anything but the immediate past, which produced them, and the immediate future, which they in turn produce. That is why the equations we use are paradigmatically sets of simultaneous differential equations in which any set of values and derivatives at any one time is sufficient to enable all other events to be derived, given sufficient computing power.

In saying that these events can be idealised to have causal impact at the time they occur, I am not, of course, arguing that there are no consequences beyond that time. On the contrary, via the temporal chain of cause and effect, the effects are transmitted over time. The crucial word here is impact. The analogy is with the action of billiard balls. Causal agency is transmitted at the time and only at the time impact occurs and the description of each impact is complete without reference to earlier or later events. That, in words, is what differential equations describe mathematically. Of course, in particular applications we may not actually use differential equations as such. Computer architecture, for example, lends itself to a different approach based on binary switching, but the principle is similar in that the state of the system's components at any one time is sufficient to predict the subsequent states, and that is what a machine analyst means when he insists that knowledge at this level is sufficient, at least in principle, to account for the system's behaviour.

Of course, the idealisation is often rather strained. The actions of forces at a distance, for example, are represented as though they were a series of 'pulses' occurring at each interval of time as the equations are integrated. In some cases we can avoid this idealisation by the mathematical method of obtaining a closed form solution of the equations. This avoids the fiction (though on some views it is not a fiction — perhaps continuous forces are really particulate) involved in the idealisation but it is an option that is only rarely available and then only for rather simple cases. It does though serve to remind us that even at the most basic level of physical explanation there is room for argument about the extent to which mathematical or computing convenience presses certain assumptions upon us as to the nature of causality.

For obvious reasons, I am also neglecting any problems of time scale arising from relativity theory. Of course it is possible for the precise time relations of two events to be changed depending on the way in which they are observed. But this never leads to any possibility of the *causal* sequence being altered. Events that can change in temporal sequence with respect to each other would be too far apart to influence each other in the time interval involved. Moreover, for simplicity I have also neglected the problem of physical indeterminacy. It would make the argument more complex but would not alter the essential conclusions. That means that I do not see the question whether physical indeterminacy is important in the behaviour of the nervous system as having much bearing on the role of intentional explanations.

By contrast with this simple temporal order, programs and intentional state accounts do not derive their explanatory power from such 'straight line' temporal sequences. This is not just because the order of a program is not necessarily, or even usually, the order in which it is obeyed. It is rather because any causal role is not representable by sets of differential equations or their equivalents. It is represented rather by the branching network of 'decisions' which can range from items that are very close to machine events to ones that involve logical rules. The causation involved then ranges from simple physical causation to logical entailment (see p. 84). I am not arguing that, by analogy, intentional behaviour is always rational in a strict sense. It does though, like programs including logical and mathematical 'decisions', involve rationality in the sense that the causation involved is often more akin to logical cause, or cause by virtue of certain rules. That is why in my first paper I took the radical view that it would be better to say that intentions do not 'cause' neural events in the sense in which neural events cause each other in a linear time sequence.

The causal role involved in a program is usually of the kind 'When $x$ is true, start doing $y$ until $z$ is true, and then repeat this until $z$ is identical with $w$.....' and so on. It doesn't matter to the program explanation either how this is implemented in machine terms, or exactly when certain conditions are true. All that matters is what one might call the temporal topology of the sequences. Moreover, forward reference to representation of possible future states (see Montefiore p. 60) is not only permitted, but is of the very essence of REPEAT–UNTIL loops.

*Second*, into this temporal matrix, which has a certain topology irrespective of how we might map out the machine events on a 'straight line' time scale, we can also introduce something that is inconceivable on a machine event time scale: we can introduce conditions and states of which it does not make sense to say that they exist in any linear time scale. These are the purely logical parts of programs or of rational intentional behaviour. Thus, the convergence property of my function *fncon* (see p. 83) certainly does not exist in a machine event time scale. It is a logical property. Such properties can not only be used in programs, they can be mixed with items that could be said to exist in a linear time scale. Thus we can write:

$$\text{While } x \text{ and if } y \text{ repeat } z$$

where $x$ might be something (like the value of a physical parameter compared to another parameter) that is true at some times but not at others (and therefore could represent something that exists in a linear time scale), whereas $y$ might be the result of a purely logical operation.

There are strong analogies here with the way in which rationality enters into intentional actions. *That* rationality can enter in is the key fact, not whether we can identify the time of a particular event. Thus, a chess player may, during an end game, have seen that if his opponent makes a particular move, he will certainly be able to force a checkmate. The realisation itself and the planning of possible future action is independent of whether or when the opponent actually makes the move in question. It depends only on the rules of chess and the ability of the player to achieve a fully rational analysis of the possibilities within those rules. Moreover, looking back on the game, the player can say that he 'intended to checkmate his opponent in such and such a way' without it necessarily being true that he is referring to a particular event in time. For one thing, the event, in the sense of actually implementing the checkmate, may not even have happened. But more importantly his realisation of the state of affairs and the formulation of an intention depended on rule-based properties that are not properly placed in any time scale.

There is a possible comeback here for the machine analyst. This would be to elaborate on Lockery's idea (listed as statement IV above) that physical differences can, indeed must, 'mirror the logical relations'. I agree, and that means that a determined machine analyst can say that to the chess player's intention to force a checkmate in a particular way, and despite its rationality, there corresponds *some* particular sequence of neural events. Indeed, they will in Lockery's sense 'mirror' the logical relations and will differ physically from all other sequences of events by virtue of that fact. But this is the kind of issue on which I am uneasy about some of Lockery's points. I find I agree with most of them provided they are not construed in a way that puts the relationships (the 'mirroring') the wrong way round. If we ask the question why the physical system that allows the 'mirror' to occur has been selected, the answer of course lies in the fact that it expresses a rationality that has been selected for precisely because the rationality itself is the advantage selected.

The point here is similar to one about selection of genes. Strictly speaking genes, as chemical sequences of nucleotides, are never selected for. Their expression in particular phenotypes is what is selected. This is not a mere quibble between two equivalent ways of representing the same thing. An identical sequence of nucleotides occurring in a genetic system that does not produce a phenotype that enables the gene to be expressed will not only not be selected for, it might even be disadvantageous and selected *against*. Strictly speaking, therefore, genes are not identical with particular chemical sequences since they cannot exist as such, and still be genes, in isolation.

Similarly, it would be senseless to suppose that a neural sequence of activity that happened to 'mirror' the logic of a chess game would have any significance as such in, for example, a fish. It might have as much significance as a cloud formation happening to look like the face of a man. (I am not arguing here against Lockery's general scheme to look for particular neuronal characteristics that mirror the logic of intentional action in animals other than man any more than I would argue against looking for similarities between the genetic code for, say, oxygen-carrying molecules in fish and men. I am saying simply that we must always bear in mind the question whether, given the animal's known repertoire of behaviour, a particular neuronal pattern of activity could bear the interpretation we seek to put on it.)

This argument can also be seen as another way of putting the point about 'local' physiological facts (see p. 87 and p. 154). What is characteristic about these kinds of problems is that in shifting from local to functional accounts two important things happen: first, as explained above, we might shift to a level that permits incorporation of properties that do not exist at all on the local scale and, second, there is no way of knowing from a purely local analysis where in the world we should draw the boundary of the system whose states and properties are relevant to the functional analysis. And the boundary problem here can be either or both spatial and temporal. The diary with its crucial entry (see the discussion between McFarland and Wilkes — p. 180 and p. 227) might be on the moon; a part of the explanation of a particular intentional act may refer to presumed behaviour of the stock markets in the year 2000.

### Final and immediate causes: what kind of complementarity?

It is of course the reference to future events somehow determining present happenings that appears to cause so much offence to the natural inclinations of traditional scientific explanation. Reading the seven outline theses in Montefiore's first chapter (p. 59), I am struck by the fact that probably only two of them would actually provoke many scientists into attempts at refutation: the first and the third. The first asserts that it is inconceivable meaningfully to dispense with intentionality; the third that present events can be determined by reference to possible future states of affairs. The other five points in Montefiore's paper would, I suspect, be thought of as essentially derivative in that if these two could be effectively countered then there would hardly be any need to discuss the others.

I will deal with the first point later. The easiest to deal with in the light of previous sections of this paper is the third: the view that present events can be determined by reference to possible future states of affairs. It will be evident from what I have written already both that I accept this part of Montefiore's discussion and that my escape from the offence to traditional modes of scientific explanation is to show that the sense of 'determined by' is not at all the same as that embodied in terms of differential equations and the like. And the reason why this intentional determination is not in conflict with causal determination is that out of the innumerable possible results of the latter a very few have been selected out precisely because they satisfy the requirement of no conflict or, as Lockery would put it, because they mirror the intentionality. That in turn is why such complementarity (as Montefiore describes it) will only be found in enormously complex structures like nervous systems. For effective selection (evolutionary or informational) implies huge redundancy. The more absolutely improbable the causal sequence required to mirror intentionality the greater must be the number of implicitly or explicitly rejected sequences.

It will be evident here that, while I accept large parts of Montefiore's first chapter, I am doubtful about accepting that the complementarity must be an uneasy one. Until the philosophical consequences of selection theory on the nature of this complementarity have been worked out, I remain on neutral ground on this crucial matter. It would be an extensive enterprise indeed to work through the arguments here that would pertain to settling the matter between me and Montefiore. Here I can only outline why, in remaining neutral, I am still attracted towards what Montefiore calls a more 'comfortable' form of complementarity and which he himself rejects.

First, we must not be too easily deterred by the sheer improbability of 'blind' causation generating sequences that mirror intentional determination. The important point to note here is that absolute improbability does not imply progressive improbability. Richard Dawkins in *The Blind Watchmaker* has put the argument very effectively in the case of evolutionary selection and has even written an impressive computer program to illustrate his point. All his arguments also apply to what I have called informational selection (indeed his computer program actually represents this more than it represents natural selection). The argument is simply that if each operation of the selector occurs on the result of the previous operation a sequence that might have required billions of independent selections will require only a few tens of selections to occur. The difference is truly phenomenal and, as more and more complex sequences are selected for, it rapidly becomes the difference between what could not possibly occur even within the lifetime of the universe and what could occur within time scales meaningful to us.

Second, we should note that one difference between evolutionary selection and what I have called informational selection is that while the former is necessarily blind, the latter need not be. Indeed it would be a major advantage for it not to be so. For if, at some stage in evolution, more rational forms of behaviour became advantageous then the emergence of a process that speeds up the construction of a repertoire of such behaviour in each individual would certainly be advantageous. What would be required to do that would be a selector that is capable of assessing the conformity of the results of neural activity to that required for intentional determination. Given the nature of biological evolution and the role of individuals, such a selector would need to be located in each individual, and would therefore be processing the results of the same physical system that also contains the selector. This might be the kind of thing, I imagine, that Montefiore is referring to when he refers to autonomous intentionality (p. 64). Certainly I agree with him that something like this is required for genuine as opposed to derived intentionality. It is also akin to what we are referring to when we talk of self-awareness. My suspicion therefore is that the answer to the question whether the complementarity is to be a 'comfortable' one, or rather an uneasy and incomprehensible one, may lie in whether it is correct to suppose that the evolution of self-awareness and consciousness has occurred precisely because of the biological advantages of a selector for rationality, and that self-aware consciousness consists, at least in part, of just such a selector.

I do not pretend to know, or even easily to envisage, how this might have come about (that is why I remain neutral on the question of the kind of complementarity we must envisage) but, if it is what has happened then the first of Montefiore's theses would fall into place even in a scientific scheme of things. As he notes (p. 59), it is not actually part of his thesis that evolution has programmed us so as 'to be unable to do otherwise than make use of these concepts (of intentionality etc.)', for his argument stems rather from the a priori conditions for rational discourse to occur, together with the obvious fact that it does occur. But if in fact it were true not only to say that we have been so programmed but also that the practical results of the use of such concepts are precisely what the evolutionary process has selected out as advantageous and that it would therefore be, biologically speaking, perverse to regard this as an illusion, then the unavoidable complementarity of physical causation and intentional determination would become much easier to live with. But we are a long way from a serious analysis of the immensely difficult philosophical and biological questions that sprout at every turn in this particular argument. Perhaps, in this book, we have mapped out some of the terrain from which an assault on this Everest of a problem can be mounted.

# PART IV
# A CHALLENGE RENEWED

CHAPTER 16

# SWAN SONG OF A PHOENIX

*David McFarland*

At this point, I should perhaps outline my basic argument. Animals are rational beings, in the economic sense. This means that the individual is designed to behave in such a way that some entity is maximised (subject to certain constraints). We may call this entity utility. Now, there must be some mathematical function with respect to which the utility of particular states and activities are judged (i.e. the dynamic equivalent of utility functions). We call this mathematical function the goal function. It describes the notional costs and benefits attributable to all possible states and activities of the animal (the actual costs and benefits are described by the cost function). The goal function specifies the design of the individual (individuals have different goal functions). It cannot be changed by learning, though it can change throughout life by preprogrammed maturation.

Specifying the goal function tells us nothing about the mechanisms by which animal behaviour is controlled, but it does tell us the design criteria. If certain proposed mechanisms violate the design criteria, then those mechanisms cannot be responsible for the control of behaviour. An important aspect of the design criteria is the trade-off principle. I claim (in my first piece) that goal-directed behaviour, a mechanism proposed for the control of behaviour, violates the trade-off principle, so I conclude that goal-directed behaviour (as I have defined it) is not possible. In addition, I claim that there is no empirical evidence for explicit representations of goals-to-be-achieved (an essential component of the goal-directed mechanism), and, moreover, the concept of goal-directed behaviour is not necessary to account for the apparent purposive behaviour of animals. Various forms of goal-seeking behaviour (as I have defined it) will do the job.

In extending this view to human behaviour, I have to furnish some explanation for the teleological imperative — that people are predisposed to attribute intention (in the narrow sense) and purpose to other people, and to animals. Moreover, I have to meet the argument that the very intelligibility of human language requires this notion of intention (since without intention there can be no meaning). These problems do not arise with the conventional action-theory view of purposive behaviour.

My suggestion is that the teleological imperative has evolved as part of a communication package designed to circumvent exploitation, manipulation and discounting by conspecific rivals. By communicating in a teleological mode, the actor can avoid being judged as honest (and exploitable) or dishonest (and discountable). Moreover, (following Trivers) the (evolutionary) strategy is more effective if the actor is self-deceiving. In other words, I am suggesting that there are two modes of cognition in humans, the behaviour-control mode and the semantic mode. The former is concerned with the production of rational behaviour, while the latter is concerned with communication, social behaviour and politics. The latter gives a commentary on the former, so if somebody says to me 'What do you think you are doing?', I should reply (using my semantic brain) that my control brain is engaged in writing this chapter. But, objects Montefiore (chapter 14, p. 240) 'any precise line between linguistic and non-linguistic behaviour turns out to be peculiarly hard to find'.

I think it is worth taking up Montefiore's point in some detail. His argument is as follows: 'What, for example of the movements of my own arm, hand and fingers, co-ordinated, of course, with those of my eyes, as I guide my pen accross the paper in the act of writing the first version of this present sentence? These movements are integral to this act as it actually takes place. This is not, evidently, to say that they might not have had their behaviourally quite different functional equivalents if I had performed the same act in terms of sentence production through use of a type-writer, dictaphone, or wordprocessor.... However, I take it to be beyond need of further argument here that some physical changes in my bodily disposition are strictly necessary to the performance of any of these functionally equivalent acts of sentence production.' (p. 240). I understand this to mean that Montefiore thinks that there are alternative ways of behaving in performing a particular act of sentence production ('if I had performed the same act' etc.). By the 'same act' he cannot mean the same behaviour. I think he must mean functionally equivalent behaviour. My first point is that there is no exactly functionally equivalent behaviour. To produce a sentence with the same meaning as another sentence is not exactly functionally equivalent, because the sentences will be of different lengths (and therefore have taken more energy, ink, paper, etc.), and because they will have different effects on the recipient by virtue of representing different linguistic styles. Even the same sentence produced in different ways (hand-written, typed, etc.) does not result in exact functional equivalents. A typed letter does not have the same effect on the recipient as a hand-written letter. Notice, moreover, that Montefiore, chose to write his sentence by hand. Evidently, he did not think this to be the functional equivalent of typing. The point is that, however function is judged, by natural selection or by human value-judgements, it is judged on the basis of all the consequences of the behaviour. These include the consequences for the writer and the (estimated) consequences for the recipient (which, of course, ultimately rebound on the writer).

Let us agree that the different ways of producing the sentence are nearly functional equivalents. What does Montefiore mean by performing the same act? I think he means that the act-outcome is perceived as being the same by the actor. That is the two sentences (with the same word order) are judged as being equivalent by the author. Note that this does not mean that the author was indifferent between them, since he chose to write in one way rather than another. I must agree, however, that the author may think that the hand-written and typed sentences will have the same effect on the reader. I suspect that Montefiore thinks that, because the same act-outcome is involved in the two cases, they are produced by the same psychological process. That is, the author thinks of the act-outcome he wants to achieve, and regards the means of achieving it (hand-writing, typing, etc.) as relatively unimportant. I take it that Montefiore would say that he intends to write a particular sentence. The ancillary behaviour (approaching the desk, etc.) and the mode of writing, are just ways of achieving the end, but they cannot be separated from the intentional behaviour. If Montefiore is implying, and I think he is, that the intention guides the behaviour, then I regard this as a form of action-theory with which I disagree. The question is, do I have a viable alternative? Before answering this question, I should address a point made by Lockery, which bears on the same issue.

According to Lockery (chapter 10, pp. 188–9), 'The TOP amounts to a calculus of behavioural choice. Given an animal's repertoire of (mutually exclusive) actions, and its current needs, environmental inputs and behavioural state, the theory predicts which actions will be expressed.' (Incidentally, I do not accept this wording, there are no needs and there are no actions, in my book. Nor do I accept Lockery's version of premise 1, on p. 187. My original wording, as indicated in his footnote 1, was correct). 'The TOP washes its hands of prediction (and explanation) once an activity is begun. In one of his examples, it predicts the circumstances under which the robot will undertake to wipe up the ink spilled on the carpet, but it does not tell us how the task is accomplished, that is, how the many actions within the cleaning activity are organised (the plan), nor how progress is monitored along the path to completion.' The short answer is that there is no plan, and progress is not monitored. I certainly do not share Lockery's view (p. 189) that 'to follow a plan is to match one's unitary acts to an internally represented "script" or action plan'.

The long answer is that Lockery is thinking in a different (and inappropriate) framework from myself. In the first place, the TOP relates to design criteria, and does not specify any mechanism. Whatever mechanism is proposed for the control of behaviour, it must meet the trade-off criteria. We do not know much about the mechanisms that exercise this control (though I could make some suggestions), but the TOTE, and other proposed versions of action-theory, will not do, because they fail to meet the design criteria. Let us consider Montefiore approaching his desk to write a sentence. According to the TOP he must, at any stage, be unequivocally free to change, on balance, to another activity. He may change because he feels a stone in his shoe. He may change because someone knocks on the door. He may change because his pencil is slightly too soft, or his ink is slightly too runny. Moreover, he may change at any point; before starting the sentence, having just started it, etc. Action theory (including the TOTE) cannot meet these criteria, because its design principle is to control by discouraging outside influences, the very opposite of the trade-off principle. Cumbersome arrangements for changing course once an action has started can be suggested, but these are inevitably going to be incapable of producing the change at the optimal point. The trade-offs must be designed to meet the optimality criteria, otherwise the device will not survive in the face of competition. Let us return now to Montefiore's main point, that the linguistic and non-linguistic aspects of writing behaviour cannot be separated. Montefiore walks across a room, sits down at a desk, picks up a pen, and writes a sentence. Let us characterise this behaviour sequence as a sequence (A) of activities ($a_1 - a_2 - a_3 -$ etc.). The size and specification of these activities is immaterial to the argument. At any point in the sequence Montefiore could have deviated from the observed sequence (viz. $a_1 - a_2 - b_1 - b_2$). In fact, he would have deviated had not the trade-off balance been such as to favour $a_3$. In other words, at each point in the sequence the control-brain surveys the alternatives and picks the best (according to its goal-function). This happens not only at the gross level (shall I write the sentence or go to the loo?), but also at the micro-level (shall I step in the waste basket or step just beside it?). Each evaluation is carried out by taking account of the subject's state (I am not yet ready to go to the loo), including his perception of external phenomena (the illumination at the desk is adequate), and the utility attached to the likely consequences of the alternative activities (if I step on the waste basket I will crush it — if I step beside it I will be off-balance). Much of this evaluation requires no cognition (in the usual sense of the word). It is simply the result of the way our bits and pieces are put together. They are tailored to achieve the optimal design. But it may, sometimes, involve cognitive evaluation of declarative representations of the consequences of potential activities (as I suggest in the case for Dickinson's rats, see p. 227). Thus Montefiore might believe (have declarative knowledge) that stepping in the waste basket will help to keep him alert while writing his sentence. This belief may tip the balance (of the trade-off outlined above) towards stepping into the waste basket.

Neither the behaviour sequence A, nor the sequence B (which includes stepping in the waste basket) involve any semantic, or linguistic processes up to the point that the sentence is formulated. If asked what he is doing with a waste basket on his foot, Montefiore could report on his behaviour. He could say 'I found myself treading in the waste basket, which conforms with my belief that it helps to keep me alert', but he is more likely to report teleologically, 'I trod in the waste basket in order to keep myself alert'. Even when alone, Montefiore may say such things to himself, aloud or otherwise, but these thoughts will not be the processes controlling his behaviour.

When it comes to formulating the sentence, Montefiore has a choice, similar in kind to all the other $a_1 - a_n$, or $b_1 - b_n$, choices.

In deciding whether to formulate the sentence one way (a), or another way (b), he takes account of the consequences of the alternative sentences. These consequences include the meaning (the expected meaning to the recipient). The intentional content of the sentence plays no part in the formulation of the sentence that is different from the part played by other (non-semantic) considerations. It is simply an ingredient in the trade-off among alternative sentences. Thus Montefiore might think that 'the consequence of sending this sentence to McFarland is that he will pick on the word $xxx$ and raise a silly objection. It would be better if I used a different construction.' This process is no different in principle from the process of deciding whether or not to step in the waste basket. In formulating the sentence there are semantic considerations to be taken into account, while in walking across the room there may be no such considerations involved. On the other hand, if Montefiore believes that by stepping into the waste basket he will send a (non-verbal) message to the next person to enter the room, then there may be semantic considerations involved in deciding whether or not to step into the waste basket. Thus Montefiore might think 'if so-and-so comes into the room and sees me with a waste basket on my foot, he might think me to be absent minded, and decide not to put me on the executive committee'. This would be a political manoeuvre on Montefiore's part, an attempt to influence the behaviour of another person. It would be a possible semantic alternative to sending a written message including the sentence 'I am not competent to be on the executive committee'.

We come now to some points raised by Noble. In his view (p. 264), if 'we can talk to each other about them (declarative representations, but *ipso facto* in this case, our intentions) then it cannot be the case that they are not responsible for our behaviour.' I disagree, while agreeing with most of the points made by Noble about responsibility and causation. First of all, I must clear up what might be a misunderstanding. Intentions in the narrow (goal-directing) sense are procedural representations which have the role of guiding our behaviour (remember that I claim that these do not exist). Intentions (to me) are declarative representations of what we believe our behaviour to be about. Thus intentions are beliefs, where beliefs are declarative representations, which we make use of when we assess the likely consequences of our future behaviour. Thus if Montefiore believes that a consequence of stepping in the waste basket is that he will be alert while writing his sentence, then this belief may influence his behaviour, and this belief may be communicated to others (I did it because I believe etc.). But the belief was not responsible for the behaviour, it was only an ingredient in the trade-off recipe. If Montefiore had not held the belief he may still have stepped into the waste basket, whereas this could not have been the case if the belief was responsible for the behaviour (if an agent is responsible for an event, then the event does not occur when the agent is absent). If Montefiore says 'I stepped into the waste basket in order to keep myself alert,' he is deluding himself if he thinks that he did it intentionally (in the narrow sense). He did it as a result of (a) standing next to it, (b) noticing it, (c) remembering his belief about it, (d) assessing the alternatives, etc.

Noble (p. 267) claims that 'it is the rationality of intentional behaviour that is relevant to its ability to carry the burden of concepts like responsibility, not its ability to compete with the physical causes of our behaviour. A diary entry (to quote the example discussed by Wilkes and McFarland) is not, on this view, simply a stimulus to be weighed with all other stimuli, it has a significance that is only apparent in the context of a rational intentional scheme. That is not to say, of course, that trade-offs of the kind McFarland envisages do not occur. It is rather to say that the significance of the diary entry does not lie merely in its being an event. It cannot therefore be a mere stimulus, coming as it were out of the blue.'

In entering a note in a diary we are (a) deciding, on balance, not to do something else at that point in time, (b) taking account of the consequences of making the entry (that it uses up space on the page, that we are likely to consult the diary in future, etc.). We may think that we have a plan in which the diary entry plays a role, but when it comes to looking in the diary, the status of the diary entry is no different from the status of the other ingredients of the trade-off that occurs at that time. Noble's point is that the diary entry was put there as part of a rational scheme. I do not disagree, but I would say that such rational schemes are common in the animal kingdom. When a dog goes for a walk, it places its urine as part of a rational scheme. It places it in locations that other dogs are likely to visit, near to the messages left by other dogs, etc. The dog does not have to have a plan that is controlling its behaviour. At each point on the route the dog decides whether or not to leave a message, depending on such factors as the suitability of the site, the size of the urine supply, the likely number of future good sites, etc. For Noble, it is not whether the behaviour is rational, but 'that rationality can enter in is the key fact' (p. 275). But rationality can enter in in many ways. For example pigeons can be trained to communicate their internal (interoceptive) states to one another (Lubinski and Thompson, 1987). Their behaviour may appear to be intentional, but the necessary rationality is inherent in the way the pigeons were set up by their trainer. Presumably, Noble would say that the trainer, not the pigeons, was responsible for the behaviour. In the case of the diary entry, Noble seems to say that the diarist is responsible, because the entry forms part of a rational scheme (or is capable of forming part of a rational scheme). Surely he must also say that the diarist is responsible for the entry, only if he is also responsible for the rational scheme.

What does it mean for me to be responsible for a rational scheme? It means that I devised the scheme, and without my devising the scheme would not exist. To devise such a scheme I must design a scenario that is rational. To design it, I must fashion it so that it maximises some entity. For Noble this entity is related to the local objective (my aim is to obtain the best exchange rate (see Wilkes, p. 180). What is the best way of attaining that objective?). For me the entity is utility, so in designing a scheme I must enter a utility maximising exercise. That is I must trade-off each element of the scheme against alternative possible elements. Moreover, I must trade-off designing each element of the scheme against alternative thought processes of a different kind. I can say that 'I intended to make a note in my diary, as part of my intention to visit the bank and obtain a better exchange rate'. My language conveniently encapsulates my goals, but unlike Noble's chess player, my rationale is not encapsulated within an intentional system.

For Noble (p. 275) 'a chess player may, during an end game, have seen that if his opponent makes a particular move, he will certainly be able to force a checkmate. The realisation itself and the planning of possible future action is independent of whether or when the opponent actually makes the move in question. It depends only on the rules of chess and the ability of the player to achieve a fully rational analysis of the possibilities within those rules. Moreover, looking back on the game, the player can say that he 'intended to checkmate his opponent in such and such a way' without it necessarily being true that he is referring to a particular event in time. For one thing, the event, in the sense of actually implementing the checkmate, may not even have happened. But more importantly, his realisation of the state of affairs and the formulation of an intention depended on rule-based properties that are not properly placed in any time scale.'

I agree with this analysis, with the exception of (perhaps) the last sentence. It seems to me that Noble sees the chess game as closed off from the rest of the person's life. The player formulates the intention in accordance with the rules (he could have formulated one in violation of the rules, but on-balance the advantage lay in staying within the rules), and if the opportunity arises, the scheme is launched. That is the player makes a critical move, the logic of which is premeditated. This I do not deny, but (a) in premeditating, certain possibilities (some of which would have violated the rules) were considered and rejected, on balance. (b) In making the move, there is an unbiased trade-off among other (chess and non-chess) possibilities. Now here the reader's intuition may indicate that a chess game has a momentum of its own; that we are often reluctant to break off in the middle of a game and do (or even pay attention to) something else. All I can say here is that this is a familiar problem in animal behaviour, called the cost-of-changing problem. Solutions to this problem, that accord with optimality theory, have been proposed (McFarland, 1989). (c) The rational premeditation is itself an optimising process (otherwise it would not be rational), the main difference between myself and Noble is that (I presume) he sees the optimality criteria as relating to winning the game, whereas I see them as a maximising utility. By his choice of optimality criteria, Noble is forced into a teleological mould. (Given that my objective is to win the game, what is my best strategy, etc. My objective controls my thinking and behaviour in a way that excludes trade-offs with other non-chess considerations.) I am not forced into a teleological mould, because my objective embraces all my thinking and behaviour, and my objective (unlike Noble's) does not have to be explicitly represented in the brain.

On this point, also, I part company with Lockery (p. 188). 'Action theorists (e.g. Brand, 1984) have identified three necessary aspects of behaviours which are intentional actions. The first is that the action must fall within the pattern of a plan.' Noble's chess player clearly falls within this category. '... a further requirement for an intentional action: that the subject knows or at least believes that he is following the plan.' The chess player may believe that he is following a plan, but whether the plan is guiding his behaviour is another matter. 'The requirements that an action fit into the pattern of a plan, and that the subject knows this, can be subsumed under what we might call the cognitive aspect of intentional action. The final essential element is the motivation to undertake the plan.' This last requirement is very ambiguous. On the one hand, the observation that the subject's behaviour follows a plan is sufficient to conclude that the subject's behaviour was motivated, since motivation is simply what moves the subject. On the other hand, I suspect that Lockery means that some kind of cognitive representation of the plan plays an instrumental role in guiding the behaviour so that it follows the plan. There is no real sense in which the plan-following behaviour could not be motivated. Lockery mentions cases of extreme coercion, but these are merely cases where the subjects chose to follow the plan (because of the coercion), rather than do something else. The subject was still motivated to follow the plan, the coercion was just another ingredient of the subject's motivational state. My problem, here, is that I find the argument of Lockery (or of Brand, 1984) for that matter) that behaviour can be explained in terms of beliefs, desires and intentions to be totally unconvincing.

Part of Lockery's justification of this approach is that recent experiments on classical conditioning in animals 'have provoked a new generation of theories of classical conditioning ... All of them are expressed in intentional terms. This is good because it suggests that representational states are at issue. Better, the intentional terms in the theories denote causes of learning and behaviour, which means that representational states are essential to these accounts. Finally, the representational states posited by the theories generally have rather complex functional roles' (chapter 10). As I have indicated (p. 227), I do not accept that these experiments do show that intention (in the narrow sense) is a necessary ingredient of the explanation of the behaviour. I accept that some declarative representational states are involved, but not that they play a special causal role.

At a later stage in Chapter 10 (p. 139) Lockery asks, 'Does the mathematical account imply states with determinate functional roles? And are these the functional roles of recognisable representational states?' To answer this question, Lockery takes a mathematical version of the Mackintosh model of conditioning, which consists of 'several mathematical formulae and supporting sentences that provide the interpretation of them'. To show that reference to intentional states is hidden in the interpretation of the mathematics, Lockery conducts a thought experiment, in which

Mackintosh discovers the mathematical version of his theory ready made in the *Journal of Arcane Cybernetics*, though applied to a different type of problem. Lockery then argues that 'Since we have already seen that an intentional state is defined by its functional role in the explanation of behaviour, we are forced to conclude that **M** refers to states identical to those referred to in (i)–(iv). Of course, **M** is just the mathematical formalisation of the original Mackintosh account of conditioning. Thus the Mackintosh account, however expressed, makes essential reference to intentional states and representational states are non-figuratively at issue in this, and related theories of classical conditioning and its modern permutations' (p. 142).

It is well known that certain variables play the same functional roles in the systems of differing hardware. Thus is is possible to devise analogous electrical, mechanical and thermal systems (Olson, 1958). The logic of this approach can be extended into the biological field (e.g. Milsum, 1966; McFarland, 1971). I can understand how we could reach conclusions concerning intentionality that were hardware-dependent, but I do not understand how we can reach conclusions concerning functional roles of intentional concepts that would apply to one set of analogous hardware and not another.

Suppose that Mackintosh was not the only person looking at the *Journal of Arcane Cybernetics*. The meteorologist, Trevor Downpour, firmly believes that control of the weather is based upon intentional principles. He is delighted when he discovers the Mackintosh formula. He realises that this formula provides an exact mathematical analogy to his data. Moreover, Lockery tells him that this analogy justifies his belief that the intentional states that he employs in his explanation of changes in the weather are non-figurative. He can use the Mackintosh formula as a shield against those of his colleagues who would pour cold water on his intentional theories.

Lockery's reply to this argument (personal communication) provides us with a suitable ending point, which keeps alive the spirit of debate that we have tried to encapsulate in this volume:

'I absolutely accept your point that I have to allow Trevor Downpour his meteorological mind. But this isn't so bad really, because there is a huge assumption implicit in your example, one that makes me seem far less a panpsychist. Your example requires a very peculiar kind of weather: one that, among other things, is sensitive to predictive relationships in the environment. To be fair, you have to allow me that Trevor is a scientist in good faith, and not insane. Let us say he notices that by organising a parade he can bring on rain ("it always rains on my parade"). Now he decides to see how "clever" the weather really is. In England he always sets off fireworks before his parades. But in America he sets off fireworks the same number of times, but in a random relation with regard to his American parades. After a summer's worth of "training" he tests each weather with a series of fireworks displays and asks which weather rains most on the crowds. He is justified in attributing a Mackintosh account only if he really gets an increase in rain in the English case. (The following summer he controls for baseline by reversing the conditions in England and America.) And by God, if the weather worked like that, I wouldn't begrudge him his intentional ascriptions one bit.' (letter dated 14 Nov. 1987).

I leave it to the reader to compose a suitable reply.

# BIBLIOGRAPHY

*Note: the pages on which each reference is cited are shown in square brackets at the end of the reference*

Adams, C.D. and Dickinson, A. (1981a) 'Instrumental responding following reinforcer devaluation', *Q. J. exp. Psychol.*, 33 B: 109–12. *[222]*

Adams, C.D. and Dickinson, A. (1981b) 'Actions & habits: variations in associative representation during instrumental learning', In: N.E. Spear & R.R. Miller (Eds.), *Information Processing in Animals: Memory Mechanisms*, Hillsdale, N.J: Erlbaum. *[223]*

Audesirk, T.E. Alexander Jr. J E., Audesirk, G.J. and Moyer, C. (1982) 'Rapid, nonaversive conditioning in a freshwater gastropod. 1. Effects of age and motivation', *Behav. Neurol. Biol.*, 36: 379–90. *[147]*

Bakal, C.W., Johnson, R.D. and Rescorla, R.A. (1974) 'The effect of change in US quality on the blocking effect', *Pavlovian Journal of Biological Science*, 9: 97–103. *[137]*

Bateson, P.P.G. (1978) 'Early experience and sexual preferences', In: J.B. Hutchinson (Ed.), *Biological Determinants of Sexual Behaviour*, London: John Wiley, pp. 29–53. *[46]*

Bennett, J. (1976) *Linguistic Behaviour*, Cambridge: CUP. *[115]*

Bennett, J. (1983) 'Cognitive ethology: theory or poetry?' (commentary on Dennett, 1983), *Behavioral and Brain Sciences*, 6: 356–8. *[115]*

Berger, T.W., Rinaldi, D.J., Weisz and Thompson, R.F. (1983) 'Single unit analysis of different hippocampal cell types during classical conditioning of rabbit nictitating membrane response', *J. Neurophysiol.*, 50: 1197–219. *[156]*

Berliner, H. and Ebeling, C. (1986) 'The SUPREM architecture: a new intelligent paradigm', *Artificial Intelligence*, 28: 3–8. *[107]*

Braitenberg, V. (1984) *Vehicles: Essays in Synthetic Psychology*, Cambridge, Mass: MIT Press. *[103, 109]*

Braithwaite, R.B. (1946–7) 'Teleological explanation', *Proc. Aristotelian Society*, XLVII: i–xx. *[45]*

Braithwaite, R.B. (1953) *Scientific Explanation*, Cambridge: CUP. *[45]*

Brand M. (1984) *Intending and Acting*, Cambridge, Mass: MIT Press. *[188, 291–2]*

Brooks, R. (1987) 'Intelligence without representation', *Proceedings of Workshop on the Foundations of Artificial Intelligence*, AI laboratory MIT, June 1987. *[103, 234]*

Butters, N. and Miliotis, P. (1985) 'Amnesic disorders', in K.M. Heilman and E. Valenstein (eds.) *Clinical Neuropsychology*, 2nd edn., Oxford: OUP, pp. 403-51. *[203]*

Byrne, J.H. (1987) 'Cellular analysis of Associate Learning', *Psych. Rev*, 67: 329-439. *[131, 145, 156, 158]*

Byrne, J.H., Castellucci, V.F., Carew, T.J. and Kandel, E.R. (1978) 'Stimulus and response relation and the stability of mechanoreceptors and motor neurons mediating defensive gill-withdrawal reflex in *Aplysia*', *J. Neurophysiology*, 41: 412-431. *[153]*

Carew, T.J. and Sahley, C.L. (1986) 'Invertebrate learning and memory: from behaviour to molecules', *Ann. Rev. Neurosc.*, 9: 435-87. *[156]*

Carew, T.J., Walters, E.T. and Kandel, E.R. (1981) 'Classical conditioning in a simple withdrawal reflex in *Aplysia californica*', *J. Neurosci.*, 1: 1426-37. *[147]*

Cartwright, N. (1983) *How the Laws of Physics Lie*, Oxford: Clarendon Press. *[206-7]*

Cherniak, C. (1986) *Minimal Rationality*, Cambridge, Mas.: MIT Press. *[158]*

Chisholm, Roderick (1966) 'Freedom and Action', in K. Lehrer (ed.) *Freedom and Determinism*, New York: Random House, pp. 28-44. *[188]*

Churchland, P.M. (1981) 'Eliminative materialism and the propositional attitudes', *Journal of Philosophy*, 82: 8-28. *[151]*

Churchland, P.M. (1984) *Matter and Consciousness*, Cambridge, Mass.: MIT Press. *[158]*

Churchland, P. M. (1985) 'Conceptual progress and word/world relations: in search of the essence of natural kinds', *Canadian Journal of Philosophy*, 15: 1-17. *[200]*

Churchland, P.S. (1986) *Neurophilosophy*, Cambridge: MIT Press. *[150, 158]*

Cohen, D. (1977) *Psychologists on Psychology*, London: Routledge and Kegan Paul. *[202]*

Colwill, R.M. (1985) 'Context conditioning in *Aplysia californica*', *Abst. Soc. Neurosc.*, 232.9. *[146]*

Couvillon, P.A., Klosterhalfen, S. and Bitterman, M.E. (1983) 'Analysis of overshadowing in honey bees', *J. Comp. Psychol.*, 97: 154-66. *[146]*

Cranach, M. von and Harré, R. (1982) *The Analysis of Action*, Cambridge: CUP. *[45]*

Croll, R.P. and Chase, R. (1980) 'Plasticity of olfactory orientiation to foods in the snail *Achatina fulica*', *J. Comp. Physiol.*, A. 136: 267-77. *[147]*

Crow, R.J. and Alkon, D.L. (1978) 'Retention of an associated behavioral change in *Hermissenda*', *Science*, 201: 1239-41. *[147]*

Davidson, D. (1970) 'Mental events', in L. Foster and J.W. Swanson (eds.) *Experience and Theory*, Amherst: University of Massachusetts Press, pp. 79-101. *[205]*

Davis, J.M. (1975) 'Socially induced flight reactions in pigeons', *Anim. Behav.*, 23: 597-601. *[217]*

Dawkins, R. (1982) *The Extended Phenotype*, Oxford: W.H. Freeman. *[30, 56]*

Dawkins, R. (1976) *The Selfish Gene*, Oxford: Oxford University Press. *[30, 96]*

Dawkins, R. (1980) 'Good strategy or evolutionarily stable strategy?' In: G.W. Barlow and J. Silverberg (Eds.), *Sociology: Beyond Nature/Nurture?* (eds.) Boulder: Westview Press, pp. 331-67. *[52]*

Dawkins, R. (1986) *The Blind Watchmaker*, Harlow: Longmans. *[44, 96, 278]*

Dawkins, R. and Krebs, J.R. (1978) 'Animal signals: information or manipulation?' In: Krebs, J.R. and Davies, N.B. (eds.). *Behavioural Ecology*, Oxford: Blackwell Scientific Publications. *[55]*

Dennett, D.C. (1976) 'Conditions of Personhood', in Amelie Rorty (Ed.) *The Identities of Persons*, Berkeley, Ca: University of California Press (reprinted in Dennett, 1978). *[235]*

Dennett, D.C. (1978a) *Brainstorms*, Cambridge, Mass: Bradford/MIT. *[132]*

Dennett, D.C. (1978b) 'Why not the whole iguana?' (commentary on Z. Pylyshyn, 'Computational models and empirical constraints', *Behavioral and Brain Sciences*, 1: 93–99), *Behavioral and Brain Sciences*, 1: 103–4. *[103]*

Dennett, D.C. (1980) 'The milk of human intentionality' (commentary on Searle, 'Minds, Brains and Programs' *Behavioral and Brain Sciences*, 3: 428–30.) *[102]*

Dennett, D. C. (1981) 'Three kinds of intentional psychology', in R. Healey (ed.) *Reduction, Time and Reality*, Cambridge: CUP. *[107]*

Dennett, D.C. (1983) 'Intentional systems in cognitive ethology: the "Panglossian paradigm" defended', *Brain and Behavioral Science*, 3: 343–90. *[105, 111, 231]*

Dennett, D.C. (1982–3) 'Styles of Mental Representation', *Proc. Aristotelian Society*, LXXXIII, 213–26. *[42, 44, 161, 170, 232]*

Dennett, D.C. (1984a) *Elbow Room: the Varieties of Free Will Worth Wanting*, Cambridge, MA: MIT Press and OUP. *[235]*

Dennett, D.C. (1984b) 'Cognitive wheels: the frame problem of AI', in C. Hookway (Ed.) *Minds, Machines and Evolution*, pp. 129–51, Cambridge: CUP. *[102]*

Dennett, D.C. (1987) *The Intentional Stance*, Cambridge, Mass: MIT Press. *[90, 212–3, 231]*

Dennett, D.C. (1988) 'Out of the armchair and into the field', *Poetics Today*, 9 (No. 1): 205–21. *[110]*

Desimore, R., Albright, C.G., Gross, G. and Bruce, C. (1984) 'Stimulus-selective properties of inferior temporal neurons in the macaque', *J. Neurosc.*, 4: 2051–62. *[129]*

Dickinson, A. (1980) *Contemporary Animal Learning Theory*, Cambridge: CUP. *[132–4, 137, 158, 219–25]*

Dickinson, A. (1985) 'Actions and habits: the development of behavioural autonomy', *Phil. Trans. Roy. Soc. London*, B 308: 67– 78. *[221-2]*

Dickinson, A., Hall, G. and Mackintosh, N.J. (1976) 'Surprise and the attenuation of blocking', *Journal of Experimental Psychology: Animal Behavior Processes*, 2: 313–22. *[134]*

Disterhoft, J.F., Coulter, D.A. and Atkin, D.L. (1986) 'Conditioning specific membrane changes of rabbit hippocampal neurons measured in vitro', *Proc. Natl. Acad. Sci. USA*, 83: 2733–7. *[157]*

Doyle, J. (1979) 'A truth maintenance system', *Artificial Intelligence*, 12: 231–72. *[104]*

Dretske, F.I. (1980) 'The intentionality of cognitive states', *Midwest Studies in Philosophy*, 5: 281–94. *[124, 158]*

Eccles, J.C. (1986) 'Do mental events cause neural events analogously to the probability fields of quantum mechanics?', *Proc. Roy. Soc.*, B 227: 411–28. *[82]*

Ericsson K. A. and Simon, H. A. (1984) *Protocol Analysis: Verbal Reports as Data*, Cambridge, Mass: MIT Press. *[104]*

Fodor, J.A. (1975) *The Language of Thought*, New York: Thomas Y. Crowell Co. *[151, 158]*

Fodor, J. (1981) 'Introduction' to Fodor, *Representations*, Brighton: Harvester Press, pp. 1–31. *[200]*

Fodor, J.A. (1981) *Representations* , Cambridge, Mass: Bradford Books, MIT Press. *[200]*

Fodor, J.A. (1986) 'Why *paramecia* don't have mental representations', *Midwest Studies in Philosophy*, 10: 3–23. *[125, 158]*

Freud, S. (1964) *New Introductory Lectures in Psychoanalysis*, London: Hogarth Press. *[203]*

Gallistel, C.R. (1985) 'Motivation, intention, and emotion: goal directed behaviour from a cognitive-neuroethological perspective', In: Frese, M. & Sabini, J. (eds.) *Goal Directed Behaviour: The concept of action in psychology*, Hillsdale, N.J.: Erlbaum. *[227]*

Gluck, M.A. and Thompson, R.F. (1987) 'Modelling the neural substrates of associative learning and memory: a computational approach', *Psych. Rev.*, 94: 176–91. *[147]*

Gould, S.J. (1980) *The Panda's Thumb*, New York: W.W. Norton and Co. *[212]*

Gould, S.J. (1985) *The Flamingo's Smile*, New York: Norton. *[97]*

Griffin, D.R. (1981) *The Question of Animal Awareness*, New York: Rockefeller University Press. *[116]*

Griffin, D.R. (1984) *Animal Thinking*, Cambridge: Harvard University Press. *[116]*

Haugeland, J. (1978) 'The nature and plausibility of cognitivism', *The Behavioral and Brain Sciences*, 2: 215–60. *[196]*

Hawkins, R. D. and Kandel, E. (1984) 'Steps toward a cell-biological alphabet for elementary forms of learning', in G. Lynch, J. L. McGaugh and N. M. Weinberger (eds.) *Neurobiology of Learning and Memory*, New York: Guilford, pp. 385–404. *[104, 147–8, 158]*

Hennessey, T.M., Bucker, W.B. and McDiarmid, C.G. (1979) 'Classical conditioning in *paramecia*', *Anim. Learn. Behav.*, 7: 417–23. *[145]*

Heyes, C. M. (forthcoming) 'Cognisance of consciousness in the Study of animal knowledge', in W. Callebaut and R. Pinxten (eds.) *Evolutionary Epistemology: a Multiparadigm Approach*, Dordrecht/Boston: Reidel. *[105]*

Holland, P.C. (1977) 'Conditioned stimulus as a determinant of the form of the Pavlovian conditioned response', *Journal of Experimental Psychology: Animal Behaviour Processes*, 3: 77–104. *[220]*

Holland, P.C. and Straub, J.J. (1979) 'Differential effects of two ways of devaluing the unconditioned stimulus after Pavlovian appetitive conditioning', *Journal of Experimental Psychology: Animal Behaviour Processes*, 5: 65–78. *[220]*

Homes, F.L. (1974) *Claude Bernard and Animal Chemistry*, Cambridge, Mass: Harvard University Press. *[33]*

Irwin, F.W. (1971) *Intentional behaviour and motivation: a cognitive theory*, Philadelphia: Lippincott. *[227]*

Iverson, S.D. and Iverson, L.L. (1975) *Behavioural Pharmacology*, Oxford: OUP.

Jennings, H.S. (1906) *Behavior of Lower Organisms*, New York: Columbia University Press. *[132]*

Joynt, R. J. (1981) 'Are two heads better than one?', *Behavioral and Brain Sciences*, 4: 108–9. *[203]*

Kamin, L.J. (1969) 'Predictability, surprise, attention and conditioning', In: Campbell, B.A. & Church, R.M. (eds.) *Punishment and Aversive Behavior*, New York: Appleton-Century-Crofts, pp. 279-96. *[132]*

Kenny, A.J.P. (1969) *The Five Ways*, London: Routledge and Kegan Paul. *[4, 93]*

Krebs, J.R., Kacelnik, A. and Taylor, P. (1978) 'Test of optimal sampling by foraging great tits', *Nature*, 275: 127-31. *[109]*

Krebs, J.R. and McCleery, R. (1984) 'Optimisation in behavioural ecology', In: Krebs, J.R. & Davies, N. (eds.) *Behavioural Ecology*, Oxford: Blackwells Scientific Publications. *[47]*

Libet, B., Curtis, A.G., Wright, E.W. and Pearl, D.K. (1983) 'Time of conscious intention to act in relation to onset of cerebral activity (readiness potential). The unconscious initiation of a freely voluntary act', *Brain*, 640. *[99]*

Lloyd, D. (1987) 'Mental representation from the bottom up', *Synthese*, 70: 23-78. *[142]*

Lynch, G. and Baudry, M. (1984) 'The biochemistry of memory: a new and specific hypothesis', *Science*, 224: 1057-63. *[157]*

Mackintosh, N.J. (1975) 'A Theory of Attention: Variations in the associability of stimuli with reinforcement', *Psychological Reviews*, 82: 276-98. *[136, 158]*

Mackintosh, N.J. and Dickinson, A. (1979) 'Instrumental (type II) conditioning', In: A. Dickinson and R.A.Boakes (Eds), *Mechanisms of learning and motivation*, Hillsdale, N.J.: Erlbaum. *[223]*

MacPhail, E.M. (1982) *Brain and Intelligence in Vertebrates*, Oxford: Clarendon Press. *[178-9]*

MacPhail, E.M. (1986) 'Vertebrate intelligence: the null hypothesis', In: Weiskrantz, L. (Ed.) *Animal Intelligence*, pp 37-50, Oxford: The Clarendon Press. *[178-9]*

Marr, D. (1982) *Vision*, Cambridge, Mass: MIT Press. *[107]*

Maynard Smith, J. (1978) 'Optimisation theory in evolution', *Ann. Rev. Ecol. Sys.*, 9: 31-56. *[47]*

McCleery, R. (1977) 'On satiation curves', *Anim. Behav.*, 25: 1005-15. *[49]*

McCleery, R. (1978) 'Optimal behaviour sequences and decision making', In: Krebs, J.R. & Davies, N.B., *Behavioural Ecology*, Oxford: Blackwells Scientific Publications. *[49]*

McFarland, D.J. (1971) *Feedback Mechanisms in Animal Behaviour*, London: Academic Press. *[293]*

McFarland, D.J. (1977) 'Decision-making in animals', *Nature, London*, 269: 15-21. *[47]*

McFarland, D. J. (1983) 'Intentions as goals', *Behavioral and Brain Sciences*, 6: 369-70. *[45, 213]*

McFarland, D.J. (1989) *Problems of Animal Behaviour*, London: Longmans. *[44-5, 53-6, 223, 291]*

McFarland, D.J. and Houston, A. (1981) *Quantitative Ethology. The State Space Approach*, London: Pitman. *[47-55, 189, 224, 227]*

Menzel, R (1983) 'Neurobiology of learning and memory: the honeybee as a model system', *Naturwissenschaften*, 70: 504-11. *[146]*

Menzel, R., Erber, J. and Masuhr, T. (1974) 'Learning and memory in the honeybee', In: Bartone-Browne, L. (ed.) *Experimental Analysis of Insect Behavior*, New York: Springer-Verlag, pp 195-217. *[145]*

Millikan, R. (1984) *Language, Thought, and Other Biological Categories*, Cambridge, Mass: MIT Press. *[107]*

Milsum, J.H. (1966) *Biological control systems analysis*, New York: McGraw-Hill. *[293]*

Mitchell, R.W. and Thompson, N.S. (Eds.) (1986) *Deception*, Albany, N.Y.: SUNY. *[56]*

Montefiore, Alan (1971) 'Final Causes', *Proc. Aristotelian Society*, Suppl. XLV: 171–92. *[4, 74, 93]*

Mpitsos, G.J. and Davis, W.J. (1973) 'Learning: Classical and avoidance conditioning in the mollusk *Pleurobranchaea*', *Science*, 180: 317–20. *[147]*

Noble, Denis (1967) 'Charles Taylor on teleological explanation', *Analysis*, 27: 96–103. *[4, 93]*

Noble, Denis (1968) 'The conceptualist view of teleology', *Analysis*, 28: 62–3. *[4, 93]*

Olson, H.F. (1958) *Solutions to Engineering Problems by Dynamical Analogies*, Princeton: van Nostrand. *[293]*

Ramachandran, V.S. (1985) Guest editorial in *Perception*, 14: 97–103. *[108]*

Raphael, B. (1976) *The Thinking Computer: Mind Inside Matter*, San Francisco: Freeman. *[107]*

Rescorla, R.A. (1971) 'Variations in the effectiveness of reinforcement and non-reinforcement following prior inhibitory conditioning', *Learning and Motivation*, 2: 113–23. *[132-3]*

Rosenblueth, A. Wiener, W. and Bigelow, J. (1943) 'Behavior, purpose and teleology', *Philosophy of Science*, 10: 18–24. *[45]*

Rohwer, W. and Rohwer, F.C. (1978) 'Status signalling in Harris sparrows: experimental deception achieved', *Anim. Behav.*, 26: 1012–22. *[56]*

Rumelhart, D.E. and McClelland, J.L. (1986) *Parallel Distributed Processing*, Cambridge, Mass: MIT Press. *[153, 193]*

Ryle, G. (1945) *The Concept of Mind*, London: Hutchinson. *[220]*

Sacks, Oliver (1985) *The Man who mistook his Wife for a Hat*, New York: Summit. *[92]*

Sahley, C. and Ready, D.F. (1985) 'Associate learning modifies two behaviors in the leech, *Hirudo medicinalis*', *Abstr. Soc. Neurosci.*, 11: 367. *[147]*

Sahley, C., Rudy, J.W. and Gelperin, A. (1981) 'An analysis of associative learning in a terrestrial mollusc', *Journal of Comparative Physiology*, 144: 1–8. *[146, 158]*

Schoenfeld, W.N. (1950) 'An experimental approach to anxiety, escape and avoidance behavior', In: P.H. Hall and J. Zubin (eds.), *Anxiety*, New York: Grune and Stratton. *[135]*

Sejnowski, T.J. and Rosenberg, C.R. (1987) 'Parallel networks that learn to pronounce English text', *Complex systems*, 1: 145-8. *[193]*

Sibly, R.M. and McFarland, D.J. (1976) 'On the fitness of behaviour sequences', *American Naturalist*, 110: 601–17. *[49, 54]*

Strawson, P.F. (1959) *Individuals*, London: Methuen. *[89]*

Susswein, A.J. and Schwarz, M. (1983) 'A learned Change or Response to inedible food in *Aplysia*', *Behav. Neural. Biol.*, 39: 1–6. *[147]*

Sutton, R.S. and Barto, A.G. (1981) 'Towards a modern theory of adaptive networks: Expectation and prediction', *Psych. Rev.*, 88: 135–70. *[154]*

Taylor, Charles (1967) 'Teleological explanation', *Analysis*, 27: 141–5. *[4, 93]*

Taylor, C. (1970) 'The explanation of purposive behaviour', in R. Borger and F Cioffi (eds.) *Explanation in the Behavioural Sciences*, Cambridge: CUP, pp. 49–79. *[202]*

Thompson, R.F. (1986) 'The neurobiology of learning and memory', *Science*, 233: 941–7. *[145, 156]*

Thorndike, E.L. (1913) *The psychology of learning. Educational Psychology 11*, New York: Teachers College. *[224]*

Toates, F. (1986) *Motivational systems*, Cambridge: CUP. *[45]*

Trivers, R.L. (1985) *Social Evolution*, Menlo Park, California: Benjamin/Cummings Publishing Co. *[56]*

Van Fraassen, B.C. (1980) *The Scientific Image*, Oxford: The Clarendon Press. *[164]*

de Waal, F. (1982) *Chimpanzee politics: power and sex among apes*, N.Y.: Harper & Row, N.Y. *[56, 214]*

de Waal, F. (1986) 'Deception in the natural communication of chimpanzees', In: Mitchell, R.W. & Thompson, N.S. (eds.) *Deception*, Albany, N.Y.: SUNY. *[56]*

Walters, E.T. Carew, T.J. and Kandel. E.R. (1979) 'Associative learning in *Aplysia californica*', *Proc. Natl. Acad. Sci.*, USA 76: 6675–6. *[147]*

Watson, J.B. (1913) 'Psychology as a behaviorist views it', *Psychological Review*, 20: 158-73. *[132]*

Wells, M.J. and Young, J.Z. (1968) 'Learning with delayed rewards in Octopus', *Z. Vgl. Physiol.*, 61: 103–28. *[145]*

Wilkes, K.V. (1984) 'Pragmatics in science and theory in common sense', *Inquiry*, 27: 339–61. *[173]*

Wilkes, K.V. (1986) 'Nemo psychologus nisi physiologus', *Inquiry*, 29: 165–185. *[173]*

Williams, Bernard (1973) *Problems of the Self*, Cambridge: CUP. *[89]*

Wilson, D.M. (1966) 'Insect walking', *Ann. Rev. Ent.*, 11: 103–22. *[46]*

Winograd, T. (1972) *Understanding Natural Language*, New York: Academic Press. *[103]*

Woodfield, A. (1976) *Teleology*, Cambridge: CUP. *[39–40, 46]*

Woods, W. and Makhoul, J. (1974) 'Mechanical inference problems in continuous speech understanding', *Artificial Intelligence*, 5: 73–91. *[106]*

Woody, C.D. (1982) *Memory, Learning, and Higher Function — A Cellular View*, New York: Springer. *[156]*

Woody, C.D., Swartz, B.E. and Gruen, E. (1978) 'Effects of acetylcholine and cyclic GMP on input resistance of cortical neurons in awake cats', *Brain Res.*, 158: 373–95. *[156]*

Ydenberg, R.C. and Houston, A.I. (1986) 'Optimal trade-offs between competing behavioural demands in the great tit', *Animal Behaviour*, 34: 1041–50. *[54]*

# FURTHER READING

Most of the suggestions for further reading will be found at the ends of chapters 2, 4, 6, 8 and 9. Those lists contain the reading material that is most closely related to the subjects of those chapters. Here we list some further books that are relevant to the debate in general.

Block, N. Ed. (1980) *Readings in the Philosophy of Psychology* 2 vols., Harvard: Harvard University Press.
Changeux, J.-P. (1983) *L'Homme Neuronal*, Paris: Fayard.
Churchland, P.S. (1986) *Neurophilosophy*, Cambridge, Mass.: MIT Press.
Dennett, D.C. (1979) *Brainstorms*, Hassocks: Harvester Press.
Dennett, D.C. (1987) *The Intentional Stance*, Cambridge, Mass.: MIT Press
Dickinson, A. (1980) *Contemporary Animal Learning Theory*, Cambridge: CUP.
Dretske, F. (1988) *Explaining Behavior*, Cambridge, Mass: MIT Press.
Hookway, C (ed) (1984) *Minds, Machines and Evolution*, Camdridge, CUP.
Parfit, D. (1984) *Reasons and Persons*, Oxford: Clarendon Press.
Woodfield, A. (1976) *Teleology*, Cambridge: CUP.

# NOTES ON AUTHORS

*Daniel C. Dennett* is Distinguished Arts and Science Professor, in the Department of Philosophy, and Director of Cognitive Studies at Tufts University. He is the author of *Content and Consciousness* (1969), *Brainstorms* (1978), *The Intentional Stance* (1987), and other books and articles in the philosophy of mind and the conceptual foundations of cognitive science. His current research is on an empirical theory of human consciousness, drawing on clinical and experimental findings and based on a model of the computational architecture of the human brain.

*Shawn Lockery* is a postdoctoral fellow at The Salk Institute for Biological Studies. A philosopher turned scientist, he is interested in the biological basis of mental states. His experimental studies include the neural basis of pattern recognition and learning in simple nervous systems. He is also exploring the use of network simulation techniques in the prediction and analysis of actual neural circuits.

*David McFarland* is Reader in Animal Behaviour in the University of Oxford, and Fellow and Tutor in Psychology at Balliol College. His main scientific work has to do with aspects of decision-making in animals. One of his hobbies is iconoclasm.

*Alan Montefiore* is Fellow and Tutor in Philosophy at Balliol College, Oxford. His interests range over moral philosophy, philosophy of education, contemporary 'continental' philosophy (particularly that done in France), the philosophy of Kant, the nature of what is sometimes called 'Jewish identity', and a whole set of topics concerned with awareness of self and others. His various publications tend, not surprisingly, to reflect these interests and their mutual interplay.

*Denis Noble* is Professor of Cardiovascular Physiology at the University of Oxford. He uses physical and mathematical methods to analyse the mechanism of the heartbeat (*The Initiation of the Heartbeat*, OUP, 1979). His interest in philosophy started in discussions with Stuart Hampshire and others at University College London in the early 60's and continued in the published debate with Charles Taylor in *Analysis* in 1967. He is deeply involved with the application of computer technology to biological research and is director of a medical software company.

*Kathleen V. Wilkes* is Fellow and Tutor in Philosophy at St. Hilda's College, Oxford. She is author of *Physicalism* (Routledge and Kegan Paul, 1978) and *Real People* (OUP, 1988); and co-edits, with W.H.Newton-Smith, *International Studies in the Philosophy of Science: the Dubrovnik Papers*. Her research interests and published papers are mainly in the philosophy of science; but she has also published papers on the philosophy of mind, on Plato and Aristotle, on moral philosophy, and on the philosophy of religion.